Nordic M...

1:Healing galdr, healing runes

Yves Kodratoff

Universal Publishers
USA • 2003

Nordic Magic Healing:
1:Healing galdr, healing runes

Universal Publishers/uPUBLISH.com
USA • 2003

ISBN: 1-58112-573-9

www.uPUBLISH.com/books/kodratoff.htm

Nordic Magic Healing

Nordic Magic Healing is made of three books.

Book 1:   *Healing galdr, healing runes*

Book 2:   *Screaming, I gathered them*

Book 3:   *Hand healing, Shiatsu and Seið: a spiritual journey*

These books illustrate my deep belief that healing must harmoniously merge rationalism and mysticism. Nordic Heathen magic and Shiatsu are very good examples of such a merger.

Our primitive being is hidden but ever present in our life, showing its demands in very strange and unexpected ways. We have to recognize and to heal the wounds that this primitive part of ourselves bears. That is what I call 'healing magic': it relies on deep superstitions and magical techniques.

These books share my experience in healing using galdr, runes, and shiatsu. They present a new healing technique that incorporates both the Japanese and Nordic approaches. Although they are far from each other physically, they are quite close in spirit.

Acknowledgments

Thanks and love to Lise Fontaine for her comments and questions which helped me so much in making this final version more precise than any original I have been writing.

Table of Contents

The cover of this volume shows the tree of the world, Yggdrasil, "High tree, splattered with white mud" as I naively see it - many colored - through the prism of my eyes.

Chapter 1: RUNES AND HEALING

Chapter 2: THE HEALING OF VÄINÄMÖINEN AND LEMMINKÄINEN

Chapter 3: SHAMANISM AND HEALING

The Shamanic Civilization
Good and Evil, Health and Illness
Do you see yourself an individual, or as a link?
Of Prudishness

Soul Theft
Bringing back souls stolen by Spirits of the Lower
World
Possession healing
Resurrections

Chapter 4: POEMS, CHARMS AND CURSES: HEALING
WITH GALDR

Chapter 5: GLOBAL PRIMITIVE MEDICINE

Chapter 1

RUNES AND HEALING

"And, all along their way - she taught him the runes, upon her white hand."
Danmarks Gamle Folkviser (in *Chants populaires scandinaves*, p. 29)

Runes are magical tools, tools for all aspects of life.
They can be used, and were used, in many ways: for war, for love, for prosperity, and so on. In this book, we are going to explore the runes and the Galdr (song) associated with them. To begin this exploration, I will first give you a glimpse of how the runes were *actively* used in the past by using examples from an area that interests me very much - healing.

The following three rune poems show us the magical use of the runes to affect someone else's health.

Those who carve without knowledge
Should not write the runes
[*for*] Great misfortune will follow
When the secrets are misused
I have seen ten letters carved
On the whale bone

They brought on the pain
That tortured the leek's lime-tree. (saga1)[1]

In this poem, "leek's lime-tree" designates a 'slender woman': the leek brings in the idea of being slender and beautiful, and lime-tree is a classical image for a woman in Skaldic poetry. Thinking of the leek you buy at the marketplace, you might get a wrong feeling. This image obviously refers to the wild leek, a beautiful slender deep-green stem rising above the other herbs.

This poem is one of Egil Skalagrimsson's, as told in the saga that describes his life. The runes that this poem refer to were carved into a whale bone in an attempt to seduce the young girl (the 'slender woman') who is spoken of in the poem, but instead they only served to make her ill. Besides the technical error of having chosen the wrong runes, this is an attempt at this kind of magic to force someone to act against their will. Whenever runes are carved for someone, this person must be made aware of what is being carved for them, they must agree with the carver, and they should participate in the creation of the poem that asks for their healing.

Using the runes is more dangerous than you might believe.
Get deeply involved when you do, magic is not nice and
funny

---

[1] Almost all the citations given here are my version of the ancient text I want to present of the reader. Most often, however, there is a classical English translation of the same ancient text. A reference such as (saga1) will be used in the bibliography, where I will give the pages of an English edition containing the translation of the same original ancient text. In general, this classical translation and mine differ. In particular, I noticed a tendency to translate ancient poetry in a pompous way that, in my opinion, kills their poetry. This is why, even when I provide a version with the same meaning as the classical translation, I tend to use simpler words.

The next poem, gives us the only example of how a healing should be done. This poem was found, written in runes, at Sigtuna on a copper plaque that dates from the end of the 11th century.

> Demon of the fever of wounds,
> Lord of the demons,
> Now you must flee,
> You have been discovered.
> Three kinds of pain on you, wolf.
> Three times the misery, wolf.
> |||, the rune of Ice.
> These ice runes will be your only joy, wolf.
> Enjoy the seið well. (rune1)

This important poem will be discussed later in detail, with particular attention given to seið, a kind of shamanic journey practiced the by Norse magicians. Clearly, the only ill wished here is for the sickness.

Unfortunately, there are many examples of what not to do: using the runes for harming others. This book will not explain, and has no desire to explain, how to practice this kind of magic. Nevertheless, it would be dishonest to try to hide this kind of use, and its traces. Busla's curse, found in the *saga of Bosi and Herraud* (where it is called a 'prayer'), is a very striking example of a harmful use, although there is no evidence that these verses were carved in runes.

> I wish you pain
> in your breast,
> that venomous vipers
> gnaw your heart,
> that your ears
> are deafened forever,
> and your eyes

become wall-eyed forever!
(edda1)

Runes: for divination or magic ?

Since many people use runes for divination, we shall now discuss their role in the ancient society.
First, the title of this book needs to be justified since the runes aren't commonly used for healing. Mystical books on runes have clearly shown that, today, their use is essentially for divination. This means that the runes are arranged in a specific system, and the seeker is asked to choose several of them. By interpreting the runes chosen, the rune reader helps people to better understand their difficulties, to better guide their life. Used this way, rune readings are similar to tea-leaf readings or tarot card readings. However, modern books on runes don't show how they can be used for healing.

The widely accepted belief in the divinatory abilities of the runes comes mostly from the widely cited Latin text written by Tacitus:

> For omens and the casting of lots they have the highest regard. Their procedure in casting lots is always the same. They cut off a branch of a nut-bearing tree and slice it into strips; these they mark with different signs and throw them completely at random onto a white cloth. Then the priest of the state, if the consultation is a public one, or the father of the family if it is private, offers a prayer to the gods, and looking up at the sky picks up three strips, one at a time, and reads their meaning from the signs previously scored on them. If the lots forbid an enterprise, there is no deliberation that day on the matter in question; if they permit it, confirmation by the taking of auspices is required. (taci1)

From this text, we might be able to conclude that the Germanic people were adept at magic, but we can't say it shows us how the runes were used. A Roman such as Tacitus would interpret divination, as he knew it in the Greek/Latin culture. Therefore, we can't be certain that he understood exactly what was going on in the Germanic culture.

Tacitus also says that in case of success, a 'confirmation' was required. Why would this be needed if the runes already did a foretelling? Besides, a bit later Tacitus describes what he considers as the most important foretelling technique: the interpretation of the "neighs and snorts" of sacred white horses.

Another reason for the confusion about the use of the runes could be attributed to the Celtic Oghams. The druids were known to use all sorts of divinatory methods, from observing birds in flight to watching the convulsions of a victim stabbed in the back. In particular, the story of Etain, well known in Celtic mythology, attests to the use of the Oghams as a method of 'seeing'. In this case, the druid Dalan uses the Oghams to discover that Etain had been married to a God. The writings about the peithynen or "the Elucidator," also known as the Druids' wheel, describe a type of divination which used branches or staves that had poems (or maxims) carved on them in Oghams. Transferring an interpretation from the Oghams to the runes is certainly possible, but there is no historical justification for doing so.

One thing is consistent in the runic texts, they all show an **active** use of the runes. In other words, they are used to act on the future, or to wish for a change in the physical world. For instance, one of the few texts that alludes to the throwing of sacred branches is *Gautrek*'s *saga*, and clearly the runes in this case aren't used to foresee the future, but to control it:

> The King, Vikar ... came up against extraordinarily adverse winds and they stayed near small islands for a long time. They threw [*some sort of*][2] 'fate' sticks in order to diminish the winds. The result was that Odin demanded that a man from the company be chosen by a draw and be hung as a sacrifice[3]. (saga2)

After these magical pieces of wood were thrown, the storm calmed itself and Odin demanded that of one of the passengers on the boat be sacrificed. The sacrifice took place several days later. This does not describe an example of divination, because clearly, the priest already knew what he wanted to achieve and without a doubt, simply waited to pay the due price, a sacrifice to the High One in this case. The runes of the Elder Futhark, like those of the Younger Futhark, serve as mediation between humans and Gods, a means of asking the Gods to grant a favor.

In *Gisli Surssson saga*, we find an example that looks casual enough, but it works in a similar way. The hero of the saga, Gisli, wants to meet up with his brother who refuses to open his door to him.

> Gisli takes a stick, carves runes on it, and throws it inside. (His brother) sees it, catches it, looks at it, then he gets up, goes out, and welcomes Gisli ... (saga3)

This is not exactly what we would call miraculous, and certainly no great sacrifice was called for. But regardless of

---

[2] Texts in brackets and in italics are my comments.

[3] The English translation found in Penguin's *Seven Viking Romances* is much less precise than the present citation, taken from a German edition of Gautrek's saga.

the price of this tiny miracle, it does show that the effect of the runes is not to foresee, but to obtain a result since, Gisli did try to speak to his brother first through the door but without any success.

We also find references to runes carved on a 'pole of infamy'. These are also attempting to alter reality. An example of this comes to us through *Vatnsdoela saga*. The goal in this case is to curse those who break a solemn promise:

> This one will be infamous to all and never find company with honest people. He will incur the wrath of the Gods and he will carry the name of Peace Violator! (saga4)

The following runic text comes from *Egil Skallagrimsson*'s *saga*:

> I place here a pole of infamy against King Eric and Queen Gunnhild and I direct this curse to the guardian spirits of this country, so that each of them will be lost, unable to find their way until they have successfully driven King Eric and Queen Gunnhild out of this land. (saga5)

This demand is far more significant than the previous one, but similar in the sense that it relates to shaping the future, and not to predicting it.

In *Gretti*'s *saga* (*Grettis Saga Asmundarsonar*), there is a sorceress who wants to ruin Gretti. In order to do so, we are told that she took her knife and carved runes on a stump. She then reddened them with her blood and muttered a magical spell. Then she turned counter clockwise around the stump and recited powerful magical spells. Since this sorceress wanted then to make sure to be able to harm Gretti, before she begins the final spell, she spies on him and listens to him speak so that she can discover his weak point. When she finally does carve the runes that will bring about Gretti's ruin, she has it all planned, and knows that she only needs to follow the proper steps to succeed.

Runes are also alluded to in other sagas. But in each case they either request that an event happen, or they assert and consecrate something (as for example in stating: "this ship is captained by X").

This active use of the runes is also found in relatively recent texts and customs, such as in *Danmarks Gamle Folkeviser* assembled by S. Grundtvig between 1853 and 1883. This collection of popular Danish poems contains 18 that mention runes. They show how to use them to calm floods, immobilize animals, seduce a partner, bring on deep sleep, ease birth, etc., but never once is there an allusion to a divinatory use of the runes. In the same way, Deichman in 1794 (cited by Léon Pineau, *Chants populaires scandinaves*, 1898, p. 144) explains two practices that were common in his time. The first, also described by Saxo Grammaticus some five centuries earlier, is that

> it's a belief today, still common in the region of Himmelsbjaerg that, if the runes are engraved on a small piece of wood and if it is placed under the tongue of a corpse, the dead will talk.

The second is:

> When Icelanders want to harm someone, they take a piece of wood, the length of two or three fingers. They engrave on it magical characters and they make their blood run upon them. After this, they go to the tomb of a corpse ... [*following*

this is a cursing ritual that I have no desire to repeat].

In any case, there is no allusion, not even a subtle one, to a divinatory use of the runes.

My purpose by this long argument is not to say that using the runes for divination is absurd, but to show that this is a more recent use that was certainly not practiced "since time immemorial" as many mystical books on runes state without batting an eye[4].

Non-runic divinatory methods

There were obviously a large number of divinatory techniques in the Nordic society. It seems that the one used most often is called *seið*[5], a kind of shamanic journey.
When knowledge of the future is what is desired, the magical means that was used was *seið* and not the runes. Many texts mention the work of a *völva* or a seeress who performs a seið to determine the future[6].

---

[4] There are so many things I would like to explain in this first chapter that it could easily become a book of its own. In order to avoid overloading it too much, I have added one appendix at the end of this chapter which is dedicated to a more thorough discussion of all the texts I have been able to gather which describe a use of runes that could have been interpreted as divinatory. (A great thank you to Marijane Osborn for sharing her notes with me on this subject!). In the end, as you will see, there are only two references describing an almost certain use of the runes for divination.

[5] To be pronounced as 'seithe'. It is also often written seidh, or seidhr. I noticed that most occurrences of this word in the meaning of 'magical foreseeing' are written *seið* in the Eddas and the sagas.

[6] Different words were used to describe similar behaviors. The interested reader may refer to the Internet paper, *Spae-Craft, Seið, and Shamanism*, by Kveldulf Gundarsson, that makes sharp differences among all these practices.

For example, in *Vatnsdoela saga*, the hosts prepared a feast according to their ancient custom for conducting a seið. This was being done so that the people could know their destiny. A Lapp völva was asked to attend the feast so that she could perform the seið. The Lapp, dressed in great gear, occupied the high-seat at the feast. People went forward to ask their future and ask questions about their destiny. For each of them, she prophesied their future.

A similar example of this use of the seið (and this is the only example I know of a seið conducted by a Scandinavian male) is found in *Gisli Sursson*'s *saga*:

> Thorgrim the Nose was paid to perform a seið that would locate a murderer, thus preventing him from getting away healthy and safe, even if others tried to help him. In return, Thorgrim was given an ox that was nine winters old.
> He began the seið, preparing for it as usual and building a scaffold. He completed the seið with all his spells and evil-doings, ... [*effectively locating the murderer.*] (saga6)

The word used for 'spells' in the original text is *ergi*. In Chapter 3, we shall discuss this concept at length, where we will show that it actually means 'impotence' or 'passive homosexuality'. This text is thus very despising towards the use of seið, but it does show that Thorgrim the Nose was able to use seið successfully to accomplish his task.

To complete this brief discussion of seið, I want to also consider the examples of seið, which attempt to modify the future, and we have many instances of those in the sagas. In particular, there are many examples where Lapp shamans have performed the seið as they were requested, correctly anticipating the future. We learn from the text that when they have been asked to perform a seið in order to retrieve an object, but they failed. Despite their efforts, they were incapable of physically modifying reality.

The role of seið is twofold: to anticipate the future and, where possible, to modify the world of physical reality. The role of the runes, as the sagas and Eddic texts illustrate, is to affect physical reality, to consecrate a possession, or to claim some power, but never to foresee the future. More discussions and references on the use of seið are given in the excellent paper of H. R. Ellis Davidson, *Hostile Magic in the Icelandic Sagas*, published in *The Witch in History*, referred in the bibliography. See also the Appendix for more detail.

Healing and using runes to heal

The focus of this book is to study the runes as they relate to health and well-being. The runes were grouped into nine rune songs according to the *Lay of Sigrdrifa* (see later in this chapter), and of these nine songs, four are dedicated to health. The runes of Branches[7], those of the physicians, are of primary importance here. Delivery runes are used to help in childbirth and they also relate directly to the medical area. Runes of Protection help in preventing sickness. The runes of Joy are also included with the healing runes because they are powerful in the prevention of sickness. The five remaining runes songs are : Victory, Undertow[8], Magic[9],

---

[7] It is usually translated by 'runes of Limbs' but this keeps an ambiguity between the limb of a human and those of a tree. I chose to follow German translations that speak of limbs of trees without ambiguity, as 'branches' does.

[8] Undertow runes are usually called Sea or Wave runes. I try to capture the threat they contain by calling them runes of the Undertow.

Speech, and Spirit. I deeply believe that each rune can be used to influence health (with the exception of Othala, and this will be explained later), complementing the rune typically assigned for this purpose. The end of this chapter will present a summary of the effect of each rune on health, and volume 2 of this book will be devoted to an in depth study of the twenty-four runes of the Elder Futhark, and their relation to health. It is interesting to note that no text describes this specific healing use of the runes. I have used the runic texts to find out the various meanings of each rune, and then from these meanings, I have associated a particular healing power to each of them.

What is striking about the ancient Northern European myths, (i.e. those referring to runes, such as the Icelandic and Irish sagas, Celtic and Germanic legends, the old-English poem *Beowulf*, etc.), is the extreme lack of details concerning health. And yet, healing must certainly have taken place. A rare example of a healing treatment is found in the Icelandic *saga of Glum the Murderer*. It tells the story of a woman whose close relative has just been killed.

> She asks to see the corpse and they show it to
> her. She then takes her relative and lays him
> gently in a cart. And when she gets back home,
> she cleans and bandages his wounds.
> She did all this so well that when she was done, he
> started to speak. (saga7)

This is an extraordinary miracle that well deserves to be told. However, when someone is simply hurt, the sagas often only explain what the end result of the injury was, and they do not discuss the care that has been provided. One of the few

---

[9] The translators of the Edda call the runes of Magic the runes of beer, but the scientific runologist W. Krause insists that they are in fact runes of magic ("Zauberrunen").

references that I could find to a doctor or healer of any kind is in the *saga of the Men of the Vapnfjord.*

> Thorvard was a man who was thought of very highly in his community and he was considered to be the best physician in the district. One evening, a man broke his leg on the farm, and Thorvard was sent for. So, Thorvard came and bandaged the leg. The man then said to Thorvard, "My wounds are to the point where, thanks to your assistance, we can take care of it by ourselves, but I know that Thorkel is hurt, that he has nobody to care for him, and that he is weakening. I ask you to join him and to heal him." Thorvard agreed to this and [*went to Thorkel's place*]. He approached Thorkel and said, "I would like to see your wound, because I have heard that it goes badly." Thorkel allowed him to see it and Thorvard spent seven nights with him, and the state of the patient improved each day. Thorvard went away, and for his care, Thorkel gave him a horse and a silver bracelet. (saga8)

This payment must have been extraordinary since the saga mentions it, but there are no details at all about how the wound was treated specifically.

Another medical treatment, though an unsuccessful one, is found in *Gretti's saga.* When Gretti is wounded, and his wound obviously starts to gangrene, his brother Illugi treats him. The saga says simply:

> Illugi watched him day and night, taking care of nothing else. (saga9)

The *saga of King Hrolf and his Champions* describes a similar type of recovery.

> King Hrolf had received two wounds to his arms,
> and a major injury to his head which caused him
> to lose an eye.
> These injuries weakened him for some time, but Queen
> Yrsa healed him. (saga10)

In the tale of *Egil and Asmund*, we are given some details about surgery. Egil lost a hand in a fight, and a friendly dwarf dressed the stump so well that "soon the pain was completely gone. In the morning the wound was healed". The dwarf then made a sword with a hilt in the form of a socket and he fixed it on Egil's arm. Later in the tale, Egil meets an old giantess who had kept the hand that was cut off, wrapped in "life-herbs." She offers to help Egil: "If you'll risk letting me reopen the wound; I'll try to graft the hand on to the arm." The tale goes on:

> She took the socket off his arm and deadened the
> arm so that Egil didn't feel any pain when she
> trimmed the stump. Then she put life-herbs on it,
> wrapped it in silk and held it firmly for the rest
> of the day. Egil could feel the life flow in. The
> old hag put him to bed and told him to stay there
> until his hand was healed. It was fully healed in
> three days, and now he found the hand no stiffer
> than it had been when the arm was still whole,
> though it appeared to have a red thread around it.
> (saga11)

This description can certainly be called a mere fantasy. Still, when taken all together, the details on the painkillers and the disinfectants (the 'healing-herbs'), the bandage and quiet time necessary for recovery, look like the tip of an impressive iceberg of medical knowledge.

In *The History of Saint Olaf*, Snorri Sturluson describes a medical treatment as it was performed on a wounded man named Tormod. The healing fails, but it shows that some knowledge of surgery was common in the Nordic world.

> Tormod then went away to a little room which he entered. Many were already there, sorely wounded men, and there was present a woman who bound up their wounds. A fire was burning on the floor and she warmed water wherewith to wash their wounds; Tormod sat down by the door. One came out and the other went in of those who were busying themselves with the wounded men. One of them turned to Tormod, looked at him and said: "Why art thou so pale? Art thou wounded and why dost thou not ask for a leech?" Then Tormod quoth a verse:
>
>> I have no fresh hue,
>> But the fair, slim woman
>> Herself hath a ruddy husband.
>> Few bother about my wounds.
>> Generous woman! The wound
>> In me was caused by
>> The deep track of Dag's spell
>> And the Danish weapons' smart.
>
> [*Dag is the name of the warrior who wounded Tormod*]
> Tormod then stood up and went to the fire where he stood for a while. The leech said to him: "Thou, man, go out and fetch me the wood which lies outside the door!" He went out, brought in an armful of wood and cast it down on the floor. The leech looked at his face and said: "Strangely pale is this man. Why art thou so?" Then quoth Tormod:
>
>> The noble woman wonders

That we are so wan.
Few grow fair of wounds;
I found them in the arrow-fall.
Through me the curved steel
Went mightily driven.
Keenly hath the perilous iron
Pierced near my heart, I think.

Then said the leech: "Let me see thy wounds and I will attend to them" . He sat down and took off his clothes. When the leech saw his wounds, she looked carefully at the wound in his side; she noticed that therein stood a bit of iron but knew not for sure what path the iron had taken. In a stone kettle she had put leeks and other grass, and cooked them together; she gave it to the wounded men to eat and so tried to find out if they had deep wounds, for she could notice the smell of the leek coming out of a deep wound. She brought it to Tormod and bade him eat. He answered: "Take it away; I have not groats-sickness." She took a pair of tongs to draw out the iron, but it was fast and would not come out; it stood but a little way out for the wound was swollen. Then said Tormod: "Cut the flesh away down to the iron, so that thou canst get at it well with the tongs; then give them to me and let me wrench it." She did as he said. Then Tormod took the gold ring off his hand and gave it to the leech, bidding her do with it what she would, "a good possession it is," he said, "King Olaf gave me this ring this morning." Tormod afterwards took the tongs and wrenched the arrow out; there were barbs on it and on these lay the fibers of the heart, some red, some white. And when he saw it, he said: "Well hath the king fed us; fat am I still about the roots of the heart!" He then fell back and was dead. Here ends the tale of Tormod. (saga12)

In *Gesta Danorum*, Saxo Grammaticus also alludes to some kind of complex healing :

> The farmer's son came then close to the patient's
> wounds, repaired the ripped parts of the stomach,
> put the innards back into the belly, and held them
> in place by knotted vines. (saxo1)

I think it safe to say that some people, at least, must have had medical knowledge, seemingly of a rudimentary kind, but we are never given any details about how healing actually takes place.

Christian texts often provide miraculous examples of healing, where the touch of a hand, or the blessing of a saint are enough to heal. For example, the venerable Bede[10] goes into great detail on the miraculous properties of the blood of a saint, or the water that washed the bones of some other one. All his stories strongly evoke paganism, but he never goes into detail about how the saints performed their miracles. Nevertheless, this is no proof of a lack of medical knowledge, since according to Bede, John, the Bishop of York, obviously demonstrates this kind of knowledge. One day the Bishop of York arrives at a convent of nuns and he is told of a young nun who is very ill. After being informed that this nun had recently been bled in the arm, he asks the Abbess when the bleeding had been practiced. When he discovers that it took place on the fourth day of the moon, he growls roughly to Abbess Heriburg:

---

[10] Bede, author of *The Ecclesiastical History of the English People*, completed his work at the end of his life in 731. Although this history is essentially aimed at the Christian crowd, the free style of the author produces in fact a very pleasant text to read, and of course, it is very instructive on the actual cultural context that Arthurian legends colorfully redesigned.

> You have acted most foolishly and unwisely to
> carry out a bleeding on the fourth day of the
> moon. I remember the Archbishop Theodore, of
> blessed memory, said that it was very dangerous
> to bleed at a time when the light of the moon and
> the pull of the tide is increasing. (bede1)

Because the Abbess then pleads with him so strongly, the
bishop agrees to go to the nun's bedside. He then utters a
prayer over the sick nun and he gives her his blessing. The
nun heals immediately, and this is as much as Bede tells us.

Fortunately, all this medical knowledge has not been
completely lost. Many medical treatises dating from before
the 17th century recorded this knowledge. For example, the
National Library of Scotland holds 83 Gaelic manuscripts[11],
of which 29 are medical treatises containing several hundred
pages of medical prescriptions. Obviously, this part of the
library doesn't interest scholars and has not often been
translated from Gaelic and the rare translations that do exist
are not published for the public. Many of these ancient
practices have been certainly lost, and many of the
christianized Heathen practices lost their credibility,
becoming merely superstition. Whenever they finally
become accessible, we will have a lot of fishing to do from
this great pond of knowledge.

The Siberian shamanic tradition is somewhat more precise
and does give us some details on the processes necessary for

---

[11] I have found these details in Mary Beith's book on the traditional
medicines of the Scottish Highlands. Later, we will use more traditional
knowledge of the Highlands. Among others, one rite, in the middle of a
Christian prayer, recommends tracing a large U on the head of the sick,
which obviously evokes the rune Uruz that corresponds to the U in the
Futhark.

recovery. However, the written records concerning their healing practices have always only described the extremely miraculous. How to treat a cold was of no concern to the authors of these great traditional texts. We have no details on treating these minor ailments, except for treatments using plants. But we do have some treatments such as those recorded by Saint Hildegard[12] in the twelfth century. I will come back to her particular charms in detail later on.

You might be asking yourself why I am not using the charms from *Galdrabok* translated into English by S. Flowers, or *Danmarks Gamle Folkviser* translated into French by Léon Pineau in 1898. The reason is because the charms presented in these works are only allusive to healing, they don't describe a precise process. They are also so much christianized ("recite three Our Fathers", for example), that I don't know how I could 're-paganize' them while still keeping their essence, as is possible with the charms of the Scottish Highlands and oddly enough those of Saint Hildegard.

One notable exception can however be found in the early chapters of Finnish *Kalevala*[13] describing how an old man

---

[12] Hildegard of Bingen, a visionary abbess of the twelfth century is quasi-unknown outside Germany except perhaps for her music. She is however very popular in Germanic countries where her precepts for good health became a sort of cult. One can hardly imagine the social recognition she enjoyed, she who allowed herself to send letters of reproach to her emperor when he mistreated the pope. She claimed to be not very cultured, that is she felt she spoke Latin badly (her work was written in Latin with the assistance of a scholar), which suggests that she was strongly cultivated in popular society, hence the magical charms she recommends. Although it is hard to believe, these charms were made public by a prominent cleric of the Catholic church.

[13] The next chapter presents this major work in detail. The Finns that I have consulted told me that 'runo' evokes for them a sung and rhythmic poem, just like those of the Kalevala.

was able to heal the first hero of the Kalevala, Väinämöinen. Väinämöinen hurt his knee with an ax, and was unable to heal himself. Later on, I will be sharing with you this beautiful text which contains a slightly christianized version of what the shamanic tradition suggests for health care. Then, we will follow Väinämöinen in his recovery. The link with the runes is simple: recovery takes place when several poems have been said, and these poems look like charms, similar to the charms we shall built with runes in chapter 4. In Finnish, the word for poem is *runo*, and Finnish dictionaries (as does Webster's) claim that it comes from Old Norse *runa*. A proper runic work would then ask for these songs to be engraved in runes on a branch. The Kalevala does not mention this, but nothing prevents us from doing so for ourselves: I am not certain that *runa* means 'song' in some primitive Germanic language, even though it is so strongly suggested by their living link to Norse *galdr* and Finnish *runo*. I am nevertheless quite convinced that we have to bind them in our present lives in order to get in touch with the mysteries.

In the last two chapters of this book I will give you a method, which follows the runic texts, for using the runes to heal. Of course, this is primitive medicine[14], based on songs, dances and pleas (also called 'supplications'). Healing is done by addressing the Spirits (or the Gods, and here, this will be Odin[15] or other Nordic Gods), by casting out bad

---

[14] The word 'primitive' tends to have become equated with naive and lacking efficiency because it seems that now only scientific techniques are considered efficient. Without losing the spirit of criticism that stems from the scientific attitude, it is clear to me that this primitive thought is very elaborate (not at all naive) and very efficient when it is not in contrast to scientific knowledge, but rather when complementing it.

[15] The 'exact' spelling of the name of Odin usually has little importance (Old Norse spells it Óðinn, in the nominative case). Some write it 'Odhinn' to stress two things. The first is that the exact letter is not a 'd', but the letter ð, specific to Old Norse, that is pronounced like the 'th' in

spirits, and by aiming to return to the patient the lost parts of his or her soul. Both the patient and practitioner must therefore attempt (humbly) to re-establish a dialogue with their primitive selves. However, this method never contradicts the application of modern health care techniques, except those that cause a long unconscious state, or that prevent patients from deciding for themselves.

My main sources of poems for pleas and charms will be: the Kalevala, whose chapter 17 is a goldmine of charms for expelling bad Spirits; the magical charms from the Scottish Highlands; the Anglo-Saxon charms; and those from Lithuania[16]. I will also use some runic inscriptions from the Middle Ages (namely: the Canterbury charm, the stick and cranium from Ribe, and the Sigtuna tablet). In a somewhat

---

'the'. The second 'n' marks the nominative case of the Old Norse so-called "strong masculine words." It is pronounced as in 'inn' with a 'n' that is very strongly pronounced at the end. In the use of the galdr that we will describe later, one sings/ howls the runes and the name of Gods, and it bodes better indeed to correctly pronounce the name of Odin. For those incapable of the 'th', do not distress too much, and that, by simple deference for the High One, they pronounce this 'dh' as a 'd', (without smacking the tongue on teeth), I am sure that Odin is not so silly, He will hear His name! In passing, I note that in the beginning of her CD, *The shades of Yggdrasil*, Freya Aswynn, a disciple of Odin if any, calls on Odin three times and that it resembles strangely the 'Om' of the Hindu because she hardly pronounces this notorious 'dh'.

[16] The Lithuanian charms, different from the chants (*dainos*) that are better known, are unpublished (in French, German or English) to the best of my knowledge. I received them from Lithuanian informants, pagan friends devoted to the rescue of the immense Lithuanian patrimony relative to Paganism. Indeed, Lithuania remained pagan until the end of 14th century and seems to have been little affected by the Inquisition. As an instance of present days pagan remains, I can witness that one of my Lithuanian colleagues, a distinguished statistician if any, who does not share my mystical choices at all, seems however very proud to assert that the last Pagan Lithuanian, one following his ancestors' religion, died as late as the 1970s.

peculiar way, the sixth main source of magical charms is the work of Saint Hildegard. Indeed, Saint Hildegard and her remedies are well known in Germany and Austria, especially because of physicians that are passionate about her work. These physicians are happy to recommend eating spelt (an ancient cereal of high nutritional quality – with which I prepare my own loaves of bread at home!), but they are a bit less enthusiastic when her remedies call for an owl beak and toad urine. And of course they all ignore the many magical invocations that she recommends. For example, she gives a general remedy as follows:

> When the leaves of the beech have not yet appeared again completely, go close to this tree, seize a branch with the left hand, and while holding a small knife in the right hand, say, "I cut your tartness, because you purify all humors that entail the man on error and injustice paths; by the living Word that made man without regret."
> With your left hand, hold a branch while you are saying this, then cut it with a steel blade and keep this branch all year long; and do this each year. (hilde1)

Saint Hildegard, working in the twelfth century and although crystallized in Christian devotions, is an image of the behaviors of her time, still impregnated with magic. Hildegard's invocations all make calls to the Christian God, obviously, but they are not any less magical in nature, and, in comparing her invocations to the ones that were current in the seventeenth century, they clearly maintain such tartness that most of their Heathen strength can still be felt. This is why I will quote all Saint Hildegard's charms, since this aspect of her work has scarcely been discussed until now.

Primitive medicine used pleas and supplications, actions of grace, and herbal concoctions to heal. Modern medicine has perfected herbal concoctions beyond anything previously imaginable, but, according to defenders of alternative medicine, it has failed on two important points. First, a complete healing is not always possible, sometimes the patient must learn to live with the sickness. Admittedly, remedies based on plants do not always give immediate results, but they provide a gentle treatment that lasts a lifetime, while modern remedies all tend to be relatively traumatic. Second, since we are also made of Spirit, the soul of the patient as much as the body and intellect have to be nursed. The healer tries to achieve this with a medicine based on magic. It addresses the souls of patients much more than their body, and it processes distant causes more than the immediate ones. Where various ceremonies of capital importance are considered infantile by rationalists, supplications and actions of grace, incantations, poems, and dances ensure a complete recovery when this is possible.

In the following chapters, you need to know the meaning of each rune in order to follow the way I suggest using them. For this reason I am providing now a brief interpretation for each rune, particularly concerning their medical use. I have tried to keep these as short as possible, since Volume 2 of this book (forthcoming), explains the meanings of the runes in much greater detail.

The Runes and Their Songs

This section is devoted to the explanations of what kind of power the runes wield. Before putting forward this power, it might be useful to put forward the possible hazards of this power.
The churches stressed a lot these dangers. For instance, Pierre de Lancre (a famous French inquisitor of the early

1600s) had this to say this about the magical ways of healing:

> As for these not understood characters
> conceived in the Hieroglyphs, engraved in
> unknown letters; all the superstitions... draw
> us toward diabolic curiosities. (lancr1)

De Lancre's writings suggest that it was the attraction to the so-called 'diabolic' that motivated the churches to ban the runes. That de Lancre was a torturer does not prevent him from having informative opinions. As a matter of fact, in the Middle Ages, the runes were no longer being used with the respect they deserve. They had become simply a way to write secret or pseudo-secret incantations, or messages. The Odense lead tablet, for example, carries Latin words written in runes (e.g. **"kristus uinkit kristus regnet kristus imperat"** which means: "Christ conquers, Christ reigns, Christ commands"), among these words, the formula **"agla"** (in runes) is found, which is known for being the first letters of the Hebrew words "attah gibbor leolam adonai," meaning "thou art strong to all eternity, Lord." This formula no longer is an invocation to the power of the rune Hagla or Hagala as was the case in earlier inscriptions. At the other extreme, one finds runic inscriptions like the Bergen inscription (on a stick of wood, probably from the beginning of the 13th century) which is some kind of obscene graffiti and can be translated as: "Jon of the silky cunt owns me, and Guttorm cunt-licker carved me, and Jon of the bumpy cunt reads me." What I want to show by citing these two examples is that over the years the runes completely lost their ancient Heathen sacredness.

The problem I see here does not come from using the runes for gaining some power over the world, since this is what the runes are made for. Nevertheless, as soon as power is gained, it can be misdirected and it can become dangerous. The formula of the Odense tablet misdirects a power originating from the ancient Heathen Gods, not from Christ. The Bergen inscription simply jokes at the power, which is possible only if you are absolutely convinced that this power does not exist. In fact, misdirecting power can take more subtle forms. For instance, I found it remarkable that so many hand healers, (and I have met many of them since I am also a Shiatsu practitioner), though their motivation is apparently very pure, are driven by an urge towards power, because obviously they think that they are doing the healing; they are not humbly waiting for the patient to heal. However, as we will see further on, one of the main principles of shamanic healing is that the Spirits heal, not the shamans, a point often largely underestimated by the shamans themselves. Again, the problem does not lie in the wish for power, but in mishandling power.

This is why we should not reject the churches' or de Lancre's opinion without thinking: Using the runes in view of gaining power is perfectly possible, but this is a choice which cannot be made lightly. Search your soul each time you use the runes, do not try to gain power, even a little, over Nature or humans without knowing the price to pay for this power.

Some of the interpretations I provide below are not usual. Next volume is devoted to explaining why I chose a particular interpretation against another one, relying on my knowledge of the Northern Middle Ages, of the runic inscriptions, on new interpretations of the various runic and Eddic poems, on yet unpublished runic verses, namely *Þrideilur Rúna, Nokvar Deylur, Malruna Deilr* (as the manuscripts spell them), and on various etymological dictionaries of the English, Old Norse, and German languages.

Fehu

Fehu is the rune of cattle or livestock; of the primitive animal force; of wealth, with all the negative aspects of wealth, but also the internal wealth that is the best aid against distress. It is to be invoked each time a sense of 'poverty' is felt, that is to say, a sense of being devoid of strength, without energy. Fehu enables the rebuilding of internal strength.

I see in Fehu the rune of the mild feminine forces, because I associate Fehu to the primitive cow who, in the Nordic myth, licked the first giant out of the original ice.

Cognates: German, *Vieh* ('cattle'); English, fee

Uruz

Uruz is the rune of the aurochs, of fertility, of the primitive feminine force, of the strength of health. It is also the fertile rain that pours upon the earth from the world tree (this is my meaning, taken from a personal interpretation of the runic poems). As the rune of the primal force of fertility, Uruz permits the healing of illnesses sent by bad spirits. It is the rune of the healing shaman who, from the Siberian tales, has been created by the Gods in order to protect the people from bad spirits.

I see Uruz as the rune of wild feminine forces, what could be inferred today as the 'masculine' side of the Goddess. I link this rune to the couple Nerthus-Njörd, with a strong emphasis on Nerthus (rune Ingwaz will be specifically associated to Njörd).

Thus the first two runes are dedicated to the feminine forces, Fehu represents the mild ones, Uruz the wild ones.

Cognates: German,   *Ur*   ('primordial',   'ancient'); German, *Auerochs* (aurochs)

Thurisaz

Thurisaz, rune of the 'thurs', the frost giants, the wild men, is the rune of primitive strength and masculine violence. It becomes the rune of protection from sharp weapons for the medieval warrior. Thurisaz can harm women with its deadly magical powers, like in the tale of Briar Rose as she is sent into a deep sleep from the prick of a spindle (thorn). This meaning has been lost in the Viking runes where, traditionally, Thurisaz is associated with the God Thor, the God symbolizing the masculine force, without the wildness associated with the Giants. Using the ancient Futhark, I devote Thurisaz only to the Thurs, Giants, and not to Thor, their fierce enemy.

This rune is generally dangerous for women. It represents brutal masculine strength. It should be used for a man (or for the masculine aspect of a woman) when there is an absence of energy. Use it with the greatest caution with women (or for the feminine aspect of a man).

Cognate: *Thurse* (in German and French) the name for giants of the frost, (and not cognate to Thor!). Runic inscriptions of the Viking Age (given in the books of Krause, Moltke, Antonsen, Makaev, see a simple version on my site: http ://www.nordic-life.org/nmh/) bear the name of Thor written as '**thur**' (in runes) while the one of the Giants is '**thurs**' or even simply '**thrs**'. This explains why some confusion took place.

Ansuz

Ansuz is the rune of the Gods who are usually symbolized by Odin.

It carries the most interesting features of Odin, but in particular, the purification that enables you to detach from your inner self. Ansuz evokes the Gods in so much as it evokes the Gods of poetry, of speech, and of liberation.

When the throat has a lump, when speech becomes difficult to hear, use Ansuz.

When you focus on your problems too much, when you need a breath of fresh air, use Ansuz.

Cognates: German and French *Ase* (called Aesir in modern English, taken directly from Old Norse), the name of the Norse Gods.

Raido

Rune of the shamanic journey.

The shamanic journey, as it was practiced originally by the Saami, is a dangerous affair, to the point that it will make a man impotent. It is therefore a rune for women.

The female rider or a woman-mare is a recurring Celtic myth. This is primarily why I recommend Raido for women who are burdened by life, who need a new start. It can also be useful for men needing to ride their own femininity, or needing to borrow femininity from a woman they are close to.

The shamanic journey and the rune Raido give the sorcerer's eye its power over the world.

Cognates: English, ride; German, *Ritt* (ride)

Kaunan (or Kenaz)

Kaunan is the rune of rot and putrescence (and not only of fire), and also of our internal fire, symbolizing the life force. It is the symbol of the narrow relationship between life and death. The internal fire is that of Life, as the heat of the boil is that of infection.

This rune helps healing the ailments magically sent by an enemy. It also provides internal heat, such as fever, to the parts of the body becoming sick or even putrid.

Related to the German *Kien* (torch), but its original meaning connects it to the idea of eruption, or chapping, which explains why Krause gives it the meaning of boil, ulcer (*Geschwur*). Moreover, the Old Norse name of this rune (*Kaun*) means boil, while it has taken the meaning of torch (*cen*) in Old English. Note that most people using the runes use it in the literal sense of 'torch, or fire', and not 'boil' or 'internal fire', as I do.

Gebo

Gebo is the rune of giving, of sharing, of friendship and equal relationships between humans. You would only utter this rune to someone who is truly very close to your heart. This rune is very important for the prevention of illness. Nothing is better for your health than to love another person. It is also the rune of the love within the constantly evolving type of marriage, it is therefore also advised for all psychological problems associated with solitude, and for trouble between partners.

Cognates: German, *Gabe* (gift); English, to give

Wunjo

Wunjo is related to physical pleasures, to the happiness of a quiet life, and not to the sort of ecstatic bliss that the mystics speak of so highly. It is the rune of the joy of living with ease in one's body. I also associate Wunjo with the pleasures and delights of making love.

Like Gebo, it does not apply to a specific illness in particular, but it treats everything by its joy of life.

Don't we have the right to a bit of tranquil happiness in this world? seems to be what Wunjo is kindly asking, in my view of this rune.

Wunjo, bliss, was eliminated in the Viking Futhark, as was Gebo.

Cognates: German, *Wonne* (bliss, joy); English, wonder

Hagla (or Haglaz)

According to Norse mythology, Hagla is the material out of which the world was formed, and in which all life finds its source. Hagla is the shamanic rune *par excellence* because it enables survival from the flames. It is the rune of hail, of purity, of the cold, of whiteness, and of the mastery of fire.

This rune is also for the shamans who come out purified from their contact with fire. Hagla is the rune that can fight against the serpents and the dragons that live inside us. As in the runic poems, the role of Hagla is to strike or attack these evil dragons.

Cognates: German, *Hagel* (hail); English, hail

Naudiz

Naudiz is linked with a sense of need, of necessity and shortage.

As the rune of necessity and fate, it represents therefore the power of the Norns. Its secondary power is to calm futile quarrels.

The acceptance of necessity and need, while submitting to the decisions of the Norns are characteristic of Germanic civilization.

This is not a healing rune, but a rune of acceptance. Knowing how to live with an illness, is one of the first wisdom of healing, and Naudiz helps us in this area.

Cognates: German, *Not* (necessity, need); English, need

Isaz

Isaz, as well as Thurisaz, Naudiz, and Hagla, is associated with the cold and therefore with the creation of the world.
Ice is the bridge that links the world of the dead with the world of the living: the poor soul of the departed is blind on this bridge, and needs a guide: the psychopomp shaman who takes the soul to its new dwelling place. Isaz represents, therefore, the bridge on which we travel to arrive in the land of the dead. Its power is in immobility, calm, and vastness. This rune prevents souls from getting lost and returning to haunt us.
Therefore, it enables the healing of ailments caused by a ghost.
Isaz, just like Hagla, is associated with the cold and also with the fight against the fevers that come with infections. In the runic poem that we saw earlier, a wolf was accused, it could have also been a serpent (though in this case, Hagla would have more likely been used).

Cognates: German, *Eis* (ice); English, ice

Jeran

Jeran, rune of the good year, of the abundant harvest, is associated with the God Frey. My first reading of *Gylfaginning* happened to be in French, in a version that said explicitly : "it is good to call upon him (Frey) for a fruitful year and for peace." This is why it has been slightly puzzling for me to see that American authors do not associate Jeran and Frey, in spite of this clear link in such a basic text as *Gylfaginning*. This confusion seems to be explained by the way the original Norse text, *til árs ok friðar*, was translated. English and German translations both give : "it is good to pray to him for prosperity and peace." However, *til árs ok friðar* means exactly "for a good year and peace" as any Old Norse dictionary will tell you. This expression is found in invocations to Frey, and has been kept, word for word, by the Christian church.

A similar ambiguity seems to have been transmitted in the Old English rune poem. The rune called *Ger* in this poem is translated by 'harvest' by Maureen Halsall, while any dictionary will tell you that *ger* or *gear* means year (and, by the way, the etymology of the English word 'year', in most dictionaries, relates it to Anglo-Saxon *ger*, and to Old Norse *ár*, and Proto-Germanic **jeran* or **jœran*).

Although Jeran actually means 'prosperous year', translators have been right to insist on the meanings they chose; however, in their translations, they lost the link with Jeran by highlighting 'prosperity' and forgetting 'year'.

This rune prevents the safe return of enemies from a shamanic journey, but its translation into positive magic helps in the safe return from such a journey.

As the rune of the prosperity of the community, it is most appropriately used for the health of the entire community rather than for an individual.

Cognates: German, *Jahr* (year); English, year

Ihwaz (or Iwaz)

Ihwaz, rune of the yew, is the rune of Yggdrasil, the world tree of Norse mythology; the rune of solitude, of the strength that we can depend upon.

The poetic Edda tells us that this is the rune females can depend on to treat their illnesses and that it is the one of masculine strength.

Celtic legends of Brittany tell us the story of how Lancelot killed Iweret, the man of the yew. The yew itself, as a powerful tree, was destroyed in our minds.

Because they stole the magical powers of women, or denied the existence of magical powers, men no longer need to depend on the "wife of another" (as says the poetic Edda) to teach them magic. They gain therefore a great independence, and as the yew tree, from majestic and powerful, they become small bushes.

Ihwaz is precious for illnesses that are the result of an imbalance.

Cognates :   German, *Eibe* (yew); English, yew; French *if* (and to the name, Yves, I am proud to say!)

Pertho

The meaning of the word *pertho* is still a mystery for scientific runologists (does it mean "fruit tree" or "table-game" or something else?), but for me, Pertho is saying either 'hall of feminine magic' or 'hall for the warrior-women'. The existence of such she-warriors is attested in a text of the 6th century, due to a historian of Goth nationality (Jordanes) who describes warlock women, called All-run or Allrunnae, who were expelled from the Goth army around the year 400, or before. Feminine magic is not reduced to the handling of maternity, even though it includes it.

It is thus the rune of Frigg, symbolizing maternity, devotion to children, and the chthonic (coming from the earth) magic of primitive mothers often illustrated by the Disir[17]. It is

---

[17] The Disir are somewhat mysterious divinities, related to the Norns, perhaps less harsh than the Norns.

however also the rune of the warrior woman who accepts maternity, but who does not reduces her life to it.

Because of its open form, I see it as symbolizing the 'open' woman, in other words, pregnant with child, but also open to knowledge, and power.

This rune carries all the strength of a mother who protects her children.

It is drawn "on the palm of the woman giving birth," therefore helping in giving birth. Tracing Pertho in the palm of the woman in labor will certainly not take away all the pain, but it will make her feel less alone, and it is a good way to communicate during labor. In any case, and although more mundane, it will be an excellent hand massage of the woman about to give birth.

Pertho, tragically, does not have a cognate in any modern language.

Algiz

Algiz is the rune of the elk, certainly, but above all else, it is the rune of intellect. This is also the rune of stupidity, insanity, therefore it is also used as a protection against these two evils through intelligence and healthy spirits. Algiz can also help to be aware when what we call insanity becomes poetical inspiration or prophetic trance.

As opposed to most people, I do not use it as a rune of protection.

The word *algiz* is cognate to the German *Elch* (elk) and the English, elk. Mystical users of the runes have given some fancy etymology relating it to 'protection'. I did not find the least trace of such a possibility in the works of the linguists.

Sowelo

Sowelo is the rune of the sun, and of a joyous victory. It seems to contain the beneficial aspects of the runes of Joy. In fact, we must remember that an easy victory is also the one that brings the least experience, that will leave you unarmed against future serious enemies where an easy victory is never possible.
The sick need to conquer illness. Using Sowelo can help defeat illness without leaving any definitive traces. The price, however, is that the patient gains nothing.

Cognates: German, *Sonne* (sun); English, sun

Tiwaz

Tiwaz is the rune of Tyr, God of the Sky, and of the victory obtained at great pain, just as Tyr defeated Fenris, the wolf, and in doing so, lost his hand. It is also the rune of the shaman blacksmith who is capable of forging a new life.
Deeply, Tiwaz is the counterpart of Sowelo: joyous victory carries negative aspects as we have already discussed, and the grievous victory, linked with Tiwaz, consequently carries wisdom, experience, and the courage to face one's fears.
As a medical rune, Tiwaz is obviously the one for victory over an illness that has been battled for a long time, the one therefore that requires some time to respond to, but that also carries a profound knowledge of a healthy body.
Tiwaz must be used when we are ready to make sacrifices in order to beat the illness.

Cognate: Tiw or Tyr, the name of a God. (God of the Sky. Also qualified as an ancient God of war.)

Berkanan

Experts agree that the birch, the tree with the most colorful leaves in the Norse forests, was the first sign of spring, and played an important role in Germanic fertility rituals. Therefore, there is a general tendency to attribute feminine power to Berkanan. In the runic poems, the association is more to feminine beauty than to her fertility.

Berkanan, the birch, is the rune of Freya, the free and independent mother who no longer carries a child, the shining beautiful woman who stuns men – and other women.

It is the typical rune of protection for a woman who wants to feel beautiful, and be active and free.

The birch is the tree of the world for Siberians, so I see it as a feminine counterpart to Ihwaz. Berkanan is the feminine aspect of the tree of the world. In this sense, this rune is for sick men who need to emphasize feminine power.

Cognates: English, birch; German, *Birke* (birch). The etymology of *Birke* also connects it to the meaning 'bright'.

Ehwaz

Ehwaz is the rune of the horse. The female rider or the mare is such a recurring myth that it is also the rune of the mare.

The horse is also one of the animals that is most used for practicing shamanism, bringing the shaman into the spirit world on its back. This is the triple sense of Ehwaz: horse, female rider, and means of travel to the spirit world. We find some runic inscriptions containing 'ehw' that are certainly an invocation of one of these three forces.

The horse was dedicated to Frey: Ehwaz is certainly close to Frey, although the rune specifically associated with Frey is Jeran.

Misguided etymology makes many confuse 'mare' (female horse), and 'mare' (bad dream) as in 'nightmare'. Linguistics assert that the two words, even though identically spelled, are different. This is why I do not link Ehwaz with any kind of bad dreams.

Cognate: Old Norse, *Eh* (horse). It seems that the root Ehw- and the word *Eh* have no derivatives in either English or German. They come from an Indo-European root *ekw- (horse) that has given *equus* in Latin and *hippos* in Greek. Thus, one can say that Ehwaz is related to French *équestre*, and to English 'equestrian', but, clearly, these words did not develop from proto-Germanic *Ehwaz.

Mannaz

Speech between individuals creates humanity like fire creates a blaze in passing from one tree to another. Mannaz, rune of humanity, of fraternity and of human activity, and therefore of communication between people, also represents the fragility and futility of man's destiny. It brings the knowledge of the Gods to humans.
It lets us fight against all the problems that arise from too much isolation, an absence of contact with other humans. In teaching us about the Gods, it also lets us fight the soul hardening that is due to our scientific vision of the universe.

Cognate: English, man and human; German, *Mensch* (human).

Laukaz

Almost everyone calls it Laguz (water), as most runescripts do. I agree with Krause who calls it Laukaz (leek). My arguments for following what some modern runologists consider to be "Krause's fancy" are well explained on my site at the end of the text called "runic inscriptions." Laukaz is the rune of the leek, garlic, onion, and all the roots with a burning taste. As pointed at by the Eddic poem *Völuspa*, stanza 4, the very first herb to grow after the Gods created our earth is *grænom lauki*: green leeks. The leek, the onion are vegetables full of water and they bear all the disinfecting properties of water. The Vikings made it the rune of water, and this is why I think, it expresses the vital, gushing strength that we find in water and in the God Thor.

Contrary to almost everyone else who links Thor with rune Thurisaz, I found many reasons in the texts to link Thor with Laukaz.

Laukaz protects against poisoning. It also includes some properties of conservation that are linked to onions since the Norse embalmed with onions.
This rune conserves, preserves, dresses wounds, and prevents their infection.

Let Thor protect us!

Cognate: German, *Lauch* ('leek'); English, leek.

Under its Old Norse form (*Lagu*), it means 'water' and its meaning is therefore related to the French, *lac*, and to English lake which was borrowed from French. Nevertheless, they are not direct cognates since the word *lac* comes from Latin, and is not related to *Lagu*.

Ingwaz

Ingwaz, rune of the God Ing is the rune of a journey toward primitive strength that will bring an abundance of good. I identify it with Njörd (in opposition to almost everyone else who attributes it to Frey, his son). Njörd brings needed wealth to those who implore him.

This rune is essentially used for recharging, or rediscovering your primitive energy.

Frey is often called "Ingvi Frey," as I do myself in chapter 4. Ingvi is also a way to say 'king' in skaldic poetry. It seems easy to see why some would attribute Ingwaz to Ingvi Frey. My main argument against this attribution is that the rune Ingwaz disappeared from the Viking Futhark (it is only found only in the Elder, or Germanic, Futhark). Frey was one of the most important Viking Gods; I cannot imagine why the Vikings would have deleted His rune.

It is cognate to the name of the God Ing.

Dagaz

Dagaz is the rune of day, with every meaning of the word. In Norse mythology, it precedes the sun, and is the son of Night, a giantess. It contains, therefore, the continuation of all the terrors of the night, besides its qualities as a messenger of light. It could well be the rune of Hel (the Norse dwelling of those not dead in battle, which has nothing to do with the terrible hell of the Christians) that prevents ghosts from returning to the world of the living.

As the rune of light, it freezes the demons and transforms them into stone. Therefore, resort to this rune when you want to put some light on a problem. I am thinking, obviously, of all the problems locked away in what psychoanalysts call the unconscious. Dagaz is the rune that chases away old demons.

Cognates: English, day; German, *Tag* (day)

Othala (or Othila)

In Othala, rune of family property and linked to ancestors, I see the rune of the seið. It can let a man practice a shamanic journey without losing his virility. Simultaneously, it honors homosexuals who accept the burden of becoming a shaman. Along with Berkanan, it is the rune of Loki, the sometimes-man/sometimes-woman God.

Classically, Othala is associated with family property and not with the other roles that I have just described.

As the rune of seið, it should not only be practiced by people in good health, but by people with extraordinary strength, those who benefit from a good balance between their diverse pulls, etc. It is not a rune to invoke at all when we are sick or weak.

Cognate to German *Adel* ('nobility'), to Old English *eðel* ('homeland'). The German *Adel und Edel*, which means 'nobility of birth and nobility of soul' helps us to get the full meaning of Othala.

Sigrdrifa's Rune Songs

A very beautiful text in the poetic Edda, the Lay of Sigrdrifa, contains the runic teachings of the Valkyrie Sigrdrifa (equivalent to Brunhild in the German myths), as they were given to Sigurdr (Siegfried in German) after he had awakened her. This text describes nine songs which indicate the nine powers of the runes. They are the runes of Joy, Victory, Magic, Protection, Birth, Undertow, Branches, Speech and Spirit. My web site explains in detail exactly how I was able to attribute a song for each of the runes, by analyzing each of the songs with attention to the minutest detail as well as the material or place where each rune should be engraved.

Here are the attributions that I have recreated:
  Runes of Joy : Jeran, Wunjo, Gebo.
  Runes of Victory : Sowelo, Dagaz, Ehwaz.
  Runes of Magic : Thurisaz, Othala, Naudiz, Algiz.
  Runes of Protection : Laukaz, Fehu, Tiwaz
  Runes of Birth: Pertho, Berkanan.
  Runes of Undertow: Ihwaz, Isaz.
  Runes of Branches : Kaunan, Uruz.
  Runes of Speech: Mannaz, Ansuz.
  Runes of Spirit: Raido, Hagla, Ingwaz.

Six runes have a double attribution :
  Thurisaz, a rune of Magic and Victory,
  Ingwaz, a rune of Protection and Spirit,
  Tiwaz is a rune of Victory and Protection,
  Hagla is of both Spirit and Magic,
  Isaz, rune of Undertow and Protection,
  Algiz is a rune of Magic and Branches.

APPENDIX TO CHAPTER 1

Runes and Divination

I found three sources that describe without ambiguity the use of staves (upon which runes **might** have been written) in order to 'perform a divination'.

In *The Book of Settlements*, (originally called *Landnamabok*, which describes how the Icelandic land was distributed among its first inhabitants, number 198 of the Sturlubok version, translated by H. Palsson and P. Edwards, University of Manitoba Press, 1972, p. 91), we find:

> There was a man called Onund the Sage who took possession of land above Merkilgill ... When Eirik was going to take possession of the valley to the west, Onund cast the *divining rod* to find out when Eirik would set out to make his claim. Onund got in first [and] shot a tinder-arrow across the river to claim the land ... (saga13)

The word translated by Palsson and Edwards as 'divining rod' is *blòtspàn* (*blòtspòn* in other versions). *Blòt* is a sacrifice and *spàn* or *spòn* (cognate with English 'spoon') has several meanings, including stick or stave. Thus, it means exactly 'sacrificial rod' with no hint at divination. The translation "divining rod" is thus misleading, even though Onund does indeed perform a divination.

In the *Ynglinga saga*, chap. 38, King Graumar goes to Uppsala to make a sacrifice:

> Then the oracle of the staves foretold him that he would not live much longer. (saga14)

The word used in this text is: *spànn* = sacrificial stave, as we have already seen.

In these two instances, each text is certainly describing a divination using sticks and runes may possibly have been written on them. It is also possible that the authors of these texts, certainly Latin knowledgeable scholars, might have been influenced by their culture, and could not accept that the sticks decided (or changed) the future rather than simply announcing future events.

In *De inventione litterarum* found in René Derolez, (*Runica Manuscripta*, p. 355) a note precedes each of the rune sections of the A and B texts:

Text A: "With these letters they [*the nordmanni, i.e. Danes*] 'signify' their songs, incantations and divinations [for] they are still given to pagan practices"

Text B: "They gave the names *runestabas* [*rune-staves*] to these letters, I believe, because by writing them they used to bring to light secret things"

Only the first of these notes speaks of divination in relation with the runes without ambiguity, as a possible use among others. Moreover, those are notes, (i.e. late additions), made by someone who can be reasonably supposed to be a scholar, hence very knowledgeable in the Latin habits, which would hamper his objectivity.

Now, if we look at the rest of the evidence, we shall see that each of them might have been describing another operation, namely a request for permission, rather than a divination.

Caesar (*Gallic Wars*) reports that one of his friends, Gaius Valerius Procillus was on an embassy to the German leader Ariovistus; they treated him as a prisoner of war and cast lots three times, in his presence, to decide whether or not to put him to death at once by burning, but each time the lots came out so that the execution was postponed.

This text shows that the lots were cast in order to ask some kind of permission to kill a man. One could see a divination

("Will nothing bad happen to us if we kill this man?"), but the text itself describes something else.

Tacitus, in *Germania* 10, p. 109, says:

> Their procedure in casting lots is always the same. They cut off a branch of a nut-bearing tree and slice it into strips; these they mark with different signs and throw them completely at random onto a white cloth. Then the priest of the state, if the consultation is a public one, or the father of the family if it is private, offers a prayer to the gods, and looking up at the sky picks up three strips, one at a time, and reads their meaning from the signs previously scored on them. If the lots forbid an enterprise, there is no deliberation that day on the matter in question; if they allow it, confirmation by the taking of auspices is required.

Most of the text hints at a divination, until you get to the last sentence which says that divination was done in another way. Tacitus goes on by describing the process by which these Germans would foresee: by interpreting the neighing of a sacred white horse. Again, the lots seem to be cast here in order to ask for permission, not to foresee.

Alcuin's *Vita Willibrordi* describes the old Frisian legal practice of determining whom "the god" judges guilty by the casting of lots three times, three days in succession. Once more, we see a practice that asks for permission, and not a divination.

Rimbert's *Life of Ansgar* tells how the Swedish king Anund suggested that the Danes cast lots to discover if it were indeed the will of the gods to destroy the town Birka, a place in which great and powerful deities had been worshipped.

The result was that "it would be impossible to accomplish their purpose without endangering their own welfare and that God would not permit this place to be ravaged by them," thus that they had to avoid taking such a course of actions. Again, the text is quite clear in showing that the Swedes asked if they could be allowed to destroy Birka, and it was denied to them.

The Eddic poems refer to the runes several times, almost always to act on someone, healing, seducing, bewitching, against evil (stanza 137 of *Havamal*) or the like. There are two instances in the *Havamal* where runes are cited without showing a direct action on reality.
One is stanza 80 of *Havamal*. Boyer's translation says, p. 183:

> That is now proved,
> what you asked of the runes,
> coming from the gods
> which the supreme gods made
> and the mighty world master stained,
> it is best to stay silent.

If this stanza means anything at all, it means that it is better not to speak of what is learned by the runes, which precludes a divination use.
The second one is stanza 111, which says (Boyer's translation p. 189):

> It is time to declaim
> from the sage's high-seat,
> at the spring of Urdr;
> I saw and I kept silent,
> I saw and I thought
> I heard the speech of men;
> I heard talk of the runes
> they were not silent about their power

at the High One's hall,
in the High One's hall;
this is what I heard: ...

And the poem goes on until stanza 164, giving good advice to a person named Loddfafnir, and teaching him eighteen possible uses of the runes, (we shall discuss these in detail when studying each rune in turn, in the second volume of this book). None of the teachings given to Loddfafnir speak specifically of the future; they are simply plain good sense (for instance: "on mountain or fjord should you happen to be traveling, make sure you are well fed"). Anyhow, this second stanza explicitly describes runes as providing good advice, which fits perfectly well with the role of 'asking for permission' I found earlier.

At this point, I hope I have given readers everything they need to draw their own conclusions. My own conclusion is that two different attested roles for the runes can be found. One is to change physical reality, the second one is as advice-givers. It looks like the runes were used to ask what was the price to pay for achieving some result. If the price was too high then they were 'forbidden' to perform the desired deeds. This use can obviously be looked upon as a foretelling, but it is of a completely different kind than foretelling, as the word is understood today.
In the context of this book, both reality modifiers and advice-givers are roles the runes can play to help us in a healing process, or to tell us what is the cost of finding back good health.

Chapter 2

THE HEALING OF VÄINÄMÖINEN AND LEMMINKÄINEN

> The runic verses [*that form the basis of the Kalevala*] will probably be the last ones to disappear from our minds; because, despite all the care that the clergy took to uproot these prejudices of the people's spirit, the Finn do not like these songs any less, and they keep them, strongly convinced that they have occult virtues, and a great power, when we turn to them in time ...
>
> ***Voyage au Cap-Nord, par la Suède, la Finlande et la Laponie***, Joseph Acerbi, Paris, 1804, t.2, p. 99.

The Kalevala is a very rich source of information and I'm going to use it here as a sort of case study for the magical healing of three different injuries or illnesses: the physical wounds of Väinämöinen; the death of Lemminkäinen, miraculously revived by his mother; and the psychological wounds of Lemminkäinen. All three examples show how important it is to recite pleas or poems during the healing treatment. I want to recapture these pleas, these poems, and associate them to a *galdr*. A galdr is of a few runes catching the deep meaning of a poem, and that are sung or screamed, as we will see in chapter four. In this chapter, we will look at the healing process as a whole. Before doing so, I'd just like to say a few words about the validity of the Kalevala.

The Kalevala is a collection of legends and songs gathered from the beginning of the 19th century, in Finland and in the region of Saint Petersburg, by a Finish doctor, Elias Lönnrot. He reconstructed this oral knowledge into 50 songs arranged as a sort of epic that scholars refer to as a Nordic Odyssey. As this beautiful text is largely unknown to the public, it gives me great pleasure to cite long extracts, that I hope will convince you of the Kalevala's extraordinary poetic qualities.

Lönnrot collected many folk chants while completing his field work in Finland, but instead of publishing them as they were, he put them together into a coherent epic. Clearly, modern ethnology no longer works this way, and many have criticized Lönnrot for having left a personal touch when gathering the poems. A summary of these criticisms can be found in *Finish Folk Poetry* which publishes a translation of some of the poems collected by ethnologists, before and especially after Lönnrot. This collection of poems, making up hundreds of thousands of verses, created the "Base of Finnish Literature." From reading the texts given in *Finish Folk Poetry*, and the criticisms of Lönnrot, the following conclusions can be made about the difference between texts of the Kalevala and those collected by ethnologists.

First of all, and this seems essential, no one has accused Lönnrot of having actually 'elaborated' on the texts that he collected. He kept them essentially in their original form. The texts collected do not themselves form a long epic like the Kalevala, but they make up most of it. The best Finnish bards always tried to join these sections to make them form a complete story exactly as Lönnrot did. He is, therefore, still within the Finnish bardic tradition, but he pushed the system to its extreme by creating one epic, uniting all the sparse themes that were collected. The mistake made by many has been to believe that this epic, authored by Lönnrot, was an exact image of Finnish folk culture. My personal conclusion is that Lönnrot's work has achieved great success, which he should be congratulated for, and shame on those who complain about it. What is true, just as Lönnrot said, is that he united, in the Kalevala, a great number of texts representing an authentic part of Finnish popular culture.

If you read the individual poems that were collected directly in the field, you will find that they match up almost perfectly with the exception of two main differences.

When the folk poem contained something coarse or vulgar, Lönnrot eliminated it and replaced it with a more acceptable version for his mid-19th century readers, and he should be reproached for these untimely modifications. The case quoted most often by those wanting to belittle him is "the ant pissing on the leg of a crane"[18]. Eliminating this description,

---

[18] Aside from my topic, and because I have been long very curious about it, I'll give you one version of this story: Väinämöinen has stolen the *sampo*, a magical music instrument, from Northland, a place named *Pohja* or *Pohjala*. He is silently fleeing away but a crane's cry awakens the people of *Pohja* and they start chasing him:

> … so on the third day
> an ant, a ballocking boy
> pissed on the leg of a crane,
> in dark Pohjala.
> The crane let out a great squawk
> Screeched out in an evil tone:
> The whole of Pohjala woke
> The evil realm was awake.

(*word for word citation*, kuusi1)

as Lönnrot did, is certainly regrettable, but it is also important to know that this happened very rarely.

The folk poems are also bristling with many Christian allusions, and Lönnrot systematically eliminated them, and for this he should be thanked, even if, in fact, it distorts the exact image of Finnish folk culture of the mid-19th century.

From the viewpoint of understanding the magical attitudes of the Nordic peoples, a viewpoint that particularly concerns us here, we could criticize Lönnrot's text. He is not a folklorist, and some poems are obviously tinged by Christianity and designed for discrediting Heathen beliefs (this, despite the selective practices of Lönnrot relative to Christianity). Despite these faults, the Kalevala is certainly the greatest text left to us, describing the shamanic customs of the people of the northern countries, even though sometimes a bit too 'modern'. The principal God, for example, is always the Sky God, whether called Ukko, or Jumala. Jumala means god in modern Finish. Ukko is rather a familiar name given to God. In modern Finish a wife may speak of her "Ukko" meaning her husband, as she would say in English "the old chap" or "the old man." This obviously evokes at once Odin who is so often called the Old One in the Edda. All this tells us that the Mother Goddess was already forgotten, unfortunately.

The Kalevala constitutes the only text of this kind written with so much detail about magical healing. The ninth song of the Kalevala, dedicated to the healing of Väinämöinen summarizes the medicine that was practiced at this time, joining magic and good sense. The fifteenth song, dedicated to the resurrection of Lemminkäinen, describes the greatest medical deed possible: how to give life back to a corpse. This last song, though hardly credible, contains characteristics that are common to the previous one, and this enables us to make some interesting generalizations. The fourteenth song, dedicated to Lemminkäinen's quest for a 'ghost elk', also describes a healing, in my opinion, of a psychic illness, using good sense, and admitting, in a way, the existence of the patient's delusions, something I think we would like to see more often these days.

The many citations of the Kalevala are my version, taken from several other versions. Bosley's translation being a kind of English standard, and for the reader's convenience, I will put references to the page of this translation that contains the same information as mine. Nevertheless, I never cited Bosley's text.

The principal hero in the epic is "the old (or eternal) Väinämöinen," as he is called in the text. Väinämöinen is searching for a companion. He meets a marvelous young woman, who is half woman half rainbow, and she agrees to follow him in his sled with the condition that he builds a boat. Väinämöinen does this, and for two days, the work goes well,

> But on the third day,
> Hiisi turned the handle,
> Lempo[19] diverted the blade
> A bad spirit shook the handle:
> The axe hit a rock
> And the edge of the blade hit the cliff
> And the axe bounced off the rock
> And the blade slid into flesh,
> In the knee of the valorous,
> In the toe of Väinämöinen. (kal1)

Thus, three demons come together to wound Väinämöinen. He reacts immediately; he turns to his magical powers to heal himself.

> He started then to sing charms
> Starting to chant:
> He said all the Origins
> And the spells in the right order.
> But he couldn't remember
> Some of the fantastic words of steel
> That could serve as a barrier,

---

[19] Hiisi and Lempo are two bad demons often met in the Kalevala.

That would serve to firmly end
These slashes from the iron,
These gashes from the blue steel. (kal2)

From this, we see the importance given to the 'Origins' that describe the sacred beginning of the world around us. The poem will come back to this point further on. Väinämöinen is missing some knowledge about the spell that would close a wound as great as his. He therefore searches throughout the countryside for help, but without much success, asking:

In this house, is there someone
Who can treat the deed of iron,
Who can stop this flood,
Who can hold this terrible blood? (kal3)

Finally, he meets someone who is able to save him:

An old man lived on the stove,
A gray beard under the ridge.
The old man muttered from his stove,
The gray beard exclaimed:
We have closed off worse things before,
We have overcome greater things before,
With the three words of the Creator,
The decrees of the profound Origins. (kal4)

After noticing the seriousness of the wound, the old man admits that he is missing knowledge of the origin of iron, knowledge that would be needed to treat a wound that serious.

I remember other words,
But I can not recall the ones
Of the Origins of iron,
Where from slag comes. (kal5)

The old man, therefore, has to know the Origins of iron in order to heal the wounds inflicted by this iron[20]. When a viper bites, the type of the venom injected is obviously important, and, more generally, everyone agrees that the cause of illness should be known in order to treat it effectively. Even in the case of an accident, this primitive medicine does not dissociate the treatment from the cause[21].

---

[20] This view lasted quite late but then became ridiculous when the religious faith associated with magic became totally forgotten. For example, until the 17th century, the notion of applying an ointment to a weapon that had been used to cause the wound creates a degenerate image of this view. A book from the middle of the 17th century explains that by plunging the weapon in the ointment, we help the blood spirit to get back to body of the wounded, and thus the wound can be healed from a distance. This book, *A Late Discourse ... touching the Cure of Wounds by the Powder of Sympathy*, from Sir K. Digby (published between 1630 and 1658), was so popular that it had 29 successive editions. This author boasts that every surgeon-barber of the time knew the formula of the ointment. Moreover, these beliefs have survived until present day through country witches.

This craze started in England in the 1630s and reached Europe in the 1640s. It is quite noticeable that amid this craziness, some minds still had a clear view of the truth. Jean-Baptiste Van Helmont, a Belgian doctor and chemist who believed in the efficiency of this kind of treatment, declared around 1640 in his *De sympatheticis mediis* : "I always noticed that this remedy (the powder of sympathy) succeeds when it is used with a hearty will ... it has almost no efficiency when the one who prescribes it, does so with a superficial thinking ... the ideas moved by the wish to do good reach far, as does the influence of the stars ..." (cited by Dr. Cabanès, *Remèdes d'autrefois*, Maloine, Paris 1913, p. 181).

I raise my horn in memory of this kindred spirit !

[21] Modern medicine does indeed look for causes, when a rational argument links the sickness or the wounds to their cause. Only rational links are accepted, mystical ones are forgotten or even despised. The kind of ancient medicine we are speaking of here takes into account very far away causes that show no obvious link to the sickness, even some that might be looked upon nowadays as ridiculous.

Let's return now to Väinämöinen, who, fortunately, knows the Origins of iron:

> Ukko, Sky God,
> Rubbed his palms together
> On his knees.
> And from this were born three daughters,
> All three daughters of a kind
> To be the mothers of rust-colored iron,
> Conceivers of the blue steel.
> The daughters ... expressed their milk upon the earth,
> Letting their breasts burst ...
> She who expressed black milk,
> From her, was born soft iron;
> The one that expressed white milk,
> From her were made all things steel;
> She who poured out red milk,
> From her we obtained cast iron. (kal6)

The old man is delighted to have gained this knowledge:

> The old man grumbled on his stove,
> The beard sang and the head shook:
> I now know the Origins
> Of iron, I know the voice of the steel. (kal7)

Before starting to treat Väinämöinen's wound, the old man addresses himself to iron, so as to become familiar, or friendly with it.

> I pity you poor iron,
> Poor iron and unfortunate slag,
> And steel, victims of sorcery!...
> Who told you to do wrong,
> Who forced you to be bad?...
> You have committed
> A horrible action yourself,

Sliced the death colored opening.
Go! Know this,
Fix these bad ways
Before I tell your mother,
Oh, that I don't complain to your parents! (kal8)

The old man knows therefore, that the 'badness' of iron is
not without reason, and linked to bad treatments that the
blacksmith made him submit to. This is how he tries to enter
into the good graces of iron. Since he knows his Origins, he
can get 'him' into trouble by complaining to 'his parents'. In
fact, he treats iron like a child who is more unruly than bad,
and he is trying to appease him. When the Spirit of iron is
appeased, then the old man can address the Spirit of blood.
Thus, the communication with iron is but a stage in the
healing. Reducing the healing to this stage only, as the magic
of the 17th century did, is to forget the greatest part of the
treatment. The following long citation is filled up with
various incantations to blood, they are a good example of the
kind of incantations you can write yourself to address a
patient's blood.

Blood, hold your spilling
Gore, hold your rippling
Stop squirting on me,
And splashing on my breast!
Blood, hold yourself well, like a wall,
Liquids, form a barrier,
Hold firmly, like an iris on a lake,
Like a reed on the moss,
Like a boulder at a field's edge,
Like a rock in the rapids!
If you need to
Move yourself a bit more,
Then let it be in the flesh,
Slide yourself along in the bones!
Inside, it is best for you

Under the skin you will be well -
Better to run in the veins,
Sliding yourself along the bones,
Than to lose yourself on the ground,
Dripping in the dust.
Your destiny, milk, is not to ooze out
On the grass, perfect blood,
Softness of the heart of man, on the grass,
On a mound, dearest of friends:
Your place is in the heart,
The lungs are your refuge;
Come back home,
Run to take refuge there!
You are neither a river for running,
Nor a pool to fill,
Nor a swamp to gurgle,
No ship will sink in you.
Stop running now, my darling,
You, the red, of falling.
If you can't stop yet, then clot!
The waterfall Tyrjä did it once,
The river Tuoni clotted,
The sea drained itself, the skies dried
During this long year of clear skies,
Of fires that none could master.
If you don't take all this into account,
We will think of other things,
Other means will be used: I cry
That Hiisi gives me a cauldron
In which the blood will be boiled,
The gore heated,
Without one drop seeping out,
Not one red drop will fall,
The blood will not be lost on the earth,
The gore will not rush out anymore.
Would I not be a man of size
To stop this flow,

Able fellow, son of Ukko,
To control the torrent of the veins,
Then heavenly father,
Jumala under the clouds,
Important to humans,
Respected by people,
Close the mouth of the blood,
Stop that which hastens outwards.
Oh! Ukko, heavenly creator,
Jumala who reigns in the skies,
Come here when you are needed,
Take this way when we call you:
Hold out your fleshy hand
And press with your chubby thumb,
Close this offending gap,
Close this cursed door;
Lay down upon it a soft leaf,
A water lily you will apply to it
To block the path of the blood,
To stop that which is moving,
That it will stop splashing on my beard,
And pouring on my clothes!
Thus he closes the mouth of the blood,
He barred the path of the gore.
(kal9)

Now that the iron and the blood have quieted down, now that the wounds have stopped producing gore, the old man dedicates himself to what we would today call proper medical action: he prepares a drug. Obviously, this medicine would have some magical properties, as we shall see later.

                ... He sent
        His son into the workshop
        To prepare a balm
        From these bails of hay,
        From the points of those with the thousand leaves

Who spills honey on the earth,
From where flows a brooklet of mead.
...
He meets an oak tree,
He asks this oak tree:
Do you have honey on your branches,
Or mead on your bark? ...
He took a few splinters of oak,
Some pieces of the brittle tree;
He took some good plants,
All sorts of herbs,
Some that we don't get here,
Growing all over far away.
He put a pot on the fire,
He made his concoction boil
All together with the bark of the oak,
With the good herbs.
The pot boiled and grumbled
In all for three nights,
Three days of spring. (kal10)

The son, responsible for preparing the balm, checks to see if what he got is good enough for treating Väinämöinen's wounds. The first time, he notices that:

The balms were not reliable,
We could not count on the remedies.
He added some plants,
Numerous herbs
That we had brought
Back from all over,
Collected from a hundred journeys,
By nine of the magical eye,
[*that is to say, nine sorcerers*]
From the heights that treat illness.
He cooked them for three more nights,
For nine whole nights.

> He removed the pot from the fire,
> Looking if the balms were reliable,
> If we could count on these remedies. (kal11)

We note that the account of days is somewhere wrong here since the medicine is cooked twice three nights, that do not account for a total of nine nights. It seems that the poet forgot one seemingly useless cooking.

Väinämöinen's son notices, finally, that the medications were effective.

> He checked the balms,
> He looked at the remedies,
> Trying them on the cracks in the rock,
> On the splits in the boulders:
> And then, the rock stuck to the rock, the boulders joined the boulders. (kal12)

Nobody can miss the magical side of this doing. Notice as well its rationality, less obvious to grasp. The balm had to be somewhat sticky, thus it should not flow on the rocks it was put upon, it should not flow in a hole between two rocks, thus 'sticking' (actually, bridging) them together.

Now that the apprentice has correctly prepared the potion, the master verifies its properties.

> The old man tries them with his tongue,
> Tasting them in his mouth.
> And he knew the drugs
> Were good, the ointments reliable. (kal13)

This phase corresponds to the many chemical and biological tests that modern medicine is supposed to undergo. Knowing the amount of protests risen (at least in France!) by consumers associations against the lack of seriousness in the way those tests are driven, I find it remarkable that this step was not forgotten by primitive Nordic medicine.

So he coats Väinämöinen
He heals the unfortunate -
He coats him underneath,
On top, splashing on the middle. (kal14)

We should note here that the ointment is applied, it seems, on Väinämöinen's whole body and not just on his wound, which hints that this balm is not looked upon as a local medicine, but as a global one, as are the modern internal medicines. A similar attitude is found in an Anglo-Saxon charm that insists on smearing the sick person on the head first, "be the sore where it may." (as8, p.113)
These actions, proper medical actions in the modern sense of the term, are potentially effective, yet the healer adds a new plea, to ask the potion to deliver its efficiency. In this plea, the healer insists that she is not the cause of the healing, but the God of the sky Jumala in this example, the Gods in many Heathen approaches, or the Spirits in the case of Shamanism.

He pronounces this speech,
He speaks these words:
"It is not my body that moves,
But the flesh of Jumala,
I don't move by my own power,
But by the power of Ukko.
I don't speak from my own mouth,
But from the mouth of the Creator.
My mouth may be soft,
Even softer is His mouth;
And if my hand is true,
Even truer is His hand." (kal15)

Relatively ironically, as do modern medicines, the ointments produce some after effects:

When the ointments were applied

And the medicines were reliable,
They made him almost lose consciousness.
Väinämöinen fainted:
He moved here, and moved there
But never found any rest. (kal16)

The old man reacts against these after effects by bandaging
the wound, doing so with a new plea. I think that we can
generalize from this example. Here he performs something
necessary, even in the absence of after effects. It is the stage
of re-education, in which the healer gives independence back
to the patient (here by a bandage). More generally, we are
describing here, all the treatments that help patients to regain
their balance once they are rid of the most serious symptoms.

So, the old man drove out the pain,
Throwing out the painful points
As far as the middle of Kipumäki Hill
[*"the hill of sickness and pain"*],
To the peak of Mount Kipu-vuori [*"the mount of pain"*]
To make the rock suffer,
To break the boulders.
He took a handful of silk,
Unrolled it into cloth,
Cut it into strips,
Made bandages out of it;
He tied this silk,
Wrapped with these beautiful strips
The knee of the valorous,
The leg of Väinämöinen. (kal17)

Once the treatment is done, the healer makes another last
plea to the Gods.

He makes this speech,
Says these words:
"Let the Lord's silk be a bandage,

The Lord's cape a blanket
For this healed knee
For these reliable legs!
Look now, Oh! Beautiful Jumala,
Keep him, true Creator,
That he will not be taken into pain,
That nothing brings back the wound!" (kal18)

The healing is thus achieved, the wound closed, in such a
way that the flesh is now even healthier than before. That is
to be expected from a treatment addressing the cause of the
sickness. Because the cause of the illness was treated, the
weakness that existed in the sick, and which enabled the
illness to settle in, is now removed. This explains perfectly
well why the state of the patient becomes better than before
the illness.

Here, the old Väinämöinen
Felt a real assistance.
Soon, there he is, healed,
And his flesh grows beautifully,
In good health underneath,
Painless center,
Sides without pains,
And on top, no scar -
More graceful than before,
Better than he has ever been. (kal19)

Here comes at last the action of grace of the patient, himself,
by which he gives thanks to the Gods who have healed him.

At that, the old Väinämöinen,
He lifts his eyes to the sky,
Handsomely looking
Up high to the sky;
He speaks these words,
He says this speech:

"From where all graces flow,
The friendly protection comes
From the sky, there above,
From the all-powerful Creator.
Be praised and exalted,
Oh! Jumala, Creator,
For the assistance
You have supplied me with
Giving me a friendly refuge
In the midst of these sharp pains,
From the sharp work of steel." (kal20)

Now let's summarize the stages of Väinämöinen's healing, since we will use this as a base for the magical treatments described later on in chapter five. This healing took place through 11 stages, each including phases of action and phases of prayer.

1.   The patient tries to use his own strength to heal himself[22].
2.   When failing to do so, he looks for someone able to heal him, a healer.
3.   The healer searches for the Origins of the illness.
4.   She makes a plea to the cause of the illness, a plea based on the knowledge of the origin of the illness.
5.   She makes a plea to the manifestation of the illness, to the symptoms.
6.   She produces drugs from a variety of herbs. A first batch is not effective. It is with the second try that the final ointment is obtained.
7.   She applies the drugs after having tasted them.

---

[22] To simplify things a bit in these stages, I have chosen to use *he* for the patient and *she* for the healer, of course the use of both is meant to be inclusive.

8. She makes a plea to the Gods so that the drugs become efficient (i.e., a plea is always necessary to insure the success of a materially satisfying drug).

9. She ends her treatment with an action enabling the sick to regain control.

10. She makes a final plea to the Gods so that the preceding action becomes effective.

11. Finally, the patient himself performs an action of grace to the Gods, to thank them for his healing.

In chapter five, we will see which of these actions take place in ordinary reality, and which in non-ordinary reality, and above all else, we will look at what role the runes can play in the process. Once again, the healing of Väinämöinen will be our constant guide in choosing ways to fight illness.

GIVING LIFE TO THE DEAD

Lemminkäinen, who is called 'fickle' in the text, is another hero of the epic. He plays the role of the 'trickster', that is to say, the role of a cheating God or hero, a bit incoherent, certainly also a bit crazy, like the God Loki of the Norse pantheon. The Kalevala describes how he is healed of his insanity before it describes how his mother resurrected him. Nevertheless, the resurrection of Lemminkäinen and the healing of Väinämöinen have interesting points in common, and so I prefer to treat them immediately one after the other, breaking Kalevala's ordering.

Lemminkäinen demands the Mistress of the North to deliver her daughter to him. As a condition for her compliance, she sends him on three wanderings, with the last one being fatal for him, since a water dragon kills him. The news of his death reaches his family magically:

> Kyllilkki, the good wife, [*of Lemminkäinen*]
> Made a speech and it expressed this:
> "Now my husband is gone,
> My beautiful Farmind has vanished
> [*he is surnamed by the name of his country*]
> In a journey without shelters
> And on road unknown:
> Blood flows from my comb
> Gore leaks from my hair brush!" (kal21)

Lemminkäinen's mother goes to great lengths to help her son. First, she wants to retrieve his corpse from Tuonela, the river of the land of the dead. She asks the blacksmith, Ilmarinen, to make her a tool that will help her.

> The blacksmith Ilmarinen,
> Eternal craftsman,

Fixed a copper rake
He forged prongs of iron;
Prongs of a hundred fathoms were forged
A helve of five hundred was prepared.
And she, the mother of Lemminkäinen
Took the metal rake,
She hastened toward Tuonela's river. (kal22)

She needs the sun's help to make sure she can complete her work without interference. To accommodate her, the sun shines very strongly, filling the land of the dead and its inhabitants with heat. By this image, we again see the healer asking help from various Spirits. This attitude of reverence in front of the Spirits illustrates the humility the healer must show all along the healing process.

She makes a prayer to the sun:
Oh! Sun, creature of God,
Creature of Creator, our light:
First send a burning light,
And then a stifling darkness,
Finally, apply all your power;
Make the exhausted people sleep
Tire the forces of the dead's dwelling,
Wear out the army of Tuoni!" (kal23)

She can now begin to drag the river to remove the pieces of her son's body.

Then the mother of Lemminkäinen
Took the metal rake;
She raked her son
From the bosom of the roaring torrent
In the flow quick like a flash ...
And with her third attempt
A bundle of entrails clung
To the metal rake.

It was not, in fact, a bundle of entrails
But the fickle Lemminkäinen,
He, the beautiful Farmind,
Hung to the prongs of the rake
By the little finger of the right hand
And by the toe of the left leg ...
But a little bit was missing-
One hand, half of the head,
A large quantity of other
Scraps, and his breath too ...
She dragged again another time
With the copper rake
The length of the river Tuonela,
The length and the width:
She found half a spine
Half of the rib cage,
And other scraps,

She has now got back all that could be retrieved, and like an
ancient Frankenstein, she begins to re-adjust the scraps of
her son's body. She begins with the bones, the sinews and
various membranes. The poem continues without
interruption, using a classical healing formula we shall
comment a bit further:

(And other scraps,) reconstructed
From all this
Something like her son, working
On the fickle Lemminkäinen,
Joining flesh with flesh,
Bone to bone adjusting,
And limbs to limbs,
The veins to veins,
Where they were torn.
She links the sinews,
Ties again the membranes,

As always, she doesn't content herself simply to act, she adds the magic of her speech to her actions, invoking the help of the Spirits, here, the "Spirit of the veins." The word 'vein' obviously must not be taken in the modern sense. The 'veins' were all the vessels that carry blood and humors, as it was used in the Middle Ages. The poem continues without interruption.

> Speaks to the sinewy threads,
> Says these sentences:
> "Soft Goddess of the veins, Suonetar,
> Beautiful weaver of the membranes
> With your sweet spindle
> Your distaff of copper
> And your wheel of iron:
> Come here when you are needed,
> Take this way when we call you,
> A bale of tendons in your arms,
> A bundle of veins under your arms,
> To relink the veins,
> To retie the ends of the membranes
> In the cracks of the wound,
> In the gashes torn!" (kal24)

She now makes a call to the Spirits of Air:

> Should not enough come of that
> There is a young smart girl on the air
> In her copper boat,
> In a small boat with a red stern:
> Come down, my beauty,
> From your rest in the air,
> Young girl, from your pure heights
> Row your boat down the tendons,
> Move it in the membranes,
> Row over the bone fractures,
> Over the fractures of the membranes!

Put back the sinewy membranes,
Put them in the right place -
Face to face the large tendons,
Eye to eye the arteries,
That the veins cover themselves again,
And the membranes be end to end!
Take then a fine pin,
Thread it with silk,
Sew with your fine needles,
Suture with your pewter needle,
Retie the ends of the tendons,
Attach them with silk ribbons!" (kal25)

Finally, she invokes Jumala himself:

Should not enough come of that
You, Jumala who lives in the sky,
Harness your foals,
Make your horses ready,
Drive your brilliant sled
Over the bones and membranes,
Over the muscles and over
The sticky sinewy membranes!
Join bone to flesh,
The sinew to the end of sinew,
Silver the broken bones,
Gild the torn tendons!
There where a membrane is torn,
Make it grow again.
There where the tendon is worn-out,
Reissue the tendon.
There where the blood has escaped,
Make it find its flow again.
There where the bone softened,
Put another bone at this place.
There where the flesh became loose,
Put more flesh in this place

And bless them in their proper place
And settle them in place,
Bone to bone and flesh to flesh
And limbs to limbs!" (kal26)

This sequence of actions, namely to set the body in back in place "bone to bone and flesh to flesh and limbs to limbs" became a classical magical formula, seemingly spread over the whole primitive European civilization. For instance, the second Merseburg charm, discussed in chapter 4, describes this action as : "… bones set right, as blood set right, as limb set right, leg to leg, blood to blood, limb to limbs, as if glued were." A Scottish charm similarly speaks of setting "bone to bone, flesh to flesh, sinews to sinews, hide to hide, marrow to marrow."

This process of revival is made of two phases. The first one brings back the body parts together and gives life to them. The second one brings back speech to the dead body.
The link between speaking and real life is so important that it deserves a digression from the Kalevala, into other legends or sagas.
The *saga of Glum the Murderer* says :

> And when she had returned to her house, she cleaned his wounds and bandaged them, did so well that he began to talk to the people. (saga15)

The healer of the saga gives speech to his patient, a brief way of saying that he was completely brought back to life.

Similarly, in the *Havamal* ("Words of the High One"), Odin boasts that he can restore the dead to life. The dead body becomes able to speak :

> If I see one who is hanged from a beam

Swinging in the wind,
Then I know engraving and coloring
The runes so that the warrior
Can now speak
And leave his gallows. (edda2)

The Celtic legend of Bran is yet another example of a magic cauldron. The warriors who died in combat are dipped in it; they come out almost alive, although they don't speak. These sorts of living dead take back their place in battle, but the legend never mentions one of them starting a normal life again.

We have another example of a partially failure attempt to resuscitate in a Celtic tale from, *The Saga of Koadalan* (cited by J. Markale, *La tradition celtique*, Payot 1975, p. 185): After the magical process intended to restore him to life, we see that Koadalan, who was cut into shreds, is entirely recreated, his body perfectly formed, except there was no life in him.

We can now come back to the Kalevala, since Lemminkäinen's mother, after recreating her son's body, sees it is still without real life, because it can't talk.

Then Lemminkäinen's mother
Remade the man, remodeled her son
Full of life like before,
Looking like he should ...
But she failed to make the man talk,
Her child did not talk. (kal27)

To bring her son completely back to life, she begins a series of treatments. She massages her son's body with a variety of original magical honeys. The first honey was taken from the land of the dead. The bee, who plays the role of a shamanic helper here, serves to find the honey from the world below.

In other words, the bee accompanies Lemminkäinen's mother in a shamanic journey to the lower world.

> Where can we get a balm now
> A drop of honey brought
> To coat those who are so weary
> To treat the unfortunate
> The kind that makes a man speak again
> That he can tell his stories?
> Oh! Bee, our dear bird,
> Queen of the flowers of the forest:
> Go find a bit of honey
> And find a bit of mead
> In the pleasant forest Metsola,
> At the cautious Tapiola's,
> From many flower petals,
> Flowers of all kinds of herbs
> To serve as a balm for the sick,
> To heal the suffering one!"
> The bee ... made the honey
> Cook on its tongue,
> Honey from six ends of flowers, of
> A hundred herbs ...
> But it was of no use, no
> Sound came from the man. (kal28)

Lemminkäinen's mother now makes a shamanic journey in the middle world, again accompanied by the bee.

> Bee, my little bird, Fly to this other side,
> Underneath the nine seas
> And again the half of a tenth one
> A world of honey
> Toward the new hut of Tuuri
> Toward the walls of Palvonen[23] ...

---

[23] It is supposed that *Tuuri* is Thor, but we know nothing about *Palvonen*.

> Here the honey is cooked,
> The balms are prepared
> In little cauldrons
> In beautiful pans
> That could contain a thumb,
> Of the size of the end of a finger ... (kal29)

Lemminkäinen's mother coats her son with these balms cooked in the fire of Tuuri. Since he is the God who throws lightning, he must therefore be identified with the Nordic God Thor, to whom I have associated the rune Laukaz, rune of preservation. Nevertheless, even the balm concocted by Tuuri is not enough to bring Lemminkäinen totally back to life:

> The mother of Lemminkäinen
> anointed him with these ointments
> With the nine balms,
> And with the eight remedies:
> Again, she received no help. (kal30)

She decides at last to travel to the upper world which is a more difficult journey, but one that brings more wisdom. In a fairly classical way, this journey is made after going through nine membranes, or facing nine difficulties (or working nine nights, as seen above) as the following text implicitly describes.

> Bee, bird of the air,
> Put yourself to flight a third time
> There up high in the sky,
> Under the nine celestial dwelling places!
> There is no absence of honey there,
> Of honey to your heart's content,
> With which Ukko other times

Sang charms and Jumala spoke
And applied a balm on his brothers,
Harmed as they were by an evil power. (kal31)

The bee does not know where to find this 'heaven' and asks which road would take it there.

You will have no difficulty in getting there
Making a beautiful and good journey there -
Under the moon, underneath
The sun, among the stars of the sky.
All day you will fly
to the moon's brow-bones.
Another day you will spin like a meteor
Toward the Great Bear's shoulder blade.
A third day, you will spring
On to the Seven Star's back.
Then, you are almost there,
You arrive turning
Where holy Jumala lives,
To the lodge of the blessed.
Here, the balms are prepared
And the creams are made
In pots of silver,
Pans of gold:
The honey is cooked in the center,
On the sides the butter is made,
To the South end, mead,
To the North, fat ointments. (kal32)

The bee gets the balm from the skies. This is the one that Lemminkäinen needs. As in the case of Väinämöinen, the healer tastes the medicine, before applying it to the patient. This concordance of process shows that this was, in fact, the classical application of a balm. Again as in the case of Väinämöinen, the balm is spread over the whole body, which is less surprising now, since the whole body was harmed.

So, Lemminkäinen's mother
Takes the balms in her mouth,
She checks it with her tongue,
Tasting if they were to her liking ...
She then applied the balm to the sick,
Tended the ill-befallen
Anointed through gaps in bone
And through cracks in limbs
Anointed below, above
Splashed on the middle.

She completes the treatment with a call to the Spirit of her son:

She then says these words,
Declaring, declaiming:
"Come out of your slumber
Leave your dreams
From these evil places, from the
Bed of bad luck!"
And so, the man gets up
Leaves his dream. (kal33)

Nevertheless, and without doubt, the treatment is not yet ended because the Origins of the illness have not yet been addressed. This is why she questions her son and he tells her that it was a so-called 'water dragon' that killed him. She then sings the Origins of the water dragon.

Alas, what a carefree person!
You ... know nothing of the hatred of the water snake,
Of the prick of the terror of cattle!
The water snake is born
From the waves, the cattle's terror,
From the good brain of a duck
From the inside of the sea-swallow's head.

On the waters spat the ogress
Syöjätär she threw a blob on the waves;
The water stretched it out,
The sun heated it until it was soft,
The wind worked to calm it,
The water's breath rocked it.
And so, the surf washed it upon the beach,
The reef took it to land.
Then Lemminkäinen's mother
lulled the one she knew
to the shape he had before
to the looks he used to have
Till he was a bit better
Even, fitter than before. (kal34)

The character of Syöjätär evokes a ferocious gapping woman, ready to devour anything she meets. It is found in Russian tales under the name of Baba-Yaga. It can also be identified with Mamm-en-Diaoul of Celtic Brittany tales, with the Sheela-na-gig shown on the capital of many churches in England, with the Devil's mother in Grimm's tales, with the Ogre mother of 'prince charming' in *Sleeping beauty*, Perrault's earlier and more complete version of better known Grimm's *Briar Rose*. (*Dornröschen*). I believe it to be the old Mother Goddess made devil.

The images of Sheela-na-gig are particularly interesting since they are most often understood as representing a woman about to devour something with her sex. I tend to believe that, on the contrary, these Sheela-na-gig represent a woman about to give birth, straining her genitals to make her work easier. The doctor, or wise woman still carries out this necessary act today, so picturing it should neither horrify nor create a scandal.

We observed 11 stages of Väinämöinen's healing. We shall now compare them to the (actually 12) stages that were just followed by Lemminkäinen's mother. This will give us the possibility of generalizing slightly form cases to medical rules inspired by the Kalevala.

The twelve steps of physical healing

The statements in italics, below, are general statements about the way healing is described in the Kalevala. Regardless of the gender of the character who is sick or healing in a particular story, we shall use our convention that the patient is a 'he' and that the healer is a 'she'.

1. *The patient tries to use his own strength to heal himself.*
2. *When failing to do so, he looks for someone able to heal him, a healer.*

These two first stages are clearly impossible for a dead person to carry out. They are replaced here by the two successive attempts that Lemminkäinen's mother made to drag her son's body from the river. The fact that she must ask for the help of the blacksmith Ilmarinen and of the sun, emphasizes the importance of asking for help. The healer as well as the sick must be aware of their social environment, and asking for help is not simply recommended, it is the very first condition of the treatment. In other words, there may be individual illnesses, but their treatment is an affair of the entire society, and the first ones concerned must be conscious of it.

3. *The healer searches for the Origin of the illness.*

This was performed at the end of the treatment, once the dead one had recovered his speech.

4. *She makes a plea to the cause of the illness, a plea based on the knowledge of the origins of the illness.*

Here, this is more of a simple declamation of the Origins of the illness. This point is particularly interesting. It shows that a plea is not really necessary, the origin must be stated, and well stated. There is magic here, clearly, but also good sense: the sick cannot heal if the deep cause of the illness remains unknown. He must absolutely know why he became sick in order to be able to control his life without falling back into the errors that made him ill in the first place. The patient must feel fully responsible[24] for himself, in particular for his illnesses. He may even declare himself guilty of the cause of his illness, but this is not the goal, which is simply to clarify and acknowledge the sickness' causes. This is how the sickness will be beneficial in a sense, since the complete healing is not meant to simply restore the old state of the sick, but to improve this state.

In the healing of Väinämöinen, we don't know if one stage was more responsible than another for this complete healing. What can be understood here is that it's the study of the Origins that gives this result. We must note in passing that modern medicine seems to abandon the whole idea of improvement through healing, since it also abandons the ambition of treating the origin of the illness. The Kalevala tells us that this reluctance to deal with the origin of the illness is likely more than a simple coincidence.

- *... (Here is a missing step in Väinämöinen's healing)*

---

[24] We find here one well-known mistake of modern medicine. Not only does it withdraw responsibility from its patients, but it treats them more as sickness cases than as sick persons. It seems that some psychology has been recently included in the normal cursus of medical studies. This hints at some awareness of the problem in high political spheres.

Here we have a supplementary stage between stages 4 and 5: the reconstruction of the physical body. This corresponds to the cleaning and eventually to the suturing of the wound. I suggest, therefore, adding this additional stage to those necessary for the healing of any illness, giving us now 12 stages.

5. *She makes a plea to the manifestation of the illness, to the symptoms.*

The plea itself is very elaborated as it asks the assistance of three types of Spirits: that of the sinewy membranes, that of air, and lastly that of Jumala. As in the case of Väinämöinen's healing, the Spirits are asked to help the patient's body heal.

6. *She makes the drugs from a variety of herbs. A first batch is not effective. It is with the second (or third?) try that the ointment is obtained.*

She also prepares some ointments. Here, it is the third attempt that is successful. The helper that prepared the remedies for Väinämöinen was the healer's son. Now, it is a bee, an insect, well known for serving as an aid to shamans for the native people of North America. I believe that we can make the hypothesis that in fact, the healer completes two tasks in parallel. One is the physical task of preparing the remedies, and it is very possible that she delegates all or part or this task to a human aid. The other is a mystical task, a shamanic journey, to bring mystical ingredients from non-ordinary reality. Both are necessary for healing.

7. *She applies the drugs after having tasted them.*

This stages are identical in the two cases. We will note the way of applying the ointments is described by the same words in the two cases.

8. *She makes a plea to the Gods so that the drug can be efficient.*

In the present case, it is not a plea, but more of an admonition to the patient himself. This stage, completely necessary, can therefore take many forms. In any case, a kind of speech must be made; the remedies are never active by themselves.

9. *She ends her treatment with an action that enables the sick to regain control.*
10. *She makes a final plea to the Gods so that the patient can again take charge of himself.*

Here, these two stages have been gathered into one. The first treatment also partially failed because Lemminkäinen was alive, but he could not talk. The application of balms here is equivalent to the bandages placed on Väinämöinen's leg. Similarly, his mother's final plea can be seen as corresponding to the successive pleas of the old man, following the application of the balm, and following the placement of the bandages. It says that healing never takes place in one step, that two are necessary. In modern medical terms, a step of recovery is necessary after taking the proper drugs. Today, this recovery step is left to the patient or to the paramedics (of a social status lower than the doctor's), while in ancient medicine the concept of paramedical action does not exist, healing is not a task to be delegated to someone else.

11. *Finally, the patient himself performs an action of grace to the Gods, to thank them for his healing.*

Nothing prevents Lemminkäinen from thanking the Gods, which would only seem proper in this context. The absence of this stage seems to me to be more troublesome than what happened in the preceding case. My impression is that the poem tells us this: he did not thank the Gods, and therefore his future life will not be good. This is in fact what the rest of the poem confirms: the behavior of Lemminkäinen becomes disastrous afterwards.

Summarizing, and by this analysis of the two treatments, the 12 stages of physical healing are as follows, but not necessarily in this order:

1. The patient tries to use his own strength to heal himself.
2. When failing to do so, he finds someone who is able to heal him, a healer, and asks for her help.
3. The healer searches for the Origin of the illness. She can ask for the assistance of other individuals.
4. She utters the Origins of the illness, in a solemn manner. This may or may not be accompanied by pleas to the cause of the illness.
5. She provides first aid to the wounded one: cleaning the wounds, cooling off fever, etc.
6. She makes a plea to the manifestation of the illness, to the symptoms.
7. She makes the drugs from a variety of herbs. It is after several tries that a satisfactory result is achieved. She performs a shamanic journey to bring back as well the spiritual components of the drug.
8. After having tasted the remedies, she applies them to the entire body of the patient (not a local treatment at this stage)
9. She utters a poem whether it is destined to the Gods, or to the sick one, to assure the success of her remedy.

10. She ends her treatment with an action that enables the sick to regain control.
11. She makes a final plea to the Gods to assure that the patient regains control.
12. Finally, the patient himself performs an action of grace to the Gods, to thank them for the healing.

To reinforce the importance of searching for the Origins of the illness, we will consider yet another example, found in Kalevala's 17th chapter:

I have no idea
I cannot guess your Origins,
Hiisi, who freed you.
Demon, from where can you come
To chew and to bite,
To eat, to chomp.
Are you sickness delivered by the Creator,
A curse of Jumala,

Or of human origin,
Shaped and brought by someone,
Put in place against retribution,
Brought up by silver?
If you are of human origin,
Caused by another man,
Be assured that I know well your family
That I will find out where you were born! (kal35)

When the Origins of the illness are unknown, the healer is unable to find a treatment and she acknowledges it. This confession is the first step in the subsequent search for the origin of the illness, and we will see further on what poetic curses can be used to determine this origin.

Now we will study the story of Lemminkäinen's insanity and his healing.

TREATING PSYCHOLOGICAL ILLNESS

In fact, the Kalevala does not say explicitly that Lemminkäinen becomes insane. However, it describes in length how Lemminkäinen must hunt a ghost elk in order to win the daughter of the Mistress of the North. This hunt strongly brings to mind some dream chasing, as often happens to people who are on the borderline of insanity. On the other hand, I attribute the handling of illnesses of spirit, foolishness and folly to the rune Algiz, as will be explained at the end of this chapter. Algiz is the rune of the elk by its name. It is also the rune of protection against these defects. Since the hunting illusion of Lemminkäinen is a ghost elk, we get closer again to a sickness of the spirit.

The Mistress of the North decides to remove this irritating suitor by sending him chasing after a wild dream. The text says explicitly that it is an illusion made up entirely by bad Spirits:

> The goblins of Hiisi listened,
> Those of the Troll[25] people noticed.
> *[That Lemminkäinen had to go chasing an elk ghost]*
> And the goblins built an elk,
> The trolls a reindeer:
> They made its head from a stump
> Its antlers, from a fork of willow,
> The feet, from driftwood, the legs
> from stakes in the marsh,
> The back, from fence poles,

---

[25] The text says *Juutas* which is an obvious transform of 'Judas', thus pointing at a Christian influence. This name is the one given by the Fins to the primitive inhabitants of Finland, described as being very large, very strong, and very wicked, as were the trolls of the Scandinavian mythology. This is why I translate *Juutas* by 'troll'.

The sinews, from dried grasses,
The eyes, from the buds of water lilies,
The ears, from water lilies flowers,
The skin from the bark of a balsam,
The flesh, from rotten wood. (kal36)

This description, since it is the way Nordic shamans would describe insanity, is certainly very important. This is why I'll give you a similar description from Finnish culture, but coming from *Finish Folk Poetry*. It is very interesting to compare the two versions:

Now Hiizi happened to hear
The evil spirit to spy:
Hiizi constructed an elk
The evil spirits conceived
Snatched the head from a hummock.
The body from rotten wood
Legs from a fence-pole
Ears from pond-lilies
The eyes from pond-lily buds.
(*word for word citation*, kuusi2)

And so Lemminkäinen begins his crazy quest, and makes a series of pleas to the forest divinities. If he can move them on his fate, then they will hand over his illusion to him, and he will regain his sanity. The treatment here is therefore purely mystical. He must recognize the strange world of the mentally ill, and contact the divinities that live in this world, before they agree to supply the mentally ill with what propelled him outside of our reality. The principle is the same as for physical illnesses; he must find the cause of the sickness and eliminate this cause, not by denying its existence (as modern psychiatry tends to do, in prescribing drugs for the sick), but by effectively supplying the sick with the object of their illusion.

Lemminkäinen follows this elk, his quest takes place in the forest, and he is a sort of hunter tracking a prey. The healing comes when the prey is finally caught. Through his quest, he also leads us to the forest God, Tapio, and to the forest Goddess, Mielikki.

He greets this world in which he will roam, and begins to ask for its benevolence.

> Greetings, mountains, greetings, slopes,
> Greetings, balsams full of sighs,
> Greetings, graying aspen,
> Greet the one that greets you!
> Be kind, forests, soft, wild places
> And you, precious Tapio, be favorable. (kal37)

He then asks the means to avoid becoming lost in this mysterious world. In the verses that follow, the "idiot", is obviously Lemminkäinen, talking about himself.

> Nyyrikki, son of Tapio
> Clear skinned man, with the red helmet:
> Carve notches in the earth
> Blaze a trail on the slopes,
> That this idiot can feel his path,
> This stranger can know
> The way that I seek
> Where I pray and beg for game! (kal38)

He then tries to flatter the feminine forest divinities so that they will help him in his quest.

> Mielikki, mistress of the forests,
> Woman of the clear skin, beautiful to behold:
> Set gold in motion
> That silver goes walking
> Facing the one who is seeking,

In the steps of the beggar:
Take the golden keys of
The ring held tight on your thigh
And open Tapio's shed
And make available this fortress
That is the forest of my hunt,
My time to search the prey! (kal39)

But the great Goddess does not condescend to answer to
Lemminkäinen's pleas. Humbly, he then asks secondary
divinities, unable to save him by themselves, to intercede on
his behalf with the higher divinities.

Small beautiful woman of the forest,
Servant of Tapio with the mouth
Tasting of mead,
Play your sweet-as-honey whistle,
Your sweet-as-mead flute,
In the ears of the pleasant,
Of the good mistress of the forests,
That she hears you already
And awakens at last.
She hears nothing now,
Hardly awakening
Although I continue to beg,
Beseeching her with golden speech. (kal40)

He then asks the main divinity of the forest to stop her
normal activities, so that she finds the time to pay attention
to him.

Mistress of the forest herself,
The good mistress of the forest,
With bracelets of gold at her arms,
Rings of gold on her fingers,
Her head adorned with gold,
Her hair coiled with gold,

Gold hanging at her ears,
Her neck encircled with beads of gold,
Soft mistress of the forest,
Old forester, soft as honey
Throw away your shoes for haying,
Take off your skirts for working at the oven,
Leave behind your work shirt[26]. (kal41)

He tries to trade the services of the forest divinities for the riches of the land, like silver and gold.

Master of the house of Tapio,
Mistress of the house of Tapio,
Old gray beard of the forest,
Generous king of the forest;
Mimerkki, mistress of the forest,
Dear old forester devoted to the hunt,
Lady of furs of the blue cloak,
Mistress of the swamp in red shoes:
Come now to exchange gold,
To trade silver! (kal42)

He is heard at last, and he pleases the God and the Goddess of the forest, and charms all the secondary divinities. They agree to seize his illusion, deliver it to him, and in doing so, freeing him from it.

He sang three times
And he pleased the mistress of the forests,
Even the master of the forests,
He delighted all the young girls

---

[26] The forest wearing a "work shirt" for haying and working at the oven evokes the lifeless forest during Winter. It puts on its feasting robe in Spring, when animals show up again.

And won the graces of all
The maids of Tapio.
They took the hunt of the prey,
The ghost elk from its shelter,
To the limits of the Demon's dwelling,
Bringing it to the seeker,
For the narrator to catch. (kal43)

Lemminkäinen is no longer sick, he starts an action of grace towards the forest divinities, and he supplies the promised compensation.

Lord of the wood, master of the land,
Beautiful man of the heather;
Mielikki, mistress of the forests
Dear generous old forester:
Come now, take gold
Pick up the silver ... (kal44)

The stages of this healing aren't as clean cut here as in the case of a physical wound, and there is no explicit healer to imitate. We will try to infer them anyway, understanding that in this example, the first stage, which is the identification of the illusion and the land where it can be found, is carried out implicitly in describing how Lemminkäinen finds himself with the Mistress of Northland, trying to obtain her daughter, and how this Mistress of Northland sets the conditions.

This medicine, that can be called 'primitive', (actually far from being primitive when one is referring to mental illness), understands very well that the one who is sick has a problem to resolve and is unable of resolving it himself. Instead of attempting to thump this problem like psychiatry has the tendency of trying to do, or instead of looking at the illness from far away, as in psychoanalysis, and in psychotherapy in general, the primitive healer identifies herself with the sick, she researches the particular problem, the unique problem, that is facing the patient, and places herself, on the path of a shamanic journey, in the places haunted by the sick in order to understand what illusion he is chasing after, and to provide it for him.

For this, she must first know the places:
   "Greetings, mountains, greetings, slopes..."
and know how to find her way:
   "Nyyrikki, son of Tapio ..."
Then, she must explain her request:
   "Mielikki, mistress of the forests ..."
and find some allies:
   "Small beautiful woman of the forest ..."
She must also understand why the God can refuse to answer:
   "The mistress of the forest herself..."
and propose an interesting compensation to them:
   "Master of the house of Tapio ..."
When the Gods have granted the request, the sick is healed, and he must not forget to thank them and keep his promises:
   "Lord of the wood, master of the land ..."

In conclusion, we can describe the healing of mental illness with nine stages:

   - Discovering the patient's illusion.
This corresponds to the stage of discovering the Origins of the physical illness: Delusions are the spiritual Origins of the illness.
   - Know the land where it lives,
   - Mark out the paths there.
These two stages are again linked to the characterization of the patient's illusion, inasmuch as it treats the environment in which this illusion evolves. Before the healer completely recognizes the Origins of the illness, she must take many shamanic journeys.
   - Explain her problem to the Gods of this land.

This corresponds to the stages of announcing the Origins of the illness.
- Make some allies.
- Understand the point of view of the divinities.
- Propose compensation.

These last three stages are completely particular to mental illness, but correspond to those of the pleas and the preparation of the ointments for the treatments of physical illness.
- Complete the healing with the help of the Gods.

This corresponds to the stage of applying the ointments on the patient's body.
- Thank the Gods and give the promised compensation.

This is the action of grace that is necessary at the end of all treatments.

The treatment of mental illness follows the major principles of all primitive treatments, that is discovering of the Origins of the sickness, and pleas to the Spirits. In the present case, it is described to us without the intervention of a healer, and we find that it is the Gods who are willing to heal Lemminkäinen. The emphasis is on the detailed exploration of the places where the illusion is found, and the intimate contact with the inhabitants of these places. This corresponds exactly with the shamanic methods of psychological treatments, which have been well described in Sandra Ingerman's books.

Like the majority of modern psychotherapies, shamanism makes the hypothesis that it is an old trauma, generally forgotten by the patient, which is the origin of the present sickness. Psychoanalysis, true to its scientific calling, tries to put the most distance possible between the sick and their doctor, and it is the responsibility of the sick to return to their past, and discover their ancient traumas, the causes of the actual illness. In some versions, the patients go even back to their ancestral past, and discover family traumas that have been transferred until them by the set of constraints felt as normal within the family relationships. The treatment ends here, and we notice, not without surprise, that psychoanalysis, like all primitive Norse medicine, considers that uttering (by the patient in the case of psychoanalysis) the Origins of the illness is sufficient to heal. It is an archaism of a modern method, all the more astonishing since other shamanic methods propose a supplementary treatment : the reintegration of the lost parts of the soul or, of a lost 'animal Spirit'[27].

Shamanism does not ask patients to go into their pasts. It is the role of the shaman to journey in the client's past, and to locate and repair the old traumas. The Origins of the illness are then supplied to the patient, but they are not the only treatment.

This is why I think we can interpret the poem about Lemminkäinen's search for the ghost elk as a shamanic journey, carried out by him or by a healer, in the land of the patient's illusions. The shaman brings the illusion back with him from his journey, and gives it to the patient. Shamanic vocabulary expresses this in the following manner: we say that the shaman searches for an animal Spirit, or a part of a soul, lost by the sick, and brings them back, and blows them into the head and heart of his patient. In this vocabulary, the quest described in the Kalevala is that of the search for a totem animal, that Lemminkäinen had lost following a trauma, and the poem describes how he is able to retrieve this mystical totem.

---

[27] This is my way of saying 'power-animals'; this enables me to avoid speaking of power, which should never be the path of a beginner.

All this shows that the Kalevala contains hidden medical knowledge that has been long since treated as ridiculous superstition, and it also shows, that it is quite interesting[28] to decode it as I have done here, even without talking about its poetic side, which is of value itself. I would have liked to have had more details about the plants used to make the potion that healed Väinämöinen, but this precise knowledge must have been the privilege of the "witches and other shamans," as we call them now, and we have eliminated them irreparably.

The poetry and magic of the Kalevala make us forget that it is also a book of natural science. It is full of medical knowledge. The fact that it is missing important botanical details reminds me of the accounts typically given by folklorists, for instance those describing the rituals of Saint John's Eve, a period of gathering medicinal plants. In addition to their monumental ignorance of aromatherapy and plant therapy, folklorists were really obsessed by the magical aspects of what was done, they ridiculed it very much, and so the rational aspect of these practices eluded them completely. For instance, they recorded that crowns had to be made out of nine different kinds of flowers, one of them being Saint Johnswort (Hypericum perforatum). They focused on the number (and deviations of this number), rather than what was really interesting like the kind of flowers that should be gathered. It may even be that there are two effects taking place : the magic of the flowers gathered on Saint John's Eve, together with the medicinal benefits of the essential oils given off from the drying flowers. Aromatherapy knows very

---

[28] ... and rather modern-looking. For an example of its modernity, just reflect on the theme of the 2nd World Congress for Psychotherapy (in 1999): *Myth - Dream - Reality*, and note that the first one, held in 1996, invited a few Siberian shamans to participate and demonstrate their art.

well that Saint Johnswort is very useful since it is an essential oil of many applications.

Hopefully you will forgive me for hammering my argument again: I believe that the medical practices of the ancients mixed magic and science in the best possible way at that time. Lots of magic (too much for my taste, I confess!) and a bit of science, certainly, but never one without the other. The current practice, that absolutely rejects magic to only accept scientific phenomena, ignores the mystical part of humans. It constitutes some sort of technological monstrosity whose limits are fortunately understood by many doctors.

Before ending this section devoted to mental illness in the Kalevala, I will address two related topics. The first one drives us into a past older than the Kalevala; it is my interpretation of rune *Algiz*, which I believe to be the rune of mental illness. The second one drives us back to modern times; it is Jung's view of the medical approaches of his time.

Algiz, rune of mental sanity and insanity

The second volume of this book deals with rune lore. We shall then see that *Havamal* states that a 'second' (rune or song) is devoted to healing. Uruz being the second rune, this gives some weight to the hypothesis that Uruz might be a healing rune, and the second volume provides more argument favoring this idea. In this case, *Havamal* speaks of a song, covering a set of runes, and we will argue in detail, with the help of the Eddic poem *Sigrdrifumal*, that Uruz probably belongs to the set of healing runes.

Once this hypothesis has been accepted, we can turn to the Viking poem on Uruz which says :

ᚾ (úr) er (is) af illu jarne;
opt loypr ræinn á hjarne.

Drizzle (*Ur*) comes from bad iron.
The reindeer often runs on icy snow.

This poem obviously links Uruz and the big animals of Northern countries such as the reindeer and the elk, thus linking the elk with medicine, at least if our hypothesis about Uruz is valid. Now, if one considers that a 'wild dream' is a "ghost elk hunt," as the one of Lemminkäinen as we just studied it, then the second verse ceases being a slightly stupid statement of fact since it would then mean both : "crazy people are often tempted by wild dreaming," and "our wild dreams push us often to wild chases." In this sense, "The elk often runs on icy snow" is a one-sentence summary of the entire Don Quixote story.

The Old Norse word *hjarn* is indeed 'hard frozen snow' but we should not forget that *hjarni* means 'brain'. In this sentence, they should take a dative form which is *hjarni* for both. We can thus suppose a kind of pun here, the physical elk running on the hard snow, and the psychological one running on the brain of the mentally sick.

As you can see, my hypotheses, how ever stretched they might look, give depth and understanding to the Viking rune poem, often called nonsensical by scientific runologists. I find it very unlikely that these runic poems would have been preciously preserved over the years if they were simple doggerels!

Moreover, the Old English runic poem says:

eolhx X ⟙ secgeard hæfþ oftust on fenne.	the elk of the sedge (*eolh* = elk) often dwells in fens.
wexeð on wature. wundaþ grimme. blode breneð beorna gehwylcne ðe him ænigne onfeng gedeð :.	grows in water. grimly wounds. burns with boils the blood of the hero who seizes it.

Here again is an allusion to the elk. This allusion can be better understood by referring to a German expression: "to be stung by the straws," which means being somewhat stupid, and to a French one: "to be slightly stung," which means being slightly crazy. As all translators agree upon, the

Old English expressions *wundaþ grimme* ('wounds grimly' as you can directly understand) and "blode breneð gehwylcne" ('blood burns with boils') refer to physical wounds. But the insane is also 'grimly wounded' and the 'burning blood' refers rather to psychological unrest than to a physical one. There is still another possibility, understanding that the "hero who seizes the elk of the sedge" will become a monster, with a hot boiling blood. I refer here to Beowulf's episode where Grendel's mother is killed by Beowulf, and his "*sweord* (sword [*Beowulf's*]) *gemealt* (had melt) ... *wæs* (was) *þæt* (that) *blod* (blood [*Grendel's mother*] *to þæs* (to cause) *hat* (hot)."

In all cases, this describes no ordinary sickness where the sick becomes weak, but a kind of sickness bringing fury, and a change of personality. In modern language, we call 'madmen' the people showing these symptoms, while they can equally be mentally sick, inspired prophets and poets, or berserk warriors.

All this argumentation explains why I associate Algiz to two different concepts: the one of what is socially known as mental disorders, thus including insanity but not exclusive to it, and the one of healing the insane.

Obviously, this argumentation prevents nobody to disagree with me and to propose another rune to associate with these concepts. This would change the exact galdr to sing, but not the principle by which runes are associated to a galdr.

What I am hinting at here is that my choices are not of the kind "follow me or leave me," the reader knows why and how to disagree, if there is disagreement.

The Kalevala never speaks of anything like using a rune, but it often refers to singing or shouting charms, we call galdr in reference to the Old Norse practice. During galdoring, the sorcerer(ess) often used runes as well. We just discussed why I would particularly insist on the use of Algiz in the treatment of mental sickness.

Carl Gustav Jung and his view of dream and reality

We will now replace our healing practice within the framework of modern, or at least more modern medicine, by looking at Jung's view of the medical approaches of his time. In his Yale 1937 lectures (published in Carl Gustav Jung, *Psychology & Religion*, Yale University Press, 1938), Jung was already complaining about the blindness that official science had towards the non rational. "The very common prejudice against dreams is but one of the symptoms of a far more serious under evaluation of the human soul in general. The marvelous development of science and techniques has been counterbalanced on the other side by an appalling lack of wisdom and introspection. (p. 18-19)" The context has changed so much since then, that what I am claiming now, with almost the same words, has a rather different meaning. Despite the similarity, there are two major differences between what Jung said and what I am saying here.

The first one is that Jung was complaining about the pure materialistic view of sophisticated people (say, people living in that social environment who were consulting psychoanalysts). I am saying that this materialistic view now belongs to everyone: sophisticated or not, educated or not, so-called naive people included. We can no longer say that "faith stands still" among simple-minded people (especially in Europe and overwhelmingly here in France), since during the last 50 years they have become just as rationalist as the so-called educated people. So in a way, it has become normal that those who believe in the mysteries of the non-rational are more or less considered as crazies. This explains why I felt it necessary to devote this book to a defense of irrationality, using the Nordic past as an example, which was full of both irrationality and good sense mixed together. My own rationality is deeply anchored because of my upbringing and way of life; perhaps this is why I am not afraid of exploring my irrational aspects in a responsible way, and of acknowledging them.

The second one is that Jung complains that the modern medicine of his time does not take the psyche into account. He stresses the importance of dreams because he believes that they say, often very plainly, what the patient really thinks; they describe psychic objects that belong to the patient's mind, and that have therefore a kind of material existence for the patient, at least (and when shared by many, they become Jung's celebrated *archetypes*). It seems to me that modern medicine today includes some of the psyche into its view of patients. I think, however that every effort is done to consider our unconscious being as rational, while its deep lack of rationality should be acknowledged, and taken into account. Although this is a funny way to put it, I want to treat the irrational rationally (by acknowledging its real properties) while at the same time I know it is irrational to ask rationality from our primitive being. My attitude is then one of extreme rationality which is able to conceive its own limits, instead of blindly applying its laws everywhere, even where they are obviously wrong. I am acknowledging a kind of deep contradiction that Jung did not discuss at all. I do believe that this contradiction is a fact of life that we have to live with, like it or not.

Conclusion for this chapter

Whether we are dealing with a physical illness or a psychological illness, thanks to the Kalevala, we can envision a patient-healer relationship, normally impossible in modern society. The healer never distances herself from his patients; she even identifies herself with them in the case of mental illnesses. Neither time nor the efforts of the healer are ever measured, which means that the patients are in principle ready to pay the price.

This asks for a kind of relationship that is no longer possible in a stressed world making haste in everything. Healer and patient must take their time, think deeply at length on the possible causes of the sickness, and perform the many steps of healing without any haste. In particular, the very early step of finding the cause of the sickness seems to have to be done again and again. The patient detects one possible cause, then the healer starts working on the grounds of this cause, and, quite often, during the treatment, the patient will recall things, or the treatment itself will induce the patient to memorize something. In particular, a good galdr stirs many emotions in the patient, and he will tend to remember and confide new facts of his life to the healer. Her job is to sort out of these confidences what is genuinely linked to the sickness at hand, to ask new questions to verify her hypotheses, and then think of a newer, deeper cause of the sickness. And the whole process can start again several times. In fact, you can see that Kalevala describes 'success stories' where the healing took place without iteration, and it might be that you found it already too lengthy. Remember it describes relatively short healing and do not hesitate to think of healing in months or even years rather than in minutes.

Chapter 3

SHAMANISM AND HEALING

> The Noaaid [*Lapp shaman*] uses the same
> method as was just mentioned, except that he
> performs several preliminary ceremonies, by
> making a number of frightening grimaces and
> contortions, which depends on the amount of
> brandy that he drinks, and the tobacco that he
> smokes during this operation ... he falls into a
> deep sleep, that the assistants take for ecstasy.
> When he wakes, he claims that his soul was
> carried to some holy mountains whose name
> he says, and tries to reveal the discussion that
> he has had with the Divinity; ... One never
> fails to follow the advice of the Noaaid ...
>
> ***Voyage au Cap-Nord, par la Suède, la
> Finlande et la Laponie***
> Joseph Acerbi, Paris, 1804, t.2, p. 263.

Shamanism is practiced in a spirit which is somewhat foreign
to our civilization, as is well illustrated by Acerbi's
condescending comments just above (see also the head
citation of chapter 4). Most of us have not had the
opportunity to have any real contact with a true shamanic
culture, so I would like to first explore the shamanic culture
before beginning this discussion on shamanism and healing.
The second part of this chapter might look a bit like a lesson
on shamanism, but the simplest way to give you a true
picture of it, is to give you some hints on how to practice it.

Finally, we will look at how Siberian shamans treated the sick using shamanism[29].

I strongly believe that the practice of shamanism is more important for the healer than for the sick. Shamanic healing should be - and in many cases it is – used together with hand healing and galdr, as we will see in both this book and in volume 3. Nevertheless, some standard shamanic practice is basic for healers. It helps them to reconnect with their primitive self and to learn the humility needed to acknowledge their own weaknesses when facing the strength of the Spirits. Therefore, there are two very important principles to be learned from shamanism: reconnecting with our primitive self, and recognizing that it is the Spirits who heal, not the healer.

As for the first principle, everything our current civilization teaches us is aimed at preventing us from acknowledging and respecting our primitive self. For most of us, being 'civilized' means despising and repressing primary instincts because they are considered aggressive and destructive. This is contrary to the shamanic view of the world where being civilized means being able to draw, at will, from primitive energy (and being able to repress destructive instincts, primary or otherwise). It is not surprising that medical doctors, who go through an intense academic training, tend to forget their primitive self when they are practicing their work. This chapter explains why our 'civilized' view is wrong, and how to include some shamanic perspective in our everyday lives. In order to avoid getting off track, I won't go into the systematic destructive attitude that our civilization

---

[29] Extracts from *Schamanengeschichten aus Sibirien*, collected by G. V. Ksenofontov, translated from the Russian by A. Friedriech and G. Buddruss, Clemens Zerling, 1987. Many of the ideas developed in this chapter were inspired by this important book.

shows towards Nature. I want to concentrate on the attitudes that mislead us when dealing with the sick.

The second principle was well illustrated in chapter two, where the "gray beard" who heals Väinämöinen emphasizes the fact that he is not the real cause of the healing, but that Jumala is. This attitude is essential for a healer who must always be aware that he or she is simply helping patients to recover their health. The Gods, and the patient, are in fact responsible for the recovery, not the healer. This is contrary to the kind of self-centeredness which is a standard for our present civilization. For instance, "me, as a person, etc." is understood in each of our statements, and it is even looked upon as impolite not to treat someone as a unique and all-important individual. In modern medicine, this attitude leads us to treat the healer as an all-powerful 'health deliverer' while the patient is reduced to the passive role of a doctor's case rather than being treated as a sick person (and this, by the way, is very impolite to patients). Within a shamanic vision of society, the healer is simply a representative of the power of the Spirits or the Gods, a receptacle that is able to use their strength, and the sick is not simply a 'patient' who waits around for the healer to cure him, but a partner who needs helps temporarily. Again, this is clearly illustrated in the Kalevala when Väinämöinen gives his healer the knowledge of the Origins of iron, and when Lemminkäinen goes after his wild prey himself, thereby curing himself when he recovers his lost Spirit animal.

THE SHAMANIC CONTEXT

I will now try to describe as briefly as possible the principal traits of shamanism. Everyone agrees that shamans are responsible for the health of their community, since they are often called 'medicine-men' (or medicine-women). Primitive thinking believed that the Spirits had the power of controlling our health. The notion of illness was always considered as linked to curse; the shaman treats both. This medical role is real, but we must understand that this is not the most essential aspect of the shaman's function as we learn from old, basic books like *Archaic techniques of Ecstasy*, by Mircea Eliade. The essential role of the shaman is that of the psychopomp, the one who accompanies those who have just died to the realm of the dead, and ensures that they don't return to haunt the tribe. However, we aren't going to discuss the psychopomp role of the shaman here, but rather his or her role as the healer, since this is the subject of this book.

The first task of the shaman healer is to determine whether or not the illness has an origin of human malevolence. If this is the case, then the shaman is certain to outsmart the trap as suggested in the following passage from the Kalevala that I cited earlier:

> I have no idea
> I can not guess your Origins,
> Hiisi, who freed you.
> Demon, from where can you come
> To chew and to bite,
> To eat, to chomp.
> Are you sickness delivered by the Creator,
> A curse of Jumala,
> Or of human origin,
> Shaped and brought by someone,

Put in place against retribution,
Brought up by silver?
If you are of human origin,
Caused by another man,
Be assured that I know well your family
That I will find out where you were born! (kal35)

If it is a matter of an "illness born of the Creator," a "curse of Jumala," then we can still do something, but it means that great risks will be taken. Note in passing that the seriousness of the illness, in the modern sense of the word, is not the way it is used here. The flu, for example, could be an illness coming from the Gods, and cancer, an old curse from a jealous neighbor. A shaman would then consider that healing this flu is nearly impossible, while curing the cancer would be an easy task.

This might look absurd at first sight, so a few explanations are needed here. My opinion is that cancer in most cases finds its origin in a 'self-curse' of the patient, and that makes its shamanic healing nearly impossible. When there is no self-cursing, or when the patient realizes his/her error soon enough, a modern-medical treatment will be effective, and the shamanic treatment will treat the deep weakness that led to the self-cursing.

As you can see, I have never believed that a few songs will cure such a deep sickness as cancer. I have only noticed that the magical and the rational are not in opposition, neither are they identical, in spite of what many people think. The rational 'hides' the magical, and the role of magical healing is to uncover the magic in order to be able to treat the patient. Discarding the rational as many 'mages' or 'seers' do presently is pure charlatanism. Discarding the magical as rationalists do is mutilation and self-mutilation.

Shamanic treatments are so deeply connected to the civilization in which they take place, that we need to spend some time studying a shamanic civilization. The way shamanism is presented these days seems to ignore the most fundamental precepts of primitive shamanism. For instance, the shamanic journey is now considered as some sort of soft drug and not like the difficult battle that it actually is. Shamans tend to be seen as 'good savages', applying an ecological medicine. The testimonies about the Siberian shamans clearly show that, on the contrary, they used all the techniques at their disposal to treat their patients, including those implying the death (in a sense, the 'sacrifice') of a third person, and that their journeys were deeply exhausting, to the point where certain practitioners would lose their virility, like in the Nordic seið. I am in no way pretending to be a specialist in current Siberian shamanism; a shamanism which has, by the way, miraculously managed to survive communism. But, I have nevertheless observed some Siberian shamans at work and I could see the frenzied competition existing among them, far from our illusions of the 'good savages'. Our occidental civilization, deeply Christian despite appearances, is so different from the civilizations referred to as primitive, that it is difficult for us to imagine the regular functioning of a healer in such a society. This is why I will now present what I find to be the most fundamental characteristics of a shamanic civilization before drawing any conclusions for a primitive medicine.

Good and Evil, Health and Illness

The first and, without a doubt, the deepest difference between the two civilizations is linked to the notion of good and evil. We could be ironic about this, since, according to the time, religion and place, that which is good can become evil; but this is not the problem I want to emphasize.

Everyone firmly knows what is evil, and knows that we must follow the path of good if we want the approval of our neighbors, or the path of evil in the opposite case. Inversely, in the shamanic world, not only are good and evil less clearly distinct, but one is necessary in order to have the other. The goal of life is not to reach some form of perfection of good; the existence of this perfection is simply not considered in shamanic civilizations. The goal of life, instead, is to manage as harmoniously as possible our urges toward what we call good and evil and to create a balance between the two.

This knowledge of good and evil (some people would say that we have had it since original sin) manifests itself in medicine by very simple definitions: good health is 'good' if possible, or, if not, at least keeping the patient alive is; sickness and death are 'bad'. And so modern medicine only tries to make illness disappear, and battles with all its strength against death. This obviously leads to excess, as in the case of those poor patients forcibly kept alive by therapeutic determination until death frees them at last.

In shamanic cultures the distinction of good and evil is far less clear, and so is the one between life and death: there are 'good deaths' and 'bad lives'. For a shaman, sickness and death are part of the normal processes of an individual's development. They are not an evil which must be fought against at all costs.

Sickness, treated correctly, should not simply bring us back to our state before the illness, but should improve on this state. Sickness, therefore, is not a nuisance that we have to relieve ourselves of, but a test that we must overcome.

Not only is the death of a patient not automatically a failure, but it is even possible that a harmonious death is the true goal. The problem for a shaman is how to avoid letting go of beings whose soul has been scattered all over their life, because they lost a part of their soul each time they experienced a shock. The patients must be helped to retrieve what is missing from their soul. Once this process has been carried out, the patients can feel sufficiently ready for death, and they will face it serenely. The death of a patient is in this case the manifestation of a successful treatment. Inversely, suffering beings are not capable of keeping their soul, such as therapeutic determination produces, from the point of view of the shaman, precisely the living dead: bodies that have been deprived of their soul through suffering.

Do you see yourself an individual, or as a link?

The second difference between the two cultures concerns our individualism. We search for personal accomplishment, recognition as an individual, in a way that is so extreme that the alternatives are considered barbaric. Who does not think of himself or herself as a person? Everyone nowadays refuses to be classified as representing a class of the society. The horror raised by the Japanese kamikaze pilots in W.W.II is a good example of our total incomprehension of a non-individualistic civilization. The shaman is certainly the most important person in the tribe, but he or she is only an expression of the will of the tribe, and, without it, shamans lose not only their powers, but even their roots of existence.

Your existence can be defined in two opposite ways.

The Occidental way treats people essentially as individuals who are of primary importance. Certainly, each individual forges bonds with other like individuals, but these links are formed individual to individual, and are subordinate to the existence of the individuals. Seeing things this way, you are the central person, and your friends, peers, and family are connected to you by links : friendship, work, family, etc.

The other one, 'Japanese-wise', sees the social links as essential, and individuals are simply the necessary parts needed to establish these links. Friendship, family, and work are central, and your personality is essentially embodied in the existing links between you and your friends, your family and your work. Obviously, to totally deny yourself as an individual is just another way of closing your eyes, and that would be strongly reminiscent of totalitarian ideologies. Nevertheless, in our society, we are so used to a crazy praise of the self, in particular under the influence of the American-Californian civilization, that we needn't be afraid to forget our ego and see ourselves as a simple link; we'll never reach the extreme of authoritarian thought. Let's leave our ego a bit, and see us from time to time as simple centers of exchange with others. This is exactly what should happen when we form shamanic circles. Each one must leave his or her ego and give more importance to the ones nearby, and to the circle as a whole, than to him or herself. Each one must stop feeling like an individual in order to become a part of the circle (I even ask participants to 'die', to accept the disappearance of their ego). Following these very 'communalist' steps, the various ceremonies of calling Spirits or dancing are more or less communal, but we end with a journey that is strongly individual. With shamanism, therefore, the balance between the two positions is well kept. In seið, as I teach it, the journey demands that the practitioner forgets him/herself totally, as when practicing Zen. Therefore, the seið recommended in the present book is even much less individualistic than the shamanism we know from the American Indians, and the balance is strongly biased towards the disappearance of ego.

Of Prudishness

The third character is the most amusing, since unbelievably, prudishness creeps back into sexual matters in a world that considers itself a model of individual liberty, and which supports, in principle, a relaxation of morals. An illustration of this deep prudishness will be supplied by your reaction to the following treatment for sterility, as practiced by Siberian shamans; a treatment that most people would now find obscene and humiliating for women.

Siberian Fertility Rite:
The session is prepared carefully by creating a special enclosure.

> During the session, the shaman joins the Spirit of Mother Earth in dancing and asks her to bring Dschalyn [pron. *Tchalun*] to each one. Dschalyn is the passion of sex. Holding his drum, the shaman simulates the neigh of a horse, turning in circles. He then cries "Choruu, choruu" like a man crying out to call his horses. At this moment, the women cry out together and imitate the sound of a mare: "Innä-sasach!" They then try to leap on the shaman and to have intercourse with him. He throws them on the ground and the men help him to get rid of the women. He whistles strongly, makes circles with his drumstick, and the women return to normal and sit down. (sib1)

I find it remarkable that this ritual doesn't describe an orgy, and indeed it does not. Instead, the link between fertility and sexual fury is not kept hypocritically secretive. It is Dschalyn who brings children and, without passion, without accepting these deep compulsions, no children. Our prudishness is not based on the refusal of sex, but on the refusal of its strength, its beauty, and its wild power. The fact that the genitals, male or female, can be sticky and smelly is often seen as shocking or horrible when in fact, it is an element of their beauty. Just talking about genital smell and stickiness can be shocking. If you are, even just a bit, put in check, then ask yourself what there is that is ugly in this reality. We want to unite with bodies without smells in such a way that we hardly touch each other, which is again made worse because of Aids. The most natural odors, as those coming from under the armpits, are fought against and considered stinky, while they should, on the contrary, be a signature of each individual's personality. Obviously, we can find the odor of some unpleasant, but why should one person be forced to please everyone? We are reduced to only show our civilized sides, and must carefully repress what is primitive. Our body smell is its intimate signature, but it must be camouflaged or we could be accused of seeming indifferent to our neighbors' feelings.

And that's not all. The sexual act itself is accepted as a sort of dance, except with respect to penetration, which is considered to be in bad taste. That pornography debases women is not acceptable, but it is also fashionable to show simple condescension towards pornography because exposing the precise details of penetration is said to be boring or ugly. This purely esthetical rejection considers implicitly that the actors are beautiful when they are dressed and ugly when they mate. Pornography as it exists is certainly presented without elegance, because the movies are filmed without love and art, but what hypocrisy it is to find these splendid young men and women ugly! In a Heathen civilization, the sexual act, the 'love making', is beautiful in itself, never shameful or sad, the sexual organs of men and women are beautiful in themselves, never disgusting or stinky.

SOME 'OBJECTIVE' FACTS ABOUT SHAMANISM

I first want to acknowledge that I have not being trained in ethnology at all, and my principal source of ethnological observations are *Schamanengeschichten aus Sibirien* and Eliade's *Archaic techniques of Ecstasy*. My other source for shamanic traditions is *The Golden Bough*, the compiled works of J. G. Frazer. One of the appeals of Frazer's books is the fact that for each of his arguments, he uses both traditional and folk stories, as well as shamanic traditions, each complementing the other. However, Eliade is objective in his descriptions, while Frazer systematically scorns all shamanic practices, often forgetting important details, which somewhat decreases the interest of his work. I have also drawn on my own personal shamanic experience, since often very simple and well-known things don't seem to be understood very well by ethnologists. My experience and my knowledge about shamanism have come primarily from my contacts with the members of the Foundation for Shamanic Studies[30] and from my participation with various shamanic circles (or 'drumming groups') in Washington, Vienna and Paris.

The shamanic journey and its balanced, controlled aspect

A shaman goes into a trance in order to carry out a journey in the Spirit world. Often the word trance is associated with a loss of control, a sort of attack of insanity. This might seems to be confirmed by the fact that in the civilizations studied by ethnologists where shamanism was a normal practice, the shaman apprentices are typically people with a problem, at least just before beginning their apprenticeship. There are innumerable reports of perfectly normal people, falling sick, and then beginning their shamanic apprenticeship. Modern

---

[30] Foundation for Shamanic Studies, PO Box 1939, Mill Valley, CA 94942, USA.

shamans in Mexico begin their training after having been hit by lightning, which is a bad omen for their mental health to say the least. Despite all this, reports always describe shamans as being particularly well balanced, tough, and well integrated into their community. In his book, Eliade makes a tour of the shamanic world and notices that in each country, from Siberia to Australia, and the Americas to Africa, shamans must be in good health. Often they are the keepers of the oral traditions, and this requires greater than average knowledge. For example, the vocabulary of the Yakut shaman contains some 12,000 words while the average person's vocabulary in that culture contains only 4,000. This is no proof, obviously, but it doesn't exactly describe shamans as a group of mentally unstable people. For the Yakuts, the shaman "must always be serious, full of tact, able to persuade his neighbors; above all else, he must be humble and have good character."

These requirements for shamans are repeated throughout the planet. Since they have often received a very violent shock in their life, there is but one solution, according to Eliade, and it is that they have had an illness or wound in the past, and that they have gone beyond their sickness, becoming perfectly healed. It is not enough to be struck by lightning, they must also survive it in good shape.

The shamanic teaching I received demonstrated this characteristic perfectly. A shamanic trance is not a delirious state by which we allow ourselves to be taken away. It is always necessary to have an alert spirit, ready to examine what is going on. In modern terms, we could otherwise interpret these journeys, at least for beginners, as taking place in the unconscious of the shaman. This enables you to start without believing in the Spirit world, as traditional shamans would describe it. Even in this case, keeping control is not easy because the unconscious is far away when the conscious remains active. The only real difficulty of the shamanic journey, in fact, is that you must always stay conscious and in control of the situation, while at the same time letting your spirit roam freely, a difficult goal that shamanic training is supposed to enable you to achieve. This attitude is like a poetic delirium, which must stay within certain limits, and also like the galdr, created to make the runes effective, combining poetry and furor in a balanced manner.

The trance state and the 'tests' showing that the state is attained

The trance state, the controlled trance, can be obtained using a variety of methods that range from the softest to the most brutal. In certain cases, the shaman is simply stretched out and melodious chanting helps to send him or her into a trance. To illustrate a similar use of such soft methods, consider the example of the seið session described in the saga of Eric the Red. The *völva* asks for an assistant to sing the chant of witches for her so she can start her work. The saga insists that particularly good results were achieved because of the quality of the singing. Another example showing that the Germanic shamans used soft methods for their journeys is found in the saga of the Earls of Orkney. One of the heroes of the saga wants to consult a seer. Once he does, the seer says:

> These believers [*the Christians*] behave in a very strange way, depriving themselves of food and sleep so as to be informed about that which they desire to know; despite all their efforts, the higher the stakes are, the less they find. People like me do not bother with self-punishment, and are able to easily find what their friends want to know. (saga16)

In many cases, the shaman or an assistant plays the drum, possibly with songs, and lets him or herself be carried away by the beat. All sorts of other instruments are possible, two pieces of dry wood would do. The Australian shamans use the didgeridoo, a hollow wooden tube in which they modulate the vibrations of their lips. It is accompanied with the beating of dry sticks of wood. All these methods are relatively soft. However, more excruciating methods are also used in order to induce a trance. Fasting for several days, often without water, sleep and heat, was the common practice for the young American Indians when they began their vision quest that would reveal the spiritual powers to them. The Sun Dance, now well re-established, is also a form of torture. Here is how it is described in Hultkranz's book, *Religions of the American Indians*. It takes place in a sort of enclosure constructed according to a precise ritual but we will not go into these details. The ceremony begins when the sun goes down, and continues for four days, stopping each night. The dancers don't eat, and in principle, don't drink (modern softened versions allow some bites of fruits each evening). Public healing ceremonies take place between 11 am and noon. The dance continues without interruption all day, after the morning prayer. This is repeated for four days. Later in the afternoon of the fourth day, the dancers receive their first water. This is the current practice, hard enough on the bodies of the participants; no drinking for several days while dancing under a scorching sun is obviously endangering their lives. *Hanta Yo* even describes a dancer who attaches a cord through the skin of his back, hangs the skull of a buffalo to each end, and doesn't stop his dance until the skull falls to the ground; when the skin on his back is completely torn. It is by these harsh means that these civilizations obtain their visions.

Taking drugs for journeying has been frequently discussed due to the popular status of Castaneda's books. What I want to emphasize on this topic is the following. It is clear that the

Indian shamans used tobacco abundantly and that certain Siberian shamans offered large quantities of vodka to their Spirits by drinking it themselves. As for using harder drugs, this would contradict all the ethnological knowledge and evidence relative to the controlled aspect of shamanic journeys. The shaman remembers the journey clearly and is able to retell it with precision. The more experienced the shaman, the more control he or she has over the journey. In one of his books, Castaneda asks Don Juan why he must take all these drugs, and Don Juan answers: "Because you are not gifted enough." Drugs, therefore, might be necessary to break through rational prejudices, but are never really useful for the trained shaman. Obviously, we can always argue this topic and I don't want to get into a debate with supporters of 'shamanic drugs'. At the very least, I want to stress that there is an important tradition that doesn't use drugs, and that their shamanic feats are not less than those using drugs.

Once the trance is reached, many testimonies describe the shaman's remarkable strength and resistance to pain. In this state, they are full of energy and can, for instance, perform incredible jumps, even when carrying loads of iron plates, as do Siberian shamans. They can also touch burning coals, swallowing them as well, self mutilate (as for example, opening their abdomen, stab themselves with a spear) without wounds or traces. I do not want to debate the objective reality of these phenomena. For one, they have certainly been attested by a number of testimonies of impartial observers, and for another, they obviously contradict rationality. I'd like to present now two testimonies coming from the Icelandic sagas that confirm the shamans' feats of power.

One of these sagas contains an indirect testimony, but it is convincing through its innocence. The goal of the story is not at all to describe the special powers of the shamans, but instead to show how the Christian faith is superior to that of the Heathens'. It is only in passing that a berserk is said to casually perform a classical shamanic feat, the one of walking through a burning woodpile. *Njal's saga* gives a few details how Iceland became Christian. It is important to know that the arrival of a *berserk* was strongly feared by the Icelandic.

The word 'berserk' is used here in its original Norse meaning: a warrior, often dedicated to Odin, able to put himself in such a state of frenzy that he becomes insensitive to weapons, fires, etc.

The evangelist, named Thangbrand, proposed a sort of bargain to them:

> "I will give you a chance to test which is the better faith. I shall kindle three fires. You Heathens are to hallow one of the fires, I shall hallow the second, and the third fire is to remain unhallowed. If the berserk is frightened of the fire that I have hallowed, but walks unscathed through your fire, then you must accept the new faith." The berserk, fully armed, hurled himself in the hall; he strode at once through the fire hallowed by the Heathens, but when he came to the fire hallowed by Thangbrand, he was not able to go through it and said that he was burning all over. He lifted his sword to hit the people seated on the benches, but the sword got caught in a beam. Thangbrand hit his arms with a crucifix and, miraculously, the sword dropped from the berserk's grasp; then, Thangbrand plunged a sword into his breast... [*and the berserk was killed*]. (saga17)

The fact that the berserk was able to walk through burning logs (not hallowed by a Christian) without any problem is so evident for the actors in this drama, that Thangbrand uses it as an argument for demonstrating the power of the Christian faith. We must emphasize that, from the point of view of shamanic performance, walking over blazing logs is, so to say, one grade higher than 'simple' walking over red coals.

The second testimony describes a 'witch-berserk', as the saga calls him, whose eye is able to dull swords. In the saga of *Gunnlaug Wormtongue*, Gunnlaug must fight against a berserk:

> "Things took a desperate turn," said the king, "because the eyes of this man dull all the weapons. Follow my advice: here is a sword with which you will battle, but cover it up and show him another one," ... [*The berserk*] asked him which sword he had, and Gunnlaug pulled his sword and showed it to him, but he had made a buckle on the sword that the king had given him, and he slid the buckle in his hand ... [*They fought*]. Gunnlaug hit back with the sword that the king gave him. The berserk did not even put himself on guard, imagining that it was the sword that he was shown, and Gunnlaug immediately gave him a fatal blow. (saga18)

The berserk didn't doubt for one second his power to dull the weapons, to the point that the king's trick caught him unaware.

This berserk's trance can be looked upon as being black magic. This is true if the berserk does not increase his spirituality by journeying in the Spirit world, and is able to perform his feats in ordinary reality only. It would be very surprising that a Christian reporting on these berserks would take note of their Heathen spirituality, and see here anything else than witchery. The existence of berserks left many objective traces in the Nordic literature and several runic poems have alluded to this state, but nowhere do we find a trace of their spiritual side.

The following section describes what normally comes from the shamanic trance, when practicing 'white' magic.

The psychopomp shaman: Death and resurrection of the shaman.

One of the roles of the shaman is to accompany the souls of the dead to their home. This is what is called the psychopomp role. In the Siberian tribes, all sorts of precautions are taken to prevent a soul from coming back to haunt its village. At the cemetery, they destroy the wagon that carried the body, and return by another road than the one taken to go there, etc., so that the soul can't find the path. When these precautions are not enough, then they turn to a shaman to take the dead to their new dwelling place. Of course this is only possible if the shaman knows the way there. This is probably why almost all the shamanic initiations, throughout the world, have at least a simulation of death followed by a resurrection, or a mystical death happening during a shamanic voyage, or a 'real' death, where the person is killed, and cut up, typically, by his or her master, before being resuscitated. Obviously, I do not know if this 'real' death is a physical death, where it could be medically determined, I only want to say that some shamans describe this death as though it happens in ordinary reality. Whether the death is virtual or real, it shows that the myth of the phoenix being reborn from its cinders is a shamanic theme of primary importance.

The following Yakut legend describes this death and its environment very well.

> The shamans were born far in the North at the root of dreadful illnesses. A larch stands there, on its branches many nests lie at different heights. The biggest shamans are pulled up at

the top of the big tree, the mean ones at half height, and the small shamans on the low branches.

It is told that at first a big bird flies, similar to an eagle, with iron feathers, up to this tree. It sits on it and lays an egg. Then, this bird hatches the egg. If a very big shaman should hatch, it broods three years, if a small, one year.

This bird is called 'animal-mother' [*Eliade gives 'bird-of-prey mother', which might well be the Russian original, but the German is 'tiermutter'*] and she appears only three times. The first time, when she carries the shaman; the second time, at the end of his evolution - of his body being cut in pieces-; for the third time, when the shaman lies in death.

When the shaman (his soul) crawls out of the egg, this bird hands over his education to a Spirit-shamaness with name Bürgästej-Udagan, who has one leg, one hand, and one eye. This shamaness lays the shaman in an iron cradle, rocks him, and fosters him with thick pieces of coagulated blood.

When the raising in the cradle is finished, the future shaman is handed over to three black emaciated spirits, who cut his flesh in pieces. At first, they put the head of the shaman on the top of a pole. Then, they scatter all over the hashed meat as an offering. Three other spirits throw the jaws of the shaman as an oracle for the origins of all needs and illnesses. If the oracle-bone falls in the normal position, it is then said that the shaman can rescue people from this illness. (sib2)

All Siberian tribes do not accept the eagle shape of the animal-mother. Here are other possible shapes for the Tungus:

> The animal-mother of a Tungu shaman has, many say so, the look of a mountain-deer with balding fur, with eight legs, grown out of the front part of the body, with backwards-deft hooves. It can also have the look of a female elk or of a bear. (sib3)

I believe this primitive mother of the Siberian shamans, the Animal-Mother, to be associated more to the rune Uruz than to Pertho. This is my personal impression, and does not come from any analysis of the texts. I feel that this primitive mother goes back so far that she doesn't have the smiling aspect of giving birth of the Disir, as Pertho would have. We are touching on mysteries going back to a very remote time, and it is Uruz that represents this primitive elementary power. The 'Idisi' of the first Merseburg charm, even though usually translated as 'Disir', might correspond better to these ancient divinities. Here is the first Merseburg charm (the second is given in Chapter 4) :

Original text (High Old German):	English translation:
Eiris sazun idisi, sazun hera duoder.	Once the Idisi [*Disir*] sat, sat here and there.
suma hapt heptidun, suma heri lezidun,	Some hefted fetters [*on the enemy*], some stopped the host [*of the enemy*],
suma clubodun umbi cuoniouuidi:	Some loosened the fetters:
insprinc haptbandun, inuar uigandun!	Jump the bonds, evade the bad wights!

What is described in the above Yakut legend case is clearly a dismemberment ritual. Other tales from other tribes describe cooking rituals, or destruction by fire like in the Celtic tales, as we will see later when speaking of rejuvenation techniques.

However, dismemberment is one of the most classic and simplest ways to 'live your own death'. I have heard many people describe their shamanic journey as a form of dismemberment. Typically, one of the Animal Spirits, an aid to the shaman, is in charge of the operation and the shaman is able to recount the operation with a great amount of detail, as for example: "My lion opened my breast and he took out my heart, etc;" This type of journey is not dangerous and so even beginning shamans can perform this journey safely.

Many journeys must also be made toward the land of the dead, where the psychopomp shaman guides the souls that have become lost in the land of the living. It is up to each individual shaman to find their way to the land of the dead, although it is not advisable to go there without very good reasons.

Along the way, the psychopomp shaman will encounter souls and he or she must then convince each one that it belongs to a dead body. Very often, these lonely souls seem to be lost simply because they are ignorant of what is going on in ordinary reality. The shaman's role is to push them gently towards the land of the dead and perhaps even argue with them to convince them to go there. To my knowledge, there has never been a struggle between a psychopomp and a soul: success is achieved through persuasion. It is possible that during the journey, the shaman meets some demons who try to prevent him or her from convincing the soul, and, as a result, some battles could take place, but never with the soul itself.

Despite the large number of ghost stories found in the Icelandic sagas, they never once describe a psychopomp rite, unfortunately. We always find that the body of the ghost is removed from its burial mound (generally, it is well conserved but "horrible to look at"), burned, and then the ashes are thrown into the sea in order to get rid of the ghost. Clearly, the goal of these sagas is to show how evil people, sorcerers in general, can create trouble even after their death, and not to describe the rites that enable the shaman to chase ghosts out from the land of the living.

An important part of shamanic training consists of a journey where the shaman travels to his or her own death, but this can only be done with the proper preparation. Most journeys last a few minutes, but these can last several hours or days. The return from this journey must be especially well prepared if the shaman doesn't want to risk losing his or her soul. Odin himself understood this risk and was afraid of losing both his ravens: "Thought, and even more so Memory." It is during these very long journeys that catastrophes can happen. A good illustration of this phenomenon can be seen in the only shamanic joke that I have ever heard told (told by Sandra Ingerman during one of her seminars in Vienna):

> It's the story of a shaman who leaves for a shamanic journey of three days. For his return, he makes an agreement with his wife that is connected to the fact that he is somewhat of a glutton for a special dish, let's say wheat cakes. So, his wife must whisper in his ear: "The wheat cakes are ready" to make him come back. But his wife is not very faithful and she takes advantage of the situation to get rid of her husband. She doesn't whisper the formula for returning and he is considered dead and is buried. One year later, having forgotten completely about her 'dead' husband, and after having just cooked some wheat cakes, she calls out to her new husband: "The wheat cakes are ready!"

Then, she hears three knocks on her kitchen door ...

I suppose that this funny story is told to somewhat lessen the serious and impressive nature of the journey to one's own death. In any case, I have never seen people joke after such a journey, instead, they are full of awe.

The only allusion to the runes playing the psychopomp role is found in the incantations of Groa. There are nine incantations and I have associated them to the nine songs Odin talked about and to the nine types of runes, (which is explained in detail on my site: http ://www.nordic-life.org/nmh/). I attribute the role of the psychopomp to the runes of Protection because they protect the living from dead souls by helping the souls go to the land of the dead. Here is what Groa wishes her son so that he completes a safe journey:

> Here is what I sing for you in the eighth place:
> If you are surprised outside
> At night on a dark path
> I wish for you to avoid
> The evil that could be caused by
> A dead Christian woman. (edda3)

I don't want to discuss here why Groa talks about a Christian woman, but it is clearly meant to protect the living from the deads' souls, which is part of the function of the psychopomp. Another possible rune for this kind of protection would be Dagaz instead of a 'rune of Protection' as you might expect. An Eddic poem says that the hero "traced the runes of Hel" on a giantess who was preventing his passage, and that the giantess was petrified by the light of dawn. Tradition says that the souls of the dead stop tormenting the living at this moment. Dagaz is then a good rune for performing this kind of magic.

The shaman, searcher of lost souls

Eliade emphasizes that everything concerning the soul is the shaman's domain and that the shamanic treatment is designed to heal corruption of the soul. According to the Buryats, the shaman sits on a rug with the patient. An arrow lies close to them and its point is attached to a red thread that links it to a sacred birch tree outside the tent. The patient's soul moves along this thread to reintegrate into the patient's body. Similar to this Buryat custom, there is a shamanic training game of searching for the patient's lost soul. Two partners journey together, one starting a bit after the other. The one who leaves first wears a red thread on the wrist. The second must try to follow the first, and uses the red thread to mark the first in the Spirit world. After the journey, the second one tells the first what he or she saw the other do and this way, they can discuss how much their journeys agree.

I would also like to share with you the experience of a modern shaman, Sandra Ingerman. She has written two books detailing her work and personal experiences in her search for lost souls. She has treated many people by 'descending' into their past to find an incident where a part of their soul was lost. Losing a part of your soul can happen for many reasons, the result of a shock, illness, an accident, or a psychological shock, but also because another individual tried to steal your soul. Ingerman's ideas on the vampire like behavior of certain parents or partners are truly original and convincing. She illustrates, in a very particular way, all that psychology has presented as evidence on the subject of co-dependence, master-slave relationships, etc. The principal of her description of a person can be summarized as follows. We carry with us our past, as everyone would say, but we carry it almost 'physically' (at least, in the Otherworld), like a long rope that hangs behind us, and throughout this past, we can find parts of our soul that we have lost and that are still lingering around the 'rope'. This is also where we will find traces of what happened when others have robbed soul parts from us. The shaman's role is to go into the client's past, following this 'rope', to repair the soul, or, when the clients have lost part of their soul, to convince the parts to return to their 'owner', or to convince the souls' thieves to return what they stole.

In ethnological texts, we find descriptions that are very similar to what Sandra describes, but never with such precision.

Certainly, there isn't one particular rune for finding the lost parts of a soul, but we can recognize that this is the medicine man or woman at work. Therefore, the runes of Branches would be used:

> You must know the runes of Branches
> If you want to be a doctor
> Who knows how to treat wounds;
> On bark you must engrave them
> On the twigs of a tree
> Whose large branches stretch toward the East. (edda4)

Here again is what Odin says, after being suspended from Yggdrasil for nine days:

> I know a second
> Which is needed by the son of Man
> The one who wants to be a doctor. (edda5)

We can also translate 'branches' as 'limbs' as French and English translations do. I prefer to follow Genzmer's German translation, as I can't see why the medicine man would have a privileged relationship with his patient's limbs, and not with their breast, stomach, or head. On the other hand, that branches are important to his art is exactly what the above text stresses. I interpret it as follows: the runes of Branches (or the runes of Trees) are engraved on the twigs of a tree whose main branches stretch toward the East.

Shamans and their helpers

Ethnologists have recorded that many animals have been known to help shamans. With the Inuit, we see the fox, the owl, the bear, the dog, the shark, and all sorts of mountain Spirits. Other texts cite many other animals, but in general they are always wild animals. All the shamanic traditions give an extreme importance to wild animals, trees, hills, to all manifestations of nature. For example, consulting the Spirits during a shamanic journey often happens through the intermediary animal companion of the shaman, and the shaman always 'possesses' familiar Spirits that are those of the animals, typically wild ones. Very often, the Spirit that is consulted for a patient's healing is an animal's.

With the Siberian people, the horse plays a particularly important role, like with Sleipnir, Odin's horse with eight feet. One Buriat legend emphasizes the horse's role in shamanic initiation.

> In addition to her 'ordinary' husband, a young shamaness must take a spiritual husband who is the ancestral Spirit of a shaman. After this mystical marriage, one of her mares brings forth a foal with eight hooves. The ordinary husband, worried about order, cuts four of the foal's hooves. The wife then cries: "Oh, my little horse, the one that I rode as a shaman!" and she disappears, flying in the air to settle in another village. (eliade1)

With the hunting tribes of the American Indians, the youth would fast alone in the mountains in order to have dreams and visions where they would meet the Spirits. These Spirits can take a relatively abstract form like that of an indistinct being, but most often they are wild animals that help or that must be fought: owl, bear, humming bird (this is the image of the Spirit of lightning), deer, rattle snake, falcon, buffalo, and many others. In fact, the nature of the animal corresponds to the ability that will be received: deer for becoming a good runner, or the magpie for becoming a good scout, etc. For the American Indians who were gatherers, animals played a less important role in the life of the tribe, but nevertheless, each of the six directions was under the protection of a particular animal. As an example, the wolf was the guardian of the East, the badger was the guardian of the South, the bear was the guardian of the West, the mountain lion was the guardian of the North, the eagle the guardian of the sky, and the mole was the guardian of the earth. Initiations were performed by six 'societies', and each of them is associated with a direction and therefore with an animal. Because these societies have remained largely secret, we don't know exactly what the vision quest was made up of, and we cannot therefore be certain that the initiate comes in contact with animal Spirits. However, we do know of twelve parallel medicine-societies that have the Spirits of the wild beasts for their patrons and that respect and dance these animals' Spirits.

It is therefore a primordial characteristic for the shaman to ask for the help of the spirits, animal Spirits, generally, but also the Spirits of natural elements: lightning, wind, rain, fog, hills, lakes, etc.

In our modern civilization, we can easily interpret the shamanic journey as a descent into the unconscious, but this, clearly, is not in keeping with the tradition at all. The shamanic tradition describes these journeys as though they were made in a 'non-ordinary' reality, during which the shaman meets the Spirits of animals, typically, to ask their advice about their own problems or those of their clients. For example, during a journey to recover the lost parts of a patient's soul, if the shamans have a difficult time, they will ask one of their animal Spirits to help them learn how to solve the problem.

The shamanic ceremony is not only made up of the journey. It also contains two important rituals. One is the calling of the Spirits where the shaman successively addresses the six directions (East, North, West, South, Zenith, Nadir). Personally, I have adopted a more Celtic rite in which the Spirits of five directions are called, the four cardinal points and the center, asking the Spirits of these directions if they wish to join in the ceremony. The other ritual, often incompletely described by ethnologists, is the dance of the Animal-Spirits ('power-animals'). All those participating in the ceremony must dance their animals, in other words, to let their Spirit fill them, and to let themselves be carried by the animal's Spirit in order to imitate them in the best way. Certainly, those physically unable to do it could perform the dance in their head without moving about, but a person in good health will, as faithfully as possible, reproduce the movements of the animal. The incredible leaps that astounded the ethnologists seem poorly described if we don't say that the shaman made them by integrating the shape of the animal into himself or herself. It is not 'because' of the trance that the shaman is capable of these physical movements, it is 'because' he or she has left his or her body and allowed it to become taken over by the Spirit of an animal who performs these jumps because it is very natural for them.

I see a strong analogy in this with the necessary poetic fury of the rune master, who must allow himself or herself to be inhabited by the strength/force of the runes in order to express magical power. Instead of 'dancing their animals', the rune masters 'sing or howl their runes' in the galdr, but the two processes are very close in terms of the state of mind, emptiness and alertness of spirit that they each demand of their practitioners. At the same time, we do not want to hide the differences that exist between the two. Shamanism is close to nature, and the runes are a human construction. While the shaman works in the middle of a wild nature, the rune master operates in the heart of a home. The shaman is in direct contact with the elements of nature, while the rune master calls on human society before addressing the elements. Runic work for me, therefore, is a form that evolved from shamanism; one we could call 'runic shamanism'. The Celts, with the Oghams, and the Germanic, with their runes, were creating magical alphabets that, contrary to their equivalents in the rest of the world, have remained strongly connected to their shamanic roots, while transcending them.

Magical Flight

There are so many testimonies, from all regions of the world, of the shamans' abilities to magically relocate themselves from one place to another over great distances, that it is useless to repeat these references. Eliade's book, for example, gives many details on this theme. Our own tradition says that witches were able to fly on a broomstick. Odin could do this thanks to his two ravens, Thought and Memory, and also by practicing seið. Freya and Frigg had 'feathered skin' of falcons and they lent them to other Gods when they wanted to fly. Similarly, Eliade cites *Fridthjofs saga* which describes two völva, in a trance on their platform, seen from a great distance, riding a whale and trying to sink the hero's boat. In the non-ordinary reality, the hero defeated them by breaking their spines, and at this very moment in ordinary reality, they fell from their platform and broke their backs.

In every testimony, the shamans are able to create an overlap between ordinary and non-ordinary reality in such a way that both interact on each other. The saga cited above gives us an example of how accidents that happened at a great distance can manifest themselves instantaneously where the body of the shaman is.

A rather particular example of an action occurring at a distance is found in Gretti's saga. A magician wanted to bewitch Gretti. To do this, she took a stump which provided

> a small flat space where she could work; then she took her knife and carved some runes on the stump that she stained with her blood while singing a magical chant. She went around the stump counterclockwise and said solemn magical verses. (saga19)

Then, she entrusted the stump to the waves that would take it, with the curse, to Gretti's house. In this case, the magician, instead of flying, uses a roundabout way to act from far away. There aren't any particular runes for flying great distances, but they certainly enable a magician to act from a distance, as Gretti's saga well illustrates.

The Mastery of Fire

Throughout the world, shamans have had to prove their mastery over fire (or cold) in order to be accepted by their community as authentic shamans. While in a trance state, they will hold burning coals in their hands, and often swallow them. Some can grab iron bars that are heated until white and not get burned. I don't know if all this is true, but it is attested by many testimonies and by ethnologists who have studied this phenomenon. Inversely, or perhaps in parallel, the Manchu cut nine holes in the ice and ask the shaman candidates to jump in and come out successively in each of the nine holes. The Inuit held an initiation that lasts five days in icy water. All this is related to a mastery of extreme temperatures, that we find again and again in all shamanic cultures. As well, outside the shamanic context, we find the same thing in the tests performed by yogi apprentices.

The rune associated with this power is described by Odin as the seventh in the Words of the High One (*Havamal*):

> I know a seventh:
> If I see the room
> With fire surrounding my bench mates,
> The flames are not so strong
> That I can't guard myself
> When I sing this charm. (edda6)

There is a striking example of this resistance to fire in the story of Saint Patrick, an Irish evangelist. In the legend, Saint Patrick fights against the magic of the local druids and a battle of magic follows. The chief of the Irish druids and Saint Benin, accompanying Saint Patrick, were each closed in a cottage that was set to flames. Obviously, Saint Benin came out without a burn and the chief of the druids was reduced to cinders (celt1).

Blacksmiths and Shamans

In studying the runic poems, we find some allusions to blacksmiths. These allusions are impossible to understand if they are not put into a shamanic context. The blacksmiths were also masters of fire, and this is why they are often associated with witches. This relationship between metallurgy and magic seems fixed around the world. I would like to focus on this very particular aspect in Yakut mythology. There is a Yakut proverb that says: "shamans and blacksmiths were born from the same nest." In the Yakut legend discussed earlier, the word 'nest' is not to be taken to the second degree since it was in a nest that the Animal-

Mother hatches the souls of the shamans. Moreover, the Yakut associated blacksmiths with eagles, and the eagle is considered the creator of the first shaman.

The following text of a Samoyedian shaman describes his death and his resurrection as a ritual brought about by a blacksmith.

> He entered a cavern and met a nude man who was working some bellows. On the fire, there was a caldron as big as half the earth. The nude man saw him and grabbed him with an enormous pair of tongs ... [*This blacksmith*] cut off his head, cut up his body into small pieces [*dismemberment ritual*], and threw everything into the caldron. His body stayed boiling in the caldron for three years [*cooking ritual*]. There were also three anvils, and the nude man forged the man's head ... (eliade2)

Not only shamans are welded as smiths, but they find also a continuous source of power in the smith's art:

> A smith Kydaj-Bachsy lives there below. Near him will shamans be welded and hardened as smiths. The big and dreadful shamans increase their strength from this source. (sib4)

We often find other stories or tales, where the shaman candidate is forged in this way, which is again another ritual, different from dismemberment and cooking. The blacksmith is responsible for creating the shamans.

These examples show the narrow connection between shamanism and metallurgy, and enables us to better understand the allusions to blacksmiths in the runic poems.

Shamanism in the Edda

Sacred Events

The Edda describes three kinds of sacred workings, which have been very well analyzed by Boyer in his book, *Le Monde du Double*.

The *nidh* is a curse made with ceremony and magical formula. We could say that when Egil plants the pole of infamy for the king and the queen, and engraves cursing runes for the Spirits of the country, he is carrying out a *nidh*. I have never seen an example of a 'positive' *nidh*, where instead of cursing someone, it is requesting a blessing. Perhaps it would have had another name. However, the principle of the action is easy to see: through magic someone wants to get something from the Spirits or the Gods.

The *blot* is a sacrifice. Best known is the Fall *blot*, called *Freysblot*. We know that this custom must have been very popular since eating horsemeat has been forbidden in Norway and Iceland because of the pagan practices associated with it. Certainly, there are other types of sacrifices, especially when a rich man died, since even human sacrifices were possible. For instance, a saga briefly describes the place where sacrifices to Thor were practiced, the victim's back would be broken. Odin is the God of the hanged, and, together with Freya, he is also the God of heroes who die in combat. Frigg was perhaps the Goddess of drowning. Curiously, no Nordic God is associated to the most common means of rebirth in shamanism: dismemberment; being cooked once shred to pieces; being forged; and consumption by fire. The rune, Hagla, is clearly linked to regeneration through fire, but the other three operations seem to have been forgotten.

Finally, *seið* is a more elaborate ceremony where a *völva* leaves her body on the platform where it rests. She then travels to the sound of a chorus of singers or to the sound of the drum. This is very close to the classic shamanic journey as it is still practiced today. We will discuss *seið* again a bit further in this chapter.

Nordic God shamans

Despite some missing details, I believe that we can accept the hypothesis that all Nordic Gods were more or less shamans. Odin can travel alone thanks to his horse, Sleipnir. Thor also has a means of traveling with his chariot drawn by two magical goats. Freya and Frigg possess the "feathered skin of a falcon." We don't know much about Frey, but likely his golden boar could be used to carry him about. Following this order, we get the runes Ansuz, Laukaz, Berkanan, Pertho and Jeran. Two other Gods explicitly linked to the runes have not been mentioned yet : Tyr (Tiwaz) and Ing (Ingwaz). The Edda barely says a word about them. However, Tyr, by sacrificing his right hand to the wolf is initiated in a way, and the runic poem describing Ing going East does describe a journey. Loki, who we will connect to Othala, travels (journeys) a lot in the Edda, even if it is by borrowing someone else's means. Finally, the prose Edda tells us that each of the twelve Gods had their own particular horse, which concurs with the fact that Freya taught seið to all of them.

Shamanism in Celtic tales (and in the Grimm tales)

Many shamanic characteristics can be found in Celtic tales as well as Grimm's, as we will see in the next volume. I want to focus now on the important theme of the shaman's death since it is recurring in the tales. This death is often made by fire, and the importance of fire in shamanic traditions is well known. Similarly, a celestial betrothed, with whom they have sexual relationships, very often initiates the heroes of these tales, just as apprentice Siberian shamans do. The heroes go into the magical country where their betrothed lives, but they don't always return. We have also emphasized the importance of Animal-Spirits that help the shaman in his or her work. We know that many animals help the heroes (of both sexes) in the various tales.

I do not want to go into detail on this theme since it seems to be already well established, suffice to say that there is a narrow concordance between shamanic themes and the tales. One difference, however, is important to note. It is found in tales that are describing the end of some ancestral power. The myth of the city of Is describes a child, the small Kristof, who begins the destruction of Is by removing the ancestral protective oak. The oldest Lancelot tale shows him cutting down Iweret, the man of the yew. Finally the end of the Cuchulain myth describes him humiliating queen Maeve. For me, these tales are relatively recent, and they relate how the archaic power, the matriarchal power, has been destroyed by a man. Therefore, they describe the end of the feminine shamanic tradition, and tell how man has appropriated the power of magic.

THREE NEGLECTED ASPECTS OF SHAMANISM

Finally, I want to focus on three characteristics of shamanism that for various reasons, have been neglected by modern shamanism as well as by ethnologists. The fact that shamanic treatment is a social operation, and not an individual one, has not been sufficiently emphasized in my opinion. It is important since this social character is responsible for the fact that it is 'white' magic that is practiced, which, indeed, does not concern ethnologists. The two other characteristics, the sexual relationship developed with partners of the Spirit world and shamanic sex changes (male to female), have been affected by the prudishness of scientists who have clearly wanted to avoid presenting a theory based on such shocking facts.

The shaman, social worker

Often, ethnologists record the social character of shamanism through allusions, but it is never discussed explicitly. For example, Eliade wants to insist on the precision of jumps made by the shaman who do not hit anyone, "although shamans ... perform their ecstatic dance in a yurt full of spectators." Similarly, he takes the opportunity to note that the spectators respond in chorus to some chants, or welcome the end of shaman's journey with shouts of joy. He also describes a ritual of soul searching with the Buryats, and specifies that the assistants are gathered by taking a slice of the population that is the same age as the patient. When he describes a Samoyed séance, he begins with: "The audience gathers about the shaman, etc." Further, he notes that with the Eskimos, the shamanic session takes place in the presence of the entire village. It seems bizarre to me, but he doesn't draw any conclusions from these facts. Recall also the seið performed by a völva in the saga of Eric the Red. The völva operates on a platform, surrounded by all the women of the household. Similarly, in the Sun Dance, as performed by some American Indians, the healing sessions are public.

Finally, I have experienced shamanic healing carried out in public, where each one asks the patient questions about the sickness, and then gives their advice. It is only after this, which can last quite a long time, that a shaman realizes the particular shamanic operation to be adapted to the patient, with the entire group of assistants helping in the effort.

In our civilization the relationship of individual to individual is privileged as compared to the relationship of an individual to a group. In using the runes, the poem shouted/howled by the rune master serves to announce to the whole community why runes have been engraved.

But again this is perhaps not what's essential. I have no other proof than my own shamanic experience to support the idea that the shamanic treatment itself is much less addressed to an isolated individual than to an individual in its social group. The treatment is not so much caring for the body or the spirit of the patient than a reintegration into his or her social environment. There are no other sicknesses than those that threaten the social body, and it is to these that the shamanic treatment is addressed. This thesis on shamanism is relatively original, and asks for a longer development, outside of the problems of healing by the runes and the scope of this book.)

The case of current shamanism is a bit less clear. I know that many modern shamans tend to perform their ceremonies with only their patient present. I believe that this is a deep error, opposing all shamanic tradition, yet well inspired by our modern individualistic habits. In this spirit, the best modern shamans will insist that their client brings at least one family member or a friend to assist with the ceremony; for example, searching for lost parts of souls.

By insisting upon the importance of our social relationships, particularly with respect to our health, both moral and physical, and on a social treatment of illnesses, I can clearly see how I am contradicting the values defended by our modern society. One value, basic to the Germanic culture, and therefore to the comprehension of the runes, is simply accepting one's destiny. Several times in the Edda, we find the story of a hero who finds out his destiny in advance, sees that it will be terrible, and yet does not seek to deviate from the line that has been traced for him by the Norns. This is an excellent illustration of a being who gives little importance to his ego. That might be frightful, but we can't understand the spirit of rune masters without leaving our ego aside. The incredible importance that we give to the individual makes us somewhat unable to understand that other civilizations have been able to make other choices, and, in my opinion, we cut off the magical vision of the world that I would like to illustrate and defend here.

ALL THAT BRINGS US TO OURSELVES DESTROYS OUR POTENTIAL TO EXERCISE MAGIC. ALL THAT PLACES US IN INTERACTION WITH OTHER HUMANS DEVELOPS THIS POTENTIAL.

Mystical marriage with a celestial partner

In many shamanic traditions, spiritual forces elect the shaman, and this is marked by accepting a spiritual partner, often along with his or her human partner. Among the Buryats, for example, it is important that the shaman candidate has sexual relationships with a 'celestial betrothed'. During his initiation, the candidate makes love with the nine wives of the God of dance, fertility and wealth. Only when his shamanic instruction has been completed does he meet his celestial betrothed and they make love. In many traditions, the shaman has a celestial partner in addition to his or her human partner. Elsewhere, we find tales that are full of stories in which the celestial partner is jealous of the human one and seeks vengeance in a more or less cruel manner. When all goes well, the shaman has children with the celestial partner as well as with the human one. If the apprentice refuses sexual relationships with a celestial partner, he or she is choosing death.

The Siegfried and Brunhild history (called Sigurdr and Sigrdrifa in the Edda) illustrates this practice very well. Siegfried is initiated twice. The first is through tasting the blood of Fafnir, the dragon, that he kills on the advice of his mentor, Regin. As a result, he is able to understand the song of birds, which puts him in contact with classical shamanism. The second time, it is with Brunhild who, as a Valkyrie, is a typical celestial partner, and she initiates Siegfried to the knowledge of the runes. Nothing in the texts suggests that Siegfried has abandoned the way of classical shamanism. On the contrary, he seems to hold some particular bonds with his horse. In fact, after his murder, his horse, Grani, announces his death to his widow, as is found in the *Second Chant of Gudrun* :

> Grani lowered his head
> Down to the grass.
> The horse knew well
> That its master had perished. (edda7)

Siegfried had made many love oaths with his celestial partner, Brunhild, yet he abandons her for another. By taking a human wife, Siegfried breaks the contract that linked him to his celestial partner, provoking his death, and this is what happens classically in the shamanic context. The epic states explicitly that it is following Brunhild's jealous plots that he will be killed. I associate the Gebo rune to the love oaths and Siegfried is guilty of breaking his oaths. But even more so, he betrayed his celestial betrothed, the wife-initiator, who I associate with Berkanan. Two broken runes can explain why it was no longer possible for him to remain alive.

Shamanism and sex changes

One last point, somewhat delicate but important, is the shamans' sex change. Seið was reserved to women in the Nordic civilizations. When he practiced it, Odin was treated as effeminate. In the rare examples of seið described in the Icelandic sagas, it is almost always women who practice it (and a man who practices seið in one of the sagas is referred to as a pederast a bit further in the saga).

Now, when we consider recorded shamanic observations, we meet an overwhelming majority of male shamans with the exception of rare isolated islets. A disturbing detail, however, is that female shamans often leave behind the reputation that they have had exceptional powers. Another interesting fact is that, even in the ethnological records, there were still testimonies stemming from the Chukchee tribe, where some had to change their sex to practice their art. They are the 'soft men' who wear women's clothing, play the role of women, and even marry men sometimes. A change as extreme as this does not, however, always seems to be required. Many intermediary stages exist, for example, where the shaman dresses as a woman, but continues to live with his wife and has children. Nevertheless, this demand of the Spirits must not be taken lightly, and those refusing it end up dead. Eliade notes that this phenomenon is rare but not exclusive to the Chukchee tribe. It is also found with certain Eskimo, and with some Indian tribes of North America, South America, and Indonesia. Interestingly, there are no symmetrical cases where a woman has to become more masculine to become a shaman.

In light of the role of femaleness in shamanism, we will now consider how this relates to the creation of the runes. When speaking of the inventor of the runes, everyone assume that this inventor is a 'he', which would be kind of obvious in a Latin or Greek civilization where the influence of women could be only marginal. However, in a Germanic civilization, the chances of this person being a male ranges about around 50-50. For instance, Tacitus shows a deep disdain for these Germanic peoples that were led by women[31], and even the brutish warlike Viking society maintained women of power.

In the Edda, we see women teaching the runes to men as a recurring partner, in particular Sigrdrifa, a Valkyrie, initiates Sigurdr to rune knowledge.

Again in the Edda, *Havamál* (the words of the High One) describes the creation of the runes. It does not claim that Odin invented the runes, but that they were invented by a somewhat mysterious *ginregin* entity, who, at the very least, is not obviously masculine.

Rúnar munt þú finna	Runes you will find
oc ráðna stafi,	And well-explained runic inscriptions,
miöc stora stafi,	Very important runic inscriptions,
miöc stinna stafi,	Very powerful runic inscriptions,
er fáði fimbulþur	They, tinted by the supreme mage,
oc gorðo ginregin	And created by *ginregin*
oc reist hroptr rögna...	And engraved by the Crier of the Gods.

Before commenting on the meaning of *ginregin*, I want to first specify the meanings of the other expressions used in this poem.

Stafi means 'stave' but it usually takes the meaning of 'runic inscription'.

---

[31] In *Germania* 45, he states: "Bordering on the Suiones are the nation of the Sitones. They resemble them in all respects but one - woman is the ruling sex. That is the measure of their decline, I will not say below freedom, but even below decent slavery." (taci2)

fimbulþur can be corrected as '*FimbulÞýr*', meaning 'supreme Tyr', Tyr is an ancient god. It could also be corrected as *fimbulþulr* to mean supreme mage, as I did.

hroptr rögna is the Crier of the Gods, a classic name for Odin.

Now, *ginregin* contains *regin* meaning 'gods', but the exact meaning of this word is unknown. It appears in another poem of the Edda, *Alvissimál*, where it is said that the *ginregin* use a different word than the Gods do to designate the night and the wind. Therefore, these divine powers are not identical to the Gods. The Nordic myths describe only one other supreme power alternative to the Gods, the Norns. They are of various origins: another famous poem, the *Völuspa* (the prediction of the prophetess - you will find a translation commented on my site: www.nordic-life.org/nmh), describes them first as giant girls (*þursa meyiar*), then simply as "girls, very knowledgeable" : (*meyiar, margs vitandi*). Another poem, *Fafnir's Lay*, says that some are gods (Aesir), some are elves, some are dwarves (Dvalin is a dwarf):

Sundrbornar mjök	Coming from far away,
segi ek at nornir sé,	The Norns are born,
eigoð þær ætt saman;	They are not of the same race.
sumar eru áskungar,	Some are of the Aesir,
sumar eru álfkungar,	Some are of the elves,
sumar dœtr Dvalins.	Some are daughters of Dvalin.

The Norns decide the destiny of the humans, as said in the *Völuspa*:

þær lög lögðo,	They made the laws
þær líf kuro	They fixed the life
alda börnom,	Of the sons of the humans
ørlög seggia	The mortals' *ørlög* (destiny).

Even the Gods themselves cannot avoid their final judgment (and condemnation!), which is called Ragnarök, and inscribed in their destiny.

This is why, I think it is reasonable to see *ginregin* as a divinity similar in nature to the Norns, thus a feminine divinity, and the inventor of the runes.

To push my hypothesis even further, the *Völuspa* says also that the Norns engraved staves, that is to say that they wrote some runic inscriptions: they had knowledge of the runes before all other divinities, which goes along well with the hypothesis that they were their inventors.

The role of the Crier of the Gods, Odin, is to engrave the runes; the role of an executor, not an inventor. Similarly, the text that describes the suffering he endured to obtain the runes clearly states that he gathered them, not that he created them.

Moreover, let us consider reports from the Goth historian Jordanes who describes sorceresses-warriors in the Goth armies. In his *Origin and deeds of the Goths*, chap. 24, he says:

> "Filimer rex Gothorum ... reperit in populo suo quasdam magas mulieres, quas patrio sermone Aliorumnas ipse cognominat ; easque habens suspectas, de medio sui proturbat, longeque ab exercitu suo fugatas in solitudinem coegit terrae …"
>
> "Filimer the king of the Goths ... spotted among his people some sorcerer women, called by the public rumor *Aliorumnas* and suspecting these, he banished them, and far away from his army he forced them to flee in the solitudes of the earth."[32]

---

[32] This my translation. Mierow's classical English translation is available on line at :
www.acs.ucalgary.ca/~vandersp/Courses/texts/jordgeti.html

In this sentence, the name *Aliorumnas* is in the accusative plural case, this is why these women were called *Alliorumnae*, and it seems to the specialists that it is equivalent to *Alliorunnae*, or *Allrunnae*. Jordanes provides no dating, but genealogies. By giving some 10 to 20 years to each king's reign, we can assume that Filimer could not have reigned earlier than year 350 AD, which means that one century earlier these war-witches were still in full power. Only their name hints at them using runes, and that with the restriction that, classically, the Goth language is said to use the word 'rune' for 'secret'. Nevertheless, these dates place us at the beginning of the full development of runic use, it would be astonishing if Germanic witches would not have known about the runes.

Without being an absolute proof, this argument nevertheless gives some substance to the fact that women were, at least, very much linked to the early use of the runes (why were no male-warriors, called *Allrunni*, expelled from the Goth army?), which also gives consistence to the hypothesis that women were linked to their discovery.

More generally, I am always surprised at the kind of barrier that exists against masculine use of magic. Recall that the *Ynglinga saga* says men could not, without shame, practice seið. Many runic inscriptions attest that practicing seið, or practicing magic became an insult. More recently, consider the extraordinary torture, which some American Indians submit themselves to, in order to have a vision. Consider also that, except in Iceland (where at any rate the repression was very weak), the Inquisition executed mostly female witches. All this hints at a kind a feminine superiority in practicing magic.

One of my strongest personal experiences happened when a shamaness, a leader of a group, asked me to be her tool in recovering the lost Spirit of a land - a hard job to do. She steered me all along, then during the proper lost Spirit recovery, I had to work alone (thus taking a kind of temporary leadership), and immediately after, I became her tool again. Feeling a land wight going through me, to return to its land, was indeed a shaking experience, and I'd never have been able to do it without being steered by a woman. And at the same time, it is interesting to note that the shamaness did not feel able to do it alone.

This explains why I tend to believe that magical power is 'normally' feminine. This does not mean that men cannot practice, but that they must call on their feminine side to do so. It also possible for them to serve a 'mistress' magician, or to serve as an intermediary between her and Spirits. I also guess that men can acquire a sort of independence with respect to feminine power through using the runes, but they must first learn their magic from their feminine side or from a woman.

THE PRACTICE OF SHAMANISM

We have described the spiritual state that is required to practice shamanism and what shamanism is for a large number of primitive peoples. Now we'll look at the details of this practice in terms of how someone can use them today.

Two realities

First you have to take what we call a shamanic journey. It begins in ordinary reality, (the so-called 'ordinary reality', that you know in everyday life) and continues in the 'non-ordinary reality', the Spirit world. If, as almost everyone these days, you have some knowledge of psychoanalysis, you could refer to ordinary reality as conscious reality and non-ordinary reality as unconscious reality. Don't be concerned with the words, the important thing is your personal experience. The work of the shaman is to create a link between these two realities, which normally ignore each other. He or she will conduct a shamanic journey in non-ordinary reality, bring back information or entities, and communicate them to the patients in order to improve their day-to-day life.

Interactions between the two realities

The first problem is therefore the interaction between ordinary and non-ordinary reality. In particular, this problem comes up when shamanism is used for healing and divination. I am not convinced that the two realities are completely on the same plane. Ordinary reality has its laws, and it seems a bit blind to ignore them, as if non-ordinary reality could supersede them. In the same way, non-ordinary reality also has an existence, we should not completely neglect, as our modern society does more and more.

However, there are objects belonging to ordinary reality alone : a gun, for example, and it seems really naive to believe that someone could struggle against a gun with the arms from non-ordinary reality. It is true, however, that the one carrying the gun is a being of both realities, and that he or she can be reached on both planes. As another example, if you have a physical particularity that you dislike, perhaps a nose that you think is too large, you can do all the magnetic passes you want over it, but you will not change its size. On the other hand, you can help yourself by using non-ordinary reality to make it a necessary part of your face's beauty.

Finally, back to the topic of this book, it is clear that not all sicknesses are caused in ordinary reality, and when this is the case, they must be treated by non-ordinary reality. It is also clear that ordinary reality plays an important role in our health! Both classical and alternative medicines deal with ordinary reality. Shamanism and runes use non-ordinary reality and must not pretend anything else. This is why I do not think that a shamanic treatment works particularly better with alternative medicine than orthodox medicine: it can complement any medicine based on ordinary reality.

Your first shamanic journey

That you take pleasure in your experience is of primary importance. The shamanic journey is a deep relaxation experience that refreshes the body, the spirit, and, I believe, the soul, as well. The journey that I am about to describe is called the journey to the lower world[33]. The only real difficulty in this journey is that you have to remain aware and to control the situation, but, at the same time, you have to let your spirit wander freely. You will understand this better in the following section. Anyway, expect a bit of failure in the beginning, as everyone does, and then you will

---

[33] There is also an upper world, and a middle world, but I don't discuss them here.

learn from your setbacks. It could be that you experience some kind of psychological problem. If this happens, and it is possible during the journey, you may feel as though you are losing your footing, as if a crisis (your crisis corresponding to your problem) was beginning. In this case, I recommend that you stop your journey using the following procedure, so that you can have your crisis in ordinary reality where it belongs. Do not start again the same day. Rest and begin again the following day or when you feel better. If you continue to have crises, then you are the one who needs to have shamanic work done on you, rather than trying to become a shaman yourself. Having said that, if you have an essentially healthy spirit, if you follow the guidelines given, and if you can let yourself go easily without seeking to accomplish something specific, it would surprise me a great deal if you had this sort of crisis.

You should begin on an empty stomach, having eaten only lightly several hours beforehand or else having been fasting, but without an idea of self-punishment. Relax your body for a few minutes, and put yourself in a serious mood. It is a good idea to light a candle to give you a bit of light. You will also need a scarf to cover your eyes, but leave the candle burning during your journey. Have a pen and a notebook ready to write down your experiences during the journey. If you are alone, use a stereo or tape player to play monotone music like drumming or the sounds from a Tibetan bowl, for example. Do not listen to the music before your journey. It is intended for shamanic work, not for your pleasure. Even better, ask a friend to play some sort of rhythm for you in a repetitious and monotonous manner, using any instrument (two sticks of wood would suffice!). Now that everything is ready, you can light your candle and begin your journey. Start your music, and listen to the beat of the music. Listen - and let it penetrate your body. This is relatively difficult with recorded music, I must admit, and far easier with the sounds of a real instrument. When you feel ready, without forcing yourself, you can begin your journey. Search your memory for places that you have seen in ordinary reality, and that, in one way or another, are deeply rooted in the earth. Personally, I use a sort of cave that I played in when I was a child. You can use any opening in the earth, even artificial holes, such as a sewer, if that works for you. Try to remember things that are sunk into the earth: springs, lakes, tree roots, a hollow tree, a large rock that seems to sink into the ground, etc. Use your conscious imagination to find all sorts of these places and compare them to each other. Try to feel which place attracts you the most.

It is possible that this comparison takes a lot of time, and that the signal to return comes before you have made your choice. This isn't serious; just stop, and start again the journey some other time.

Once you have chosen your place, use your imagination again to consciously 'go' to this place, and to go through this hole into the earth, or, as the case may be, to crawl along the roots, or to flatten yourself and to slide yourself through the crevices at the base of the rock, etc. Again, by using your conscious imagination, force yourself to descend, see yourself descending. After this you should stop using your conscious imagination, except when you want to further go down. In principle, you have to keep going down until you find a place that pleases you, and then you have to explore it. Now it is time to stop imagining images, and to let them to come to you. During your descent, all sorts of images might appear to you. Let them come to you. If an image steps in on its own, then use your conscious mind again to look at it, to analyze it, and to find relationships with other images or other landscapes. Let the images come to you, without using your conscious imagination to make them appear, but, at the same time, maintain a critical spirit that analyzes what it sees. This is the difficult part of the journey; keeping your active, conscious imagination, while simultaneously allowing yourself to let unconscious images come to you for examination. Sometimes we tend to reject unconscious images because of self-distrust, or even conversely, to exaggerate the sensations with our imagination. This isn't very serious in the beginning, and with experience you will learn to let the images come to you without losing awareness. For example, suppose that you see an animal, and when you 'look' at it, you recognize it, or you notice that it is a strange animal, or perhaps you see only part of it. It is possible that it is a chimera (an animal compound of several different animal parts), or an animal known to you alone. It's possible that you see no animals, only landscapes or locations. What you see can be attractive, repulsive, beautiful or horrible; let yourself explore them. It is entirely possible that you only 'see' very indiscriminately, or that you only experience other sensations (touch, feel, etc.). In this first journey, try to have the least amount of interaction with what you see or experience; simply observe them consciously. Avoid trying to touch them or to change them, and especially to swallow them or to allow them to penetrate you. If one of these objects approaches you, or attacks you, stand firm and do not struggle against it. Escape it by consciously imagining a way to escape it (for example, you could grow some wings and take off). Do not try to bring anything back with you at the end of the journey.

After awhile, the rhythm of the drum will change, and it will be time for you to prepare yourself for your return. Take one last look around, and gently leave the place. When the rhythm becomes rapid and continuous, use it to carry you as you return. Complete your return quickly enough, but be sure to pass all the same places that you passed along your way. Therefore, at the end of your journey, you should find yourself right back where you started from. The problem with the 'return' is that it is a bit stressful the first time. You might wonder if you will be able to return. First of all, remember that you must not lose your conscious awareness during your journey, that you must stay the master of yourself, and to behave as a neutral observer, not as someone 'possessed'. If you respect these instructions, which is easy if you are able to accept losing some intensity in the experience so you can remain imperatively aware the entire time, then there is no need to have any fear.

However, if you are still a bit anxious, prepare a thought for yourself that will strongly attach you to ordinary reality, like the taste of strawberry ice-cream for example, or any other sensation of ordinary reality that you like. If you feel trapped in non-ordinary reality, then, simply think of this sensation and the charm will break easily. If you aren't working alone, then there is no problem, the worst case would be that someone will need to shake you to make you return.

Having said all this, a calm and voluntary return, making sure to go past by all the same places that you passed in descending is an important part of the journey. All that you meet during this return is also very important.

Rest for a while, remove the scarf, and take notes of your experience, or relive it again in your mind. If you did meet some extraordinary forms, or interesting sounds, it is good to make note of them (or record them for sounds) as quickly as possible. We think that we won't forget them, but then, in fact, we do. If you dream in the nights following your journey, write down your dreams, they could very well be connected to your journey. Don't continue to travel alone like this, find an experienced shaman, or get in touch with a 'drumming circle' (or a shamanic circle).

This first journey is only so that you can familiarize yourself with the lower world. If you like this experience, I recommend that you repeat it under the supervision of an experienced shaman. Take good notes of your first experience, especially if you want to continue, because you will need them with whoever teaches you shamanism and it will help you find your way in the lower world. It is possible that you meet up with some difficulties during your journey, that you are attacked by images, or that the images are scarce. Don't panic, just experience it calmly, or escape with the use of your active imagination. You will have to journey like this several times before you are able to control your journeys yourself.

To give you an example, and to share an experience with you that was both unexpected and without much pleasure, here is how my first journey went. After it was over, I felt that it was a failure because of the journeys the other participants said they had experienced, and the wonderful things they said they saw. I wasn't able to go far into the earth because I ran into a kind of large pond of human excrements, and I spent all my time trying to avoid this lake in order to get around it. I always failed, and found myself in front of the lake each time I tried to find another way to go down into the earth. So, I did not go to the lower world during my first journey. Don't judge what you meet in your journey, simply try to do what you have to do: go down into the earth, find a comfortable place, explore it, and do what you can to accomplish this task despite the difficulties you might face. If you run into some problems, that's fine, facing them while continuing to accomplish your task is what is important.

Daydream or journey?

Practicing the shamanic journey raises some problems. What bothers most beginners is knowing whether their experience is a daydream or an 'authentic experience'. Saying that a daydream is an authentic experience doesn't completely satisfy me, although it's true from a factual point of view. I think that shamanism is much more than simply a method to teach you how to daydream pleasantly. I have asked you to use your conscious imagination (to daydream, in other words) when you are looking for the opening in the earth and when you need to escape an object that seems aggressive to you. For everything else, you mustn't 'dream' your experience, you have to wait for objects to spontaneously appear to you, and if nothing comes along, then that's too bad. It's not very useful to tell wonderful stories about non-ordinary reality, but it is very important that you are able to wait to see what manifests itself to you. Now, it is another problem to know if non-ordinary reality is your unconscious or if it actually reflects another reality that exists just as surely as your every day reality. As I mentioned earlier, this isn't a big problem in the beginning, let yourself be carried by your sensations. Clearly, it is very interesting to have access to unconscious information and that can help you to make wise choices for your every day life. But, this is not at all the only type of information that one gleans from the shamanic experience. In addition to daydreams (which are very pleasant) and information about our unconscious choices (which are very useful), sometimes we also receive information that comes from what we can truly call non-ordinary reality, and the difference between these three sources of information can be strongly felt. Personally, the rare times that I have received this non-ordinary information, I was able to easily tell the difference between it and information from my unconscious, but it is up to each individual to figure it out. To help make it clear, I will tell you, excuse my coarseness, how I express my experience: "When you daydream, it is pleasant; when Spirits speak you, you get kicked in the ass; when it's the Gods, you get thrown into the ice."

The journey of the experimented shaman

With experience, this journey will become increasingly easy, and increasingly deep in the sense that more and more you will be able to leave ordinary reality far behind you while being able to keep a precise memory of the journey, and you will acquire techniques to return to ordinary reality. During the course of your journeys, you will become familiar with many animals. Some are really non-ordinary doubles of your personality (I call them 'Animal-Spirits'), and others will simply be helpers for performing certain tasks. At the same time, you will learn, according to your task, to also journey to the upper world. Your Animal-Spirits will become increasingly familiar to you and they will help you to carry out your tasks in non-ordinary reality. Don't think that all this happens in some sort of tranquil beauty. Animal-Spirits are not always very amiable: for example, it would be very classical that you experience dismemberment, where your favorite animal will tear you to pieces. It is highly likely that you meet bad spirits that attack you, and it will be necessary for you to learn to defend yourself.

Finally, your main responsibility will be to help the spirits of the dead find their kingdom, and you will have to take long journeys to the land of the dead, and to your own death. All this is far from being pleasurable, although it does enrich your personality. **It is also a painful, arid and often dangerous path.** Even though I feel it is important for everyone to have some shamanic experiences, if only to discover this other reality, **I would not recommend that anyone become an experienced shaman unless they feel a pressing need to.** Unfortunately, I do not see any other options for those who desire to heal with runes: some operations happen in non-ordinary reality, and so you must know it.

Seið

In fact, the form of shamanic journey that must be practiced in association with runes, galdr, and my own hand-healing[34]

---

[34] Detailed in the third volume of this book : *Hand Healing, Shiatsu, and Seið: a spiritual journey.*

is the Nordic shamanic journey, seið. For many who practice the Asatru religion, which is described at the end of this book, seið is nothing other than the shamanic journey that we have just discussed. I can't agree with this since seið has some very specific properties.

The contempt for seið that is found in the Nordic texts, in many sagas and in runic inscriptions has always puzzled me. One example from the sagas is the seið performed by Thorgrim the Nose in *Gisla saga Surssonar*, which is usually translated as : "Thorgrim the Nose performs the seið, prepares himself as usual, builds a scaffold and devotes himself to his sorcery, with all its spells and evil-doings."
We also find the following two examples of runic inscriptions (among several others, as shown in the section 'runic inscriptions' of my web site).
One of them states : "Let him practice seið, this one that will desecrate this stone!" (rune2)
The other one was found at Sigtuna on a copper plaque from the end of the 11th century. It attacks a "demon of the fever of wounds," and concludes by wishing the practice of seið to this demon (rune1).

We find the same thing in a well-known text, *Ynglinga Saga*: "When performed, seið is followed by such an *ergi* [*that is, impotence or passive homosexuality*] that it is held as shameful for a man to practice it, it is therefore performed by the priestesses." (saga20)

I would like to propose a hypothesis that solves this riddle. First, Snorri must have made a small mistake in saying that seið 'is followed' by ergi, since *Gisla saga Surssonar* says that ergi is actually part of the preparation to seið. The exact text of this saga, which describes the preparation of a seið by Thorgrim the Nose, "with all its spells and evil-doings" is *medh allri ergi ok skelmiskap*. The word *skelmiskap* is well translated as 'evil-doings' but *ergi* never meant 'spell', as seen above. The text says explicitly that part of Thorgrim's preparation to seið was to be *ergi*, that is to have another man practice sodomy on him. In other words, we can hypothesize that preparation for seið included, actually, sodomy of the sorcerer about to practice seið. I am quite aware that I have no solid proof for this hypothesis, since it can always be claimed that the author of *Gisli Sursson's saga* was speaking of *ergi* as an allegory, not as something happening physically. I will answer that the saga's author had a good amount of other insulting words at his disposal, and when he chose *ergi* it was obviously deliberate, and he could not ignore the physical meaning of the word. Thus, I think it very reasonable to at least postulate that the saga's author wanted to point out such a 'horrible deed' as Thorgrim the Nose being buggered before performing his seið. This means that the saga's author believed sodomy was automatically associated to seið; it obviously does not mean that such was reality.

Passive homosexuality is well-known for being a very shameful behavior in the Nordic civilization. This is true to the point that insulting a man by saying that he was ergi was one of the non-pardonable things that could not even be settled by money-paying. Therefore, seið would be so despised that saying "you practiced seið" was just a 'polite' way to say, "You have been passive homosexual," one of the worse existing insults. It seems also that slaves were systematically submitted to sodomy, as a way to mark their loss of human status. If this is true, we understand even better why being buggered was so shameful, it was not linked to any despise of homosexuality, but to the social significance of it: this was how you made a slave lose his or her status of human being.

This all becomes a bit clearer when we compare the exchange of insults between Odin and Loki in the *Lokasenna* (the sarcasms of Loki), where Loki is making fun of Odin, very clearly saying that Odin had to have received a sodomy to perform magic. Boyer's French translation is the only one that treats this passage honestly. Boyer explains very clearly in his notes that the text is referring to what he calls passive homosexuality. However, his translation: "M'est avis que c'était couillonnade" ("I am of the opinion that it was gonadery") does not follow his explanations. Sorry for being so crude, but there is so much hypocrisy going on about this topic that I am rather gross than imprecise, one should say : "And that, it is what I call being sodomized." An exact rendering would call for even cruder words. Moreover, passive homosexuality designates a state of the masculine libido, whereas *argr* designates the physical act of sodomy, and the *argr* person could have been forced to undergo this treatment, or to practice it occasionally, without his or her libido being involved at all. First, Odin brings up the fact that Loki once took the shape of a mare and gave birth to a colt. There is in fact a myth that relates this adventure. Odin says:

> You spent eight winters under ground,
> And over there you gave birth to babies,
> You have been milked like a cow
> And that, for me, is to be *argr*
> (*oc hvgða ec þat args aþal*)

It is clear that Odin associates *argr* to a man who plays a woman's sexual role. But Loki answers tit for tat:

> You practiced magic in Samsey
> There you played the drum like a sorcerer,
> And you journeyed as the sorcerers do,
> And that, for me, is to be *argr*
> (*oc hvgða ec þat args aþal*)

In both cases, precisely the same words are used by Odin and Loki, and, even though the dictionary definition for *argr* gives the imprecise meaning of 'extreme vice', it is certainly about a man in the position of playing a woman's sexual role. This accusation was one of the rare insults, or crimes, that could not be erased with financial

164

compensation in the Viking civilization. Now we can better understand why magic, typically feminine, could have been considered an insult in a world that didn't allow for an 'imprecise' sexuality.

Why would the preparation for seið include such a practice? There is one simple answers. It is obvious that a sorcerer claims being beyond any bounds of normality, and being *ergi* broke a strong Viking social code. More precisely, the men had to claim becoming feminine in order to perform seið. This is supported by the fact that priestesses practiced it, that Freya is the one who taught seið to the Aesir, as stated in *Ynglinga saga*, and that most cases of seið reported in the sagas are performed by women. A less direct proof is found in Siberian shamanism, where many shamans became 'soft men', as they are called, and they start assuming the social role of a woman (up to the point of marrying other men). In this context, it is also possible that the sorcerer preparing for seið had to rely on his feminine side - without physically undergoing sodomy - and that this kind of 'exalted womanishness' could have been considered as shameful by itself, hence the insult associated to the practice of seið. Obviously, we will never know how it was happening, but my own guess is that it would depend on the performer.

No other details have been left to us on the practice of seið except what I have already shared with you. The word associated with passive homosexuality, 'ergi', obviously expresses a form of passivity that, if it isn't sexual, gives us an idea about the manner in which seið was practiced. While Siberian or Indian shamans are very active, fighting with bad Spirits and searching for allies, it seems that seið, on the contrary, requires a deep passivity, associated with a receptivity, a listening to Spirits that can make you accept your inferiority. I suppose that it is the vigorous virility of the Vikings that made them adamantly reject the approach that dated from time immemorial, where the Mother Goddess reigned, without doubt, under the name of Nerthus, with Njörd as her consort, as some texts present it.

We now need to discuss the reconstruction of seið that I want to use in this book and whether or not this preparation has to be part of the reconstruction. A reconstruction is made to adapt old ideas and actions to our modern society in such a way that it becomes well accepted into it. The purpose of the sodomy was to break a social code by making the man more feminine. I do not believe that a modern man will believe himself more feminine because he received sodomy. It would not be looked upon as an act of mystical release of feminine values, as it should be, if it were to have any significance in the context of seið. Obviously, some homosexuals are very 'feminine', or at least fake feminine appearance, but many others go in the opposite direction of 'super-virility' in order to express their needs!
On a different level, our society accepts better what has been described as 'typically feminine' for centuries: steadiness, slow adaptation, apparent passivity (i.e., reluctance to strike back at once), acceptance of differences, etc. These qualities are now considered better than the old 'masculine aggressive' features.

I therefore think, that our modern seið should turn to the reason for sodomy in Viking seið: that men accept the existence of 'feminine' values into themselves, and that they recognize these values as more powerful during seið sessions. In passing, and even though it is not my direct problem, let me emphasize that many women also need to rethink and better accept their own femininity!
A woman can rediscover a score of 'feminine' values that will lead her to practice seið, if not "to the perfection" as the Edda says, at least very well. This might be a bit harder for a man, especially if this man is naturally unable to accept any kind of passivity. In that case, I would suggest that this man does not fight his own nature. Instead of being buggered, this

man should ask the help of a woman to perform his journey, so that she can 'lend' him her femininity. Not all women will accept this role, but many are compassionate enough to consider it a nice, non-sexual, exchange of love.

To summarize, the passive behavior recommended for the practice of seið no longer requires passive homosexuality. It demands instead the acceptance of the virtues of passivity, a request that is hard on modern men and women. Each has to let his or her femininity blossom inside, with or without the help of a woman who will lend her femininity. Sexual habits have very little to do with the whole process.

I would not recommend that a person begin practicing seið without first having had a good experience of classic shamanism. Those who have had this experience can try seið. Instead of fixing a goal and going to a place to meet Spirits, the seið asks that you relax deeply, that you stop having any wants or needs, regardless of what they might be, and that you put yourself in the total silence of your internal voice. Then, you can open yourself up to the influence of your environment and to your unconscious, balancing both these influences. This state is quite similar to the practice of Zen. With Zen, however, the ultimate goal is to reach this state. With seið, it's the state where you can begin to work: where you begin to complete the purpose of the seið. Placing yourself in a state of silence and internal balance gives the seið a very strong power as compared to ordinary shamanism. As a result, this work is completely exhausting, as the Nordic texts tell us. I have personally observed that the seið does not really arouse any sexual excitation, and that is somewhat of an understatement. However, the issue of homosexuality seems a bit gratuitous to me, the tenderness needed after seið can be found with your usual partner, without having to modify any sexual habits. It is, however, very possible that a man who wants to practice it 'to perfection', as described in the Ynglinga saga, might have to.

In other words, men more devoted to magic powers than to their sexuality might well lose all their virility. I use seið very rarely, when I want to ask the Gods to perform a miracle for a patient, not to perform myself the miracle, and so my experience is not truly complete in that respect.

In the third volume of this book, *Hand Healing, Shiatsu and Seið: a spiritual journey*, I come back to seið at length and the way it explores and modifies the energy states of the patient, which is my personal approach to the practice of seið.

Before leaving this topic, there are still two points I'd like to discuss: whether or not women were treated the same way as men with respect to seið; and an analysis of runic inscriptions that sheds some light on the problem discussed here.

Women and seið

It seems that women did not have to prepare for seið as men did, simply because they did not need to become more feminine and this is coherent with my hypothesis.

Let's look at the one instance where a woman is accused of the practice of receiving sodomy. It is found again in the Lokasenna. Loki accuses Freya of having had sex with everyone in Asgard:

> "Enough, Freya! I know well ...
> With all who sit here, elves and gods,
> With each you have played the whore." (edda10)

After that, Loki accuses her of having had sex with her brother as well, with these words:

> "You enticed in your bed your own brother, remember,
> And then, Freya, you farted." (edda11)

Loki uses allusive words, but it is clear that when a woman needs farting after having sex, even nowadays, it means that she received sodomy, and that is precisely what Loki is accusing Freya of. He has already said that she has been "everyone's whore," without excluding Frey (nor Njörd!). If Freya would have been so preparing her seið, we could count on Loki to have made fun of her as well. In short, my argument goes as follows:

    1 - Freya is indeed shamed for having received sodomy

    2 - She is not shamed for performing seið

    3 -Therefore, she did not receive sodomy before performing seið.

Being ergi: a curse or a boasting?

Although the following information does not prove anything, it certainly reinforces the feeling that ergi was important in seið practice. Two 'famous' stone inscriptions, that are rarely compared, bear almost the same inscriptions.

The stone of Stentoften (Sweden, mid-7th century) bears the following inscriptions (it included other inscriptions as well, but they are of no interest here, see Krause and Moltke for a complete description):

I 5: **hideR runono felaheka hedera ginoronoR**
I 6: **heramalasaR arageu weladud sa þat bariutiþ** (rune3)

which is translated by (each word is in the order of the inscription):

I5: the row of glancing runes I preserved here, runes carrying magic

I6: without rest, by ergi, abroad, a malicious death to the one who this [*monument*] destroys.

A slightly younger inscription, from the Björketorp stone (Norway, 2nd half of the 7th century) also shows:

B1: **haidRruno ronu**
B2: **falahak haidera g**
B3: **inarunaR arageu**
B4: **haeramalausR**
B5: **uti aR weladaude**
B6: **saR þat barutR** (rune4)

In order to compare the two, first notice that the last 'g' of B2 makes a "**ginarunaR**" with the beginning of B3. Notice also the change in the order of the words: "**ginoronoR heramalasaR arageu**" on Stentoften becomes "**ginarunaR arageu haeramalausR**" on Björketorp. The "**arageu**" of Stentoften is clearly part of the curse put on whoever harms the monument. Therefore, the translation given above is unambiguous. This is not so clear for Björketorp who puts "**ginarunaR**" together with "**arageu**," leading to a possible ambiguity where the runes are active either 'by' or 'because of' the "**arageu**." I mean that it can also be translated by:

B1: the row of glancing runes
B2: I preserved here,
B3: runes carrying magic by ergi.
B4: Without rest abroad,
B5, B6: a malicious death to the one who this [*monument*] destroys.

In this interpretation, the rune master does not curse with ergi, but he, on the contrary, brags about being able to "activate the power" of the runes through ergi. Being proud of having power, whatever the means are, must not be a feeling reserved to our days, and the 7th century Norwegian rune master could well have been inverting two words of Stentoften's text just for this purpose. Obviously, I have no further proof for my interpretation, and it is also obvious that it contradicts what all the experts are saying. But with the assumption that science tends to assimilate things that look alike, and since the Stentoften inscription is not ambiguous at all, then I think it is safe to assume that runologists simply attributed the same meaning to Björketorp. The Björketorp inscription later became a kind of archetype of how much ergi was hated in the Viking civilization.

Now let's be a bit less 'scientific', and consider that the Björketorp rune master could not really ignore Stentoften's stone since the two inscriptions are so similar. This hypothesis being accepted, what could have pushed him to inverse the order of "**heramalasaR**" and "**arageu**," thereby introducing an ambiguity? Many reasons are possible, but an obvious one is that he wanted to emphasize the role of being ergi when manipulating magic, and he did so by subtly opposing his predecessor who was only cursing by ergi. However highly speculative, my hypothesis at least explains this seemingly tiny difference between the two stones.

Dances and Positions

Shamanic dances are one way for shamans to welcome the Spirit of their Animal-Spirit into their body. It might seem that they are more or less clumsily imitating the gestures and sounds of the animal, when in reality, they are opening their bodies to their Animal-Spirit, enabling it to rediscover the sensations of a living being. The bodies of shamans are not perfectly adapted to the souls of their animals and so there is certain clumsiness in their dances. The main element of this process is a kind of exchange between the shaman, who gives his vitality to the Spirit, and the Spirit, who gives its wisdom to its shaman friend.

Runes also have a Spirit, and each rune is associated to either a natural phenomenon, an animal or a God who might have the desire to feel alive again. I haven't met anyone practicing rune-dancing, but it might be something worth exploring. What has been attempted, by a German mystic and disciple of Guido List from the 30's, F. B. Marby (of whom we must say that he spent 8 years in Nazi concentration camps on the grounds of "anti-nazi occultism"), is the practice of hieratical positions which shape the person's body as close as possible to the rune's shape, placing the arms and legs in a position such that the body represents the shape of a rune. This is supposed to make the Spirit of the rune enter the body of the practitioner. I have never found any evidence of such a practice in any of the ancient texts, but, nonetheless, I have tried these positions and I found them to be uncomfortable and far from the shape of the rune, more so for a body like mine that isn't very supple. These positions left me with more stiffness than enlightenment. Perhaps I am too coarse and insensitive to appreciate the mystical effect of subtle pain from an uncomfortable position!

De Lancre also talks about the dances of western witches and his testimony (coming from the witches that he interviewed) seems to lean toward dances with little mysticism:

> They dance in a row, two by two, and back to back, and sometimes in a circle, with their backs turned to the center of the dance; girls and women each holding their Demons by the hand, who teach them traits and gestures so lascivious and indecent, that they would horrify the most shameless ladies. With songs of a composition so brutal, and in terms and words so licentious and lewd, that eyes are disturbed, ears are twisted, and understanding is troubled, to see such monstrous things that are met there. (lancr2)

I think that the 'reversed' nature of this dance simply shows us that the dancers wanted to do things differently to oppose the conformity of always facing the center of the circle. The witches that De Lancre burnt were already so christianized that their behavior was only an attempt to reject Christian behavior, and not an authentic Heathen practice.

To end this chapter, I'd like to share some cases of Siberian shamanic healings that have so far only been available in Russian and German. These will hopefully give you more information than simple abstract descriptions.

Soul Theft

Soul theft is a concept that has been well described in magic. The following is an example of the mystical transmission of sickness, as described by De Lancre, although he writes in a contemptuous manner, his comments are detailed enough to be interesting:

> That if we heal with these nonsensical manners, it is only for a short time and if by chance it is necessary for the sickness that is ousted by the sorcerer to be given to another, it will be given to one of more importance and therefore their death will be a hundred times more important than that of the first who needed the sickness removed. (lancr3)

Siberian shamans have practiced soul theft and in order to save one client, another human is sacrificed. It's a relatively ordinary process.

> The shaman, while on his way to the house of the dead person that he must revive, meets a Spirit that tells him: "I see my relative who has been raised in the same nest as I. I did not know anything about your arrival, and I have come here after your client's death. There is a third life in him. Try to give him life by shamanism, but don't forget to give me something in return since

I have not received anything in three years." The shaman ends up at the house of the dead and begins to dance ... He dances in direction of the rising sun and he asks the Spirits what they would like in exchange for giving life back to one of the dead. He beats the drum ... Abruptly, flesh and blood appear on the drum. 160 kilometers away there lives a man who will die in three years and who doesn't really care one way or the other about it. "I will take the life of this man and give it to the dead. 16 kilometers away there also lives someone who will soon die, I am going to take his life to bring life to my patient." (sib5)

Notice that, contrary to what De Lancre says, the stolen soul is from someone who seems less important to the shaman than his or her patient. However, I am not, obviously, suggesting the practice of soul theft as the average treatment. Rather, it is the opposite action that is important, giving back lost souls. Because of the media, we learn, astonishingly, of the great number of mistreated children, physically or sexually, by their relatives. Shamans knew all too well the evil process by which a parent, often in the name of love, robs children of parts of their soul. In fact, it is almost impossible to deeply love someone, child or adult, without exchanging parts of each other's souls. If this exchange is not balanced, especially if the parent has already experienced a loss of his or her soul, then this will result in deep wounds that are unconscious on both sides. In addition to this, each accident, each painful relationship causes the loss of parts of our souls. It is the role of the shaman to go into his or her client's past, to notice any thefts or losses of soul that the client has experienced, and to search in non-ordinary reality where these missing parts have gone in order to negotiate their return or restoration. The following text is priceless for the apprentice shaman because it clearly shows how to proceed, especially, for those wanting to learn to heal magically. They must slowly read this text, analyzing each word and then think deeply about it.

To find souls stolen by Spirits of the Lower World

When a bad spirit of the North seizes someone's spirit, the shaman performs a session and brings to their country various gifts for the spirits. With these spirits, a crooked-faced girl lives. She serves as a watcher. When the shaman comes near, shouts sound there:
"There, he comes, that shaman with a heavy load, with valuable offerings. Livestock he brings, behind him he pulls animal offerings with a leash …"
"Ei, there is our eldest son (the shaman is called their son probably because his soul was raised with them). Jump, welcome him! …"
Then, they scream: "Suu, saa!" (these are the screams used for catching livestock). Then, the livestock that was brought is driven into a hurdle.
The shaman says to them, both that the human-prince has become sick and that he has sent these offerings… "Hand back his soul to me!"
These ladies are satisfied of the gifts and order to release the soul. They say:
"Ei, go and open the door of the prison where the soul of the sick person lies!"
It might happen that the spirits don't want to release the soul. Then the shaman shows anger and despair … he turns around the hearth, changes himself into a wasp and flies in the cowshed. A blue-shiny bull lies there. The wasp stings the bull's nose. The bull snorts, and the soul, that was caught in the nostrils of the bull, falls out. The shaman immediately catches it and hastily flies away with it. (sib6)

In this way, the shaman can recover a lost part of the patient's soul, but he or she must be full of humility, bring presents and convince the Spirits softly. Only when the soft approach is failing, can guile be tried. In the above case, the bad spirit had stolen the soul of its victim. Now see what happens in the case where a bad spirit takes over the soul of the patient.

Possession healing

Here are three examples of possession healing, where, unfortunately, only the most superficial aspect is described. Possession is recognized by the fact that the patient attacks the healer.

> After the shaman has danced, the possessed gets up and would have jumped on the shaman if he had not stepped back and immediately blown on the face of the possessed who then falls unconscious on the ground. The shaman hits the patient lightly with his drum stick and says: "It is time for you to wake up." The patient then has tea with the shaman and behaves normally. (sib7)

> The shaman opens himself to his spirit helpers, and ... the patient gets up howling. He lunges at the shaman who leans backwards and blows on the face of the patient who then falls unconscious to the ground. The shaman knocks him slightly on the front with his drum stick and says: "It is time that you wake." The patient wakes, and the shaman suggests that he drink a cup of tea, and the patient drinks it. (sib8)

During a marriage ceremony, twenty-five people lost so much of their spirits that they had to be chained. A shaman was asked to come. He demanded the presence of nine riders mounted on white horses. The shaman then took tepid water in his mouth and sprayed the patients who healed immediately. (sib9)

Resurrections

The Siberian shamanic tradition claims that its shamans have the ability to resurrect, as the Kalevala does with Lemminkäinen's mother. Unfortunately, only the superficial aspects of the miracle are given.

When the shaman arrived at the patient's house, his father announced that she had died two days earlier. The shaman replies that it makes no difference. He remains the night at this house and tries to make her come back. A sister of the dead girl insults the shaman by telling him that he can not wake up her sister since she has been dead for three days. However the father agrees for the session to take place during the night. The shaman puts his hands in the flame of a burning fire and he caresses the dead body three times. He absorbs the pain himself and the dead begins to breathe and to open her eyes. The shaman says that the patient is beginning to revive and that all will end well. The next night, he performs another session and the state of the patient improves again. During the last session, the shaman takes revenge on the woman who had mocked him. He tells her to lean over while opening the oven, and everyone can see that she isn't wearing any underwear, to her great humiliation. (sib10)

Aside from the vengeful aspect of the shaman, he "absorbs the pain himself," which means that he identifies with his client before taking on the patient's illness. This is a well-known approach of those practicing holistic healing methods, but it is also very dangerous. No one should behave as this Siberian shaman whose desire to prove himself causes him to neglect this danger. In the forthcoming third volume, on Seið and Shiatsu, I show how seið can take place to the beat of the patient's life, and how to open the patients' soul just enough to help them without risking your own life.

Here is another example, described again in a rather superficial way:

> A man had a son who died of tuberculosis and five shamans had not been able to do anything for him. A new shaman arrives who asks that they take the silk from under his saddle and place it in the middle of the yurt, and that they give him some milk to drink. He prepares his session and asks that they cook the milk. During the shamanic session, the dead breathes, asks for the milk and drinks it. The patient asks if he has been unconscious or dead. The shaman tells him that he has regained the force of life and that he will live again for at least three years. (sib11)

Chapter 4

POEMS, CHARMS AND CURSES:

HEALING WITH GALDR

> The cold told me a tale
> The rain blew me some poems:
> [*the word used is runoja. runo = poem*]
> Another tale came to me in the winds,
> Carried by the swell of the sea;
> Birds added words,
> The tree tops, sentences.
> [*Kalevala,* song 1]

> The Carocs in California … have two kinds of shamans,
> the root-healers, who treat with drinks and bandages,
> and the barking-healers, who suck out the sickness. The
> last ones, mostly feminine, howl like a dog in front of
> their patients, and bark for hours.
>
> [*Bartels*, p. 64]

Why should the charms be sung?

Before going into details about how to use galdr in healing, I
want come back again to discussing the bonds between
magic and poetry in Nordic civilizations. Throughout the
Kalevala, the words 'to sing' or 'to declaim' are used to
mean 'to cast a spell', which shows us that even the

vocabulary itself does not dissociate magic and poetry. In English, we still use 'enchantment' and 'incantation'; this maintains that a spell was sung. The following examples show the importance of this aspect of magic.

When a young shaman, Joukahainen, wants to compare his powers with those of the old mythical shaman, "the eternal" Väinämöinen (also called Vaïno in the text), his family tries to discourage him in this way:

> The father forbids his son
> The father forbids it,
> The mother won't allow it
> That he goes into Vaïno's land
> To confront Vaïno:
> There you will be sung to and shouted at, face
> In the snow, head in the winds,
> Fists hardened in the air
> Until what your hands can no longer turn,
> Until what your feet can no longer move. (kal45)

This text says, poetically, that Väinämöinen will cast a spell on him, enchant him, and take away all his powers. The young man answers by asserting his own magical powers:

> I want to confront myself,
> To take the measure of men.
> I will sing the one who sings me
> And declaim the one who declaims me,
> I will sing the best of singers
> So that he will become the worse singer -
> To his feet shoes of stone,
> Wooden pants at his thighs,
> Stone anchored to his chest,
> Mittens of stone on his hands,
> On his head, a stone helmet. (kal46)

"I will sing the one who sings me" means that he is counting on answering with magic against all magic put on him. He confronts Väinämöinen, and defies him by insulting him. Finally, Väinämöinen overcomes the young shaman:

> Väinämöinen becomes angry
> Hearing that, full of anger and shame.
> He begins to sing
> He begins to declaim...
> The old Väinämöinen sang:
> Lakes rippled, the earth trembled,
> Mountains of bronze were shaken,
> Robust rocks moaned,
> Cliffs split,
> Rocks cracked on the shores.
> He sang the young Joukahainen -
> Sang him in the marsh up to his calves,
> In reeds to his thighs,
> In heathers up to his neck. (kal47)

Throughout the Kalevala, as in this example, magic is sung and magicians are called singers, at least a dozen times. At the end of the Kalevala, Väinämöinen, conquered and humiliated by Christ, leaves performing his last magical task:

> He went to the shore,
> He began to sing
> His last time to sing -
> He sang a copper boat
> A ship covered with copper ...
> He went at full speed
> In the copper boat,
> In the copper barge,
> There where Earth-mother raises,
> And where the skies lower. (kal48)

This singing is the same as the galdr we have been discussing, it means both song and howl. Galdr is the poems, chants and howls which are associated to runes in order to give substance to your blessing. Obviously there are galdr for curses (which have been preserved the most in the texts), but we won't discuss them here. The poems that we will study will all be invocations designed for healing a patient.

Whether it is Odin, the cold or the sounds of Nature that inspire them, the sounds associated to the galdr must resonate in your whole body, and with the universe. No book can teach this. All I can do is try to make you feel the poetry of the text from which the galdr will be taken, trying to create a vibration between you and the world around you.

Honestly, I must confess that what I am going to teach in this chapter has not come exclusively from me. What Freya Aswynn teaches with respect to the galdr was so similar to my thinking - even before we met, that it is difficult for me to separate what comes directly from Freya, and what is truly my own. Now that I have had the pleasure of receiving her teachings, I see that all those who want to practice the galdr for healing should get her CD[35] demonstrating the use of galdr, *The Shades of Yggdrasil*. In any case, I hope that I have not betrayed her in this chapter and I am infinitely grateful to her for making me hear and feel the harmony between Nature and the singer as the runes are invoked.

As we already said, galdr is classically a poem, or a spell, sung or howled by the poet. In the runic context, we will give it a specific meaning which is connected to the four next conditions.

---

[35] Contact : Freya Aswynn, BM Aswynn, London WC 1N 3XX. It only costs 10 British pounds.

When we want to ask something from the Gods, we need to first reflect at length about what we really want to ask. Mythology is full of stories where the hero clumsily asks the Gods a favor, for example to have the power to transform all that he touches to gold, and then once granted, it becomes a curse. Similarly, many tales teach us to carefully plan our wishes so that the three wishes that can be granted to us during our life do not become trite. You must reflect, both consciously and unconsciously by interpreting dreams and shamanic journeys in order to deeply know the true wish to make.

The wish must then be expressed poetically, as a text that can be written in your own language. Languages that are specifically runic, such as Primitive Old Norse for the ancient Futhark, Old Norse for the younger Futhark, and Anglo-Saxon for the British Futhark, must have been useful since their words could be directly transcribed in runes. I do not believe we have to go back to these languages to write a poem that pleases the Gods, and this is why I will write them here in English. The poem clarifies the poet's request which will insure the accuracy of the demand.

Then the poem has to be transcribed in runes. Capturing the meaning of the poem in a few runes is also a problem of the galdr, where, once again, the poet's wish is refined and made exact. The poet must identify completely to the poem and to the runes associated with it so that he or she can really feel their deep union.

These runes are then sung solemnly, preferably during a ritual so that the sounds add their vibrations to how the poet feels about his or her problem. The sounds can be sung with a moderated strength, especially in a ceremony invoking several runes, or the whole Futhark. It can be a chant which is more or less howled when you want to demand that the rune shows its power. Half-tone variations are frequent, and this chant can sound 'off key' to our profane ears. The chant can be greeted by a surge of energy, coming from the three different non-ordinary realities: the lower world, the middle world, or the upper world. The form of the chant could be a bit modified for those who are sensitive to these variations in energy. It is of course also possible to ask without demanding, and then the chant will be a bit more 'melodic', in the non-mystical meaning of this term.

Carrying out the four stages described above is exactly what it means to practice galdr.

Heathen/Christian Charms

We are now going to look at several texts that invoke a deity who is not linked to runes, such as the Christian God, or the Finnish Jumala. In order to better explain these somewhat obscure texts, and put them in a Germanic environment, I will provide you with a rewriting of these texts, making them invocations to northern Gods and to the runes. I would like to stress that I do not believe in stereotyped magical formulas. I am personally convinced that each situation and each patient calls for an original poem. The ancient texts that I am including here constitute a good foundation from which you will be able to develop your own runic poems, and I will show you how you can adapt them to your needs. Of course, the versions that I am giving you are not to be memorized, they are only examples. I suppose I could be accused of 'stealing' formulas from other civilizations and simply adapting them to the Nordic civilization, but the transfer to the Nordic civilization is made so easily that, very likely, I am only returning them to their source, giving back to Odin what was intended for Odin.

Obviously, many charms are purely Christian, and cannot be translated to a Nordic God invocation, and then rewritten in runes. The following, which is an example of such a charm, was intended for treating tooth-aches:

> St Peter sat on a marble stone,
> Jesus Christ came to him alone,
> "Peter, what aileth thee to weep?"
> "My Lord and God, it is the toothache."
> "Rise up, Peter, and not you alone,
> But everyone who in this charm doth have belief
> Will from the toothache never lack relief."
> (scot1)

This charm, in rhymester verse, can be seen as a pious vow and does not call on any Heathen power. I have included it to make perfectly clear the huge difference between this charm, a naive, 'charming' and certainly inefficient one, and the Heathen charms of the Scottish Highlands, Lithuania, the Kalevala, and Saint Hildegard, that we are about to see.

The next charm illustrates the deep influence that Christianity has had on Heathen magic (cited by J. Cicenas, see the bibliography at the end of this volume). It was used by a Lithuanian 'witch' who sang it in a mix of Lithuanian and Polish, clearly showing the Christian influence (of Polish origin) on a tradition having continued to maintain its Heathen roots.

> The lord Jesus was crossing the sea,
> Crossing the lake, and he stopped on the Jordan.
> Let the blood of this wound stop!
> Jesus, Jesus, amen!
> Plukst!

The ending, an onomatopoeic form equivalent to our 'plop!', still shows the pagan influence within a typically Christian charm and carries analogical magic (as Christ has stopped in a place, so the blood has to stop also).

Here is another example of a popular charm that is very Christian (cited by K. Thomas, *Religion and the Decline of Magic*, Penguin 1991, p. 214) but still maintains some Heathen elements. Since it speaks of a fruit of the earth, it is easy to translate.

> Hallowed be thou Vervain, as thou growest on the ground
> For in the mount of Calvary there thou was first found.
> Thou healedst our Saviour, Jesus Christ, and staunchedst his bleeding wound,
> In the name of the Father, the Son, and the Holy Ghost,
> I take thee from the ground.

This invocation is clearly being made to give power to the vervain that is being gathered. The author of this incantation credits this plant with having treated Christ's side. Odin's side was also pierced by a lance while he hung on the Tree of the World and we will use this analogy to transpose the poem. Thus, 'Mount Calvary' can become the base of Yggdrasil, the Tree of the World, where Odin hung for nine days. This tree, as says the Eddic poem *Völuspa*, "stands above the well of Urdr" which evokes the Norns (who live near this well) thus rune Naudiz.

Jesus Christ 'obviously' becomes Odin (rune Ansuz), the Father becomes Bur (Odin is one of Bur's sons, rune Uruz), and the Son is again Odin, to respect the original poem. Finally, Yggdrasil (rune Ihwaz), which is also an abstract representation of the deity, replaces the Holy Ghost. In the transposition, I have directly integrated the galdr associated to the poem :

> Hallowed be thou Vervain, as thou growest on the ground
> For near the well of Urdr there thou was first found.
> *Naudiz! Naudiz! Naudiz!*
> Thou healedst the Old Shouter and staunchedst his bleeding wound,

Odin!
By Bur and Odin, by the power of Yggdrasil,
Uruz! Ansuz! Ihwaz!
I take thee from the ground.
Uruz!

Thus the galdr itself is reduced to Naudiz three times, Odin, Uruz, Ansuz, Ihwaz, Uruz. The poem explains the meaning of the galdr to come. In practice, I'd declaim the poem first, and shout the galdr afterwards.

In this chapter I will only be presenting charms coming from a Germanic civilization. To avoid letting the reader believe that this style of charms is unique to this civilization, I will offer one example of a Rumanian healing charm against anxiety. I will not make a galdr out of it.

Even though is charm originates from a Latin country, and in spite of the allusions to a unique God, it is still very pagan.

An example of a non Nordic Heathen healing charm

From the huge forest

came the huge man
covered with hair,
 dreadful,
with his hairy arms,
with his hairy legs,
with his eyes bulging,
with his crooked teeth,
with his fat cheeks,
with his crooked sight,
by night he came
And (name of the sick person) was
found down,
very sick, with a burning fever
and he came out of need,
to fill (name of the sick person) with
fear,
count his days,
cut in his lifetime.

But I was there to call upon him
and I called out to him :
- "What are you looking for there,
man?"
- "Well, I came to (name of the sick
person)'s house,

to this human who belongs to me,
to shrink his veins,
to suck his blood,
to shorten his days,
to eat his heart,
to decrease his lifespan,

by fright,
by pain,
by grief,
and by deep sickness,
by need and by hatred,
to give him a sickness

that forbids him from having a long
life."
- "Hey ! horrible one so ugly!
You must listen to me,
you must leave (name of the sick),
If you don't go
from the tip of his nose,
from his soft cheek,
from his arms and legs,
and their joints,
with the broom, I'll sweep you,
with the rake, I'll rake you,
over the sea I will throw you,

over 99 seas,
over 99 lands,
where you will melt and melt again,

as melts the foam of the waves,
as melts the salt in the water,
as melts the dew in the sun,
as melts the dried poppy seed
cut in four pieces ...
Go then to the center of the seas,

there you will see a small black dog,

shrink instead its veins
suck its blood,
cut its days,
bring it the sickness,
that will soon kill him.

Thus (name of the sick person) will
remain intact,
pure and shining
As he was made by God."

This is my charm
But the healing comes from God !

This charm bears a good number of similarities with Nordic charms, as we shall now see them.

Three runic charms

I would like to begin now with a presentation of some charms that were written in runes. By studying all of the existing runic inscriptions (given completely on my website), we see that very ancient inscriptions were always concise. Their galdr was made up of an allusion to magical authorities that cannot be expressed in any particular language. Later runic inscriptions, like the Ribe stick (see below), use the runes to write out the words, as the letters of an alphabet. In keeping with the ancient customs, I suggest keeping the words in the form of a poem, and creating the galdr as a chant by selecting a few runes that summarize the poem's meaning.

The *Canterbury charm* is found in an Anglo-Saxon manuscript written in 1073. It has been translated as:

> Kuril wound-causer, go now, you are found.
> Thor hallow you, Lord of Troll, Kuril wound-
> causer. Against blood-vessel pus. (rune5)

This charm illustrates once again the importance that was given to the cause of the sickness. Here, the healer has given it a name, Kuril, showing that you can try to name the patient's sickness. The name of an imaginary monster that frightened the patient in his or her childhood could serve very well here.

Notice that the end of the runic text states the medical role of the charm. It can be useful to state explicitly, at the end of a charm, the sickness it is intended to treat.

Finally, the text contains what could be seen as a contradiction since the rune master is asking Thor to hallow the sickness. In fact, what we see here is a sort of subtle paradox that is found often enough in runic texts: faking good wishes, while actually meaning the worse. Thor hallows by striking with his hammer, and he always strikes a troll (or a Thurs) with his hammer in order to break its skull, as the Edda often tells us. Thus, this wish contains the curse: "Thor break your skull with his hammer!"

The same type of 'poisonous wish' is found in the Sigtuna amulet (seen earlier). The rune master wishes that the 'wolf' who is responsible for the sickness "enjoy the seið well!" He is in fact cursing the wolf since practicing seið was seen as a shameful conduct during the course of which I think the shaman had to be buggered, thereby losing the status of a free man, as explained in chapter 3.

This charm calls on Thor, and therefore on rune Laukaz; the relationships between Thor and the Thurs are also evoked, and so the rune Thurisaz must also be used. I am going to hypothesize that the name Kuril is linked to Anglo-Saxon *cyre* and to Old High German *kuri*, both meaning, 'choice', 'decision'. The Norns are the ones who decide for us, and therefore I suggest associating Naudiz to the elaboration of the galdr for this charm. So, one possible galdr is:
Naudiz! Laukaz! Thurisaz! Naudiz!

We will now consider the *Ribe stick* charm. It is a long poem written in runes, and it dates from the beginning of the fourteenth century.

Earth I pray guard
and the heaven above,
sun and Saint Mary
and himself the Lord God,
that he grants me hands to make whole

and healing tongue
to cure the Trembler
when treatment is needed.
From back and from breast, from trunk and from
limb, from eyes and from ears; from every place
where evil can enter.
A stone is called swart; it stands out of the sea.
On it lie nine Needs. They shall neither sleep
sweet nor make warm until you are better of it;
for whom I have caused runes to utter words.
Amen. And so be it. [*ends with a sign of cross*].
(rune6)

This text is remarkably clear and shows how shortcuts can
be used in charms. The Trembler is malaria that was well
known in this period (Cromwell might have died from it, for
example). Hands "to make whole" are physician's hands
able to 'reconnect the pieces' of a body, and the "tongue that
heals" is obviously referring to the possibility of healing
magically with incantations.
The Gods who are linked to the Earth are Frey (linked to the
generosity of the Earth) and Frigg (who is able to command
the elements of the earth), leading me therefore to use the
runes Jeran and Pertho. The God of the sky is Tyr,
associated to Tiwaz. Sowelo corresponds to the sun, and I
associate the evocation of Mary with that of Freya, and
therefore to Berkanan. God 'himself' can correspond to Odin
(Ansuz) or also, for me at least, to the sacred couple,
Nerthus – Njörd, to whom are associated Uruz and Ingwaz.
The tongue that heals is the one of the words that heal,
which are associated to Ansuz. The Trembler is a sickness
giving fever, so I will associate it to Kaunan. The reference
to "nine Needs" calls of course for an evocation of Naudiz.
The words "amen, and so be it" were used as a way to
hallow the whole charm, and so a call to Thor and to his
hammer can be used to end the charm. This explains my

choices for the following 're-paganized' version of this charm.

> Earth I pray guard
> *Jeran! Pertho!*
> and the heaven above,
> *Tiwaz! Tiwaz!*
> the sun and shining Freya
> *Sowelo! Berkanan!*
> And the sovereign couple.
> *Uruz! Ingwaz!*
> that He and She grant me hands to make whole
> and healing tongue
> to cure the Trembler when treatment is needed.
> *Ansuz! Kaunan!*
> From back and from breast, from trunk and from
> limb, from eyes and from ears; from every place
> where evil can enter.
> A stone is called swart; it stands out of the sea.
> On it lie nine Needs.
> *Naudiz! Naudiz! Naudiz! Naudiz! Naudiz!*
> *Naudiz! Naudiz! Naudiz! Naudiz!*
> They shall neither sleep sweet nor make warm
> until you are better of it; for whom I have caused
> runes to utter words.
> *Thor help - me! Thor hallow my charm! Thor*
> *protect [name the patient]!*

The next charm is engraved on the *Ribe skull* fragment, which dates before the year 800. It has a hole that clearly served as passage for the cord that held it to the neck of its owner. The runic inscription has been translated as:

> Ulfur and Odin and Hydyr! Help Bur against
> pain and strikes of dwarves [= *of fever*]. [*signed*]
> Bur (rune7)

This charm is purely pagan, and can be used without change. I am going to suggest however an interpretation that gives meaning to the charm for us living in the 21st century. The classic etymology of the name Ulfur is that it clearly evokes the wolf, as in the Anglo-Saxon *ulf* or *wulf* (wolf) or to the Old Icelandic *ulfr* (wolf). The name Hydyr makes me think instead of a root that evokes something secret as in the Anglo-Saxon *hydan* meaning 'hidden'. This is why I suggest another interpretation of the names of the divinities associated here to Odin by evoking two hidden aspects of Odin. One of them is the wolf and (this is only an example) I have chosen the other to be his blood brother, Loki, the God who, in the shape of a mare, gave birth to Odin's horse, Sleipnir.

Finally, I interpret "strikes of dwarves" as fever, since, as we will see, Anglo-Saxon has preserved this meaning: the arrow of dwarves means fever, hence the use of rune Kaunan.

Here now is the poem with my modifications, and the galdr that is associated to it.

> Odin, Wolf and Mare,
> *Ansuz! Fehu! Ehwaz!*
> Help [*name of the patient*] against pain
> And the fever of dwarf arrows.
> *Kaunan! Kaunan! Kaunan!*

Some Heathen charms of the Scottish Highlands

Druidic Charms

The first two examples come from Celtic legends and they simply allude to the use of incantations in Celtic medicine.

As we have already seen, healing druids treated those wounded with poisoned weapons by bathing them in white cow's milk. It is said that these healers knew :

> "every leaf, every charm and every *sreod* (sneeze) and the language of birds, and every omen." (celt2)

The sneeze is referring to a particular way of making sounds that we could think of as being close to the Nordic galdr.

The second example comes from the story of Cuchulain which states that charms had to be recited for the healing, but it doesn't give the charms themselves.

> After their combat, when Cuchulain and Ferdia rested from their wounds, (people of the medical art) came to watch over them, to keep them, and to care for them through the night. Their bumps and cuts and gashes were so horrible, and their wounds so many, that nothing could be done for them, except to put magical amulets on them, and to recite charms and incantations in order to heal the openings and stop the flow of blood. (celt3)

Charm against ulcers and infections in general

> I save those who are sick unto death from flatulence, from spear-thong, from sudden tumor, from wounds caused by iron, from ul (?) which fire burns, from egg (?) which dog eats; be it the blood (?) that wanes, three nuts that crack (?), three sinews that weave (?), I strike its disease, I vanquish bloods, weeping of bloods. Let it not be a chronic tumor. May what it goes

upon be healed. I put my trust in the remedy which Diancecht left with his people in order that whatever it goes upon may be healed.' - This is always put in your palm full of water when washing, and you put it in your mouth, and you put the two fingers next to your little finger into your mouth, apart from each other. [*The question marks are in the original. Except for 'ul', which I still do not understand, I will discuss below explanations for the other seemingly mysterious sentences.*] (scot2)

Diancecht is the medicine-God of a mythical people of Ireland, the Thuatha De Danann. He heals those wounded in combat and revives the dead by dunking them in the "Fountain of Health" after having sung incantations that, unfortunately, have not reached us.

There isn't much to transform in this purely Heathen incantation which is designed to present the healer to his or her patient and to heal ulcers. The healer brags about knowing the universal remedy (that was "left by Diancecht"). From its description, it must be a disinfectant potion taken internally, but its exact composition is unknown. In modern medicine, we use antibiotics for this. This is why I think that this poem can be used for taking antibiotics, in spite of the strong dislike many show towards them. The two fingers parted in the mouth, the ring and middle fingers, form a Kaunan inside the patient's mouth. The name Kaunan means boil, and it is the rune associated with the putrefaction of flesh. This is why singing Kaunan at the end of the poem is a good idea.

I must say again that I believe it is never good to recite a standard formula, regardless of how powerful it may be. The healer has to make his or her own formula and assimilate it in order to give it power before applying it to the patient. I will now give you my personal interpretation of the above charm, not as a new standard, but simply as an example of what can be done. The charm must be revised for each patient.

> *Fehu!*
> Death draws near your body
> *Uruz!*
> Steel cuts you,
> *Thurisaz!*
> The lance of fire pierces you,
> *Ansuz!*
> Your flesh blisters
> *Raido!*
> The ulcer that burns gnaws you,
> *Kaunan!*
> *Futhark!*
>
> The dead flesh is to be thrown to the dogs.
> *Kaunan!*
> I will nurse your blood that weakens,
> *Uruz!*
> Your membranes stretched,
> *Kaunan!*
> Your wisdom cracked,
> *Algiz!*
>
> I will knock your sickness,
> Your humors will obey me,
> Your blood will smile again,
> Your tumor will shrink,
> Your sickness will flee.
> *Ehwaz! Ehwaz! Ehwaz!*
>
> I have faith in the runes,
> That the powerful Norns created,
> *Naudiz!*
> That the Old Shouter howled.
> *Odin!*

Water is the first of balms
Where we will trace runes.
Laukaz!
Never drink without
Protecting yourself with Kaunan.
Kaunan! Kaunan! Kaunan!

I think that the choice for each rune is easy to understand given the text accompanying it. By considering the meanings of the runes given in Chapter 1, you should see immediately why I have placed each rune after each section of the text. A word of explanation is needed for the rune Raido that accompanies 'flesh that blisters', since this is not Raido's normal role. I simply want to maintain each verse of the original charm, and at the same time put them in an order that enables me to sing 'Futhark' at the beginning. The three Ehwaz that follow "the fleeing sickness" are expressing the fact that this sickness must only be a simple nightmare that will pass when you wake.

Charm for surgery

This charm is designed for helping the surgeon in his or her work. It shows several versions in different cultures, for instance, the Kalevala has also given us examples of this charm. The Scottish version of it says:

Calum Cille rose early,
He found his horse's bones
Leg crosswise;
He set bone to bone,
Flesh to flesh
Sinews to sinews,
Hide to hide,
Marrow to marrow ;
Christ, as you healed that,
May you heal this. (scot3)

Calum Cille is the Scottish name of Saint Colomba who evangelized Scotland. The second Merseburg charm calls on Odin, and this is why I believe that Odin can easily replace Calum Cille and Christ. I thus suggest the following version of the charm:

> Odin woke early
> Seeing Sleipnir, bones crossed, [*Sleipnir is the name of Odin's horse*]
> Feet broken.
> He replaced them, bone to bone,
> Flesh to flesh,
> Tendon to tendon,
> Skin to skin,
> Marrow to marrow;
> Odin, as you healed this,
> Will you also heal that?
> *Odin! Ehwaz! Ansuz! Mannaz! Odin!*

The charm is intended to apply to a human being the work Odin did on Sleipnir. The rune of the horse is Ehwaz, the one of Odin is Ansuz, the rune of humans is Mannaz, and this is why I composed a galdr with the name of Odin framing the three runes summarizing the poem: Ehwaz, Ansuz, Mannaz. The galdr will be then: Odin! (in a calling tone), Ehwaz! (as if pointing at something), Ansuz! (in a tone seeking to connect), Mannaz! (in a tone of supplication), Odin! (in a tone of consecration).

A similar charm is found in Germanic literature in the *Merseburger Zaubersprüche*, a manuscript dated from the 10th century. There are two Merseburg charms. The first one was given in Chapter 3, and here is the second one :

> Phol and Wodan rode in the wood,
> There to Balder's foal, the foot was set right.

There Sunthgunt uttered it , [*and*] Sunna, her sister.
There Fija uttered it, [*and*] Volla, her sister.
There Wodan uttered it, as [*only*] he understood it:
So bones set right as blood set right as limb set right:
Leg to leg, blood to blood, limb to limbs,
as if glued were.

Wodan is the West-Germanic name or North-Germanic Odin, and we do not know who is Phol.

Here now are two charms that begin identically, but they can be rewritten in two different ways.

First charm of protection against bad spells

Eye will see you,
Tongue will speak of you,
Heart will think of you -
The Three are protecting you -
The Father, Son and Holy Ghost.
(name of sufferer inserted here)
His will be done. Amen. (scot4)

Finding which runes to associate to this charm is not difficult. Typically, the rune associated with sight is Raido, the one that gives power to the eye of the sorcerer; the rune associated with language is, of course, the rune of Speech, Ansuz. The rune associated with the heart in the sense of welcoming another human is Mannaz. Finally, in the Christian version, Amen is being used to hallow, which is Thor's role (his hammer, Mjöllnir, also hallows). This poem can be rewritten as:

The eye sees you,
Language speaks to you,
The heart welcomes you -
Let Raido, Ansuz and Mannaz protect you -

Raido! Ansuz! Mannaz!
(Add the name of the patient here)
Thor ensure this!
Thor! Thor! Thor!

To engrave the runes, I suggest using the runes in the poem, which are Raido, Ansuz and Mannaz, the runes for the name of the patient, and finally, Laukaz, a rune I associate to Thor. Therefore, one row of runes must be engraved containing Raido, Ansuz, and Mannaz. Then a second row of runes must be engraved naming the patient, and finally 'to sign' the poem, engrave Laukaz three times. The galdr associated with this poem involves singing the first row of runes in a commanding tone that will call the spirit of these runes. The second row is sung with a woeful and pleading tone, since it represents the patient. Lastly, Laukaz is sung three times in order to hallow the preceding runes.

Another possible version associates the three Christian powers with the three Gods of Uppsala that Adam of Bremen described : Odin, Thor and Frey. This gives:

The eye sees you,
Language speaks to you,
The heart welcomes you -
Let Odin, Thor and Frey protect you -
Odin! Thor! Frey! [or their runes: *Ansuz, Laukaz, Jeran*]
(Put the name of the patient here)
Thor ensure this!
Thor! Thor! Thor!

Second charm of protection against bad spells

The second charm is a typical Gaelic one. Using strands of wool, it physically braids colored wool strands and mystically braids white and black magic around the patient.

The strands are red, white, and black (or blue), and are wound around the part of the body affected by the sickness, and the charm, beginning like the first one, is said three times.

> An eye will see you,
> Tongue will speak of you,
> Heart will think of you,
> The Man of Heaven blesses you.
> The Father, Son and Holy Ghost.
> Four caused your hurt -
> Man and wife,
> Young man and maiden.
> Who is to frustrate that ?
> The three persons of the most Holy Trinity,
> The Father, Son and Holy Ghost.
> I call thee Virgin Mary and St Brigit to witness
> that if your hurt was caused by man,
> Through ill-will,
> Or the evil eye,
> Or a wicked heart,
> That you [name] may be whole,
> While I entwine this about you.
> *In nomine Patris, ...* (scot5)

We are going to consider the preceding interpretation while modifying it. "The eye sees you, Language speaks to you, The heart welcomes you" are represented by the runes Raido, Ansuz, and Mannaz, as we have already said. The blessing of the man of the sky makes me think of Tyr, known as the "God of the sky." The holy Trinity is preserved only superficially to be able to allude to four divinities, since four persons covering all age groups cause the pain. In Christian philosophy, it is impossible, at least in principle, to use Christ's name to cause sickness. The Nordic Gods are much less strict on the difference between good and evil, and, like with the runes, they can be invoked to perform the so-called 'black' magic. The poem refers to "Old man and Old woman" (man and wife in the text) and "Young man and maiden," the two couples that I associate with Odin and Frigg, (runes Ansuz and Pertho) and Frey and Freya (runes Jeran and Berkanan). This amounts to saying that they have been the cause of the sickness. Then the healer invokes them again, but this time to ask them to undo the pain.

In the Nordic version that I have created from this Gaelic charm, I have balanced the four ways of communicating: the eye, the word, the heart, and the curse/blessing. The result is that the poem emphasizes once again the symmetry of the Gods' actions, favorable or unfavorable.

> The eye sees you,
> Language speaks to you,
> The heart thinks of you,
> *Raido! Ansuz! Mannaz!*
> Tyr blesses you.
> *Tiwaz! Tiwaz! Tiwaz!*
> Four have caused your pain -
> Odin and Frigg,
> *Odin! Frigg!*
> Frey and Freya,
> *Frey! Freya!*
> Undo your curse!
> Odin and Frey,
> *Odin! Frey!*
> With Frigg and Freya as witnesses
> *Frigg! Freya!*
> If a human has called this pain on you,
> By bad eye,
> By bad word,
> By wicked heart,
> Or by curse of Tyr,
> *Raido! Ansuz! Mannaz! Tiwaz!*

You, (name of the patient),
You will become whole again,
While I surround you with this.
Ansuz! Jeran! Pertho! Berkanan!
Uruz! Uruz! Uruz!

The galdr runes summarizing this charm are therefore:
- Raido, Ansuz, Mannaz, Tiwaz, which are invoked as powers of white magic. Ansuz is calling the power of Speech.
- Ansuz and Pertho, Jeran and Berkanan, which are invoked in a spirit of black magic, where Ansuz here is calling on Odin.
- Ansuz and Jeran, Pertho and Berkanan, invoked in a spirit of white magic, Ansuz is again calling on Odin.
- Raido, Ansuz, Mannaz, Tiwaz, invoked as powers of black magic, and here Ansuz is calling the power of Speech.
- Uruz, invoked at the end because the poem is designed for healing pains that have been caused by witchcraft. I chose to sanctify it with Uruz rather than with Thor, as I did earlier.

Kaunan can also be used since it 'returns to sender' the evil sent by witchcraft. If you want, to take revenge, then Kaunan can be sung. The spirit in which Kaunan is sung is very important here. If you simply want to send back the pain in order to be to rid of it, then Kaunan is invoked without any hatred in your voice. If, on the other hand, you want to call for revenge, the intonation must be more aggressive.

A charm for removing styes

This charm comes from yet another source. It has been recorded by Carmichael in his book on Scottish charms.

Why came the one stye without the two styes here? Why came the two styes without the three styes here? Why came the three styes without the four styes here? Why came the four styes without the five styes here? Why came the five styes without the six styes here? Why came the six styes without the seven styes here? Why came the seven styes without the eight styes here? Why came the eight styes without the nine styes here? Why came the nine or one at all here? *Repeat Pater Noster nine times.* (scot6)

Obviously, the nine Pater Noster can be replaced by nine Futhark, in order for it to be a Heathen charm again.

In his book, after reporting this charm, Cameron tells us that while he and his sister were visiting a hospital, his sister complained about the pain of a stye on her eye. Another visitor, of Highland Scottish origin, suggested that she repeats a charm, a close variant of Carmichael's, which she had inherited from her mother. A few minutes after the charm had been chanted, the stye burst and the pain disappeared. Cameron concludes that such a coincidence of events "would have impressed the medieval mind and convinced people of the efficacy of charms." This could also show how the stubbornly rational mind is unable to see the marvelous even when it knocks at the door.

Next, we will look at a very similar charm, form the Anglo-Saxon period, but instead this one counts backwards from nine to zero.

Anglo-Saxon charms

Translators and dictionaries give the meaning 'charm, incantation' to the Anglo-Saxon word, *galdor*. Since this chapter is dedicated to galdr, I have left galdor as it is, rather than translating it, since it obviously means the same as galdr. This shows again how much magic is linked to poetry and song.

I have been especially interested in Cameron's translations because he is a biologist, and not an Anglo-Saxon specialist. This might have hampered his ability to understand the language, but it gives him a deep knowledge of the topic itself; for instance, the herbs used in these charms, and their modern use in herbal medicine.

Many of Anglo-Saxon charms were created from a mixture of Anglo-Saxon, Latin and Greek which makes them less interesting for our purposes. The most interesting ones, still full of Heathenism, are found in a text called *Lacnunga*, which is the source of the first four charms we will study. The last two are found in two manuscripts called "Royal 12D" and "Royal 4A" of the British Museum.

For removing various skin diseases

This charm has a structure that is very similar to the one for removing styes that we saw in the Scottish charms.

> For kernels: Nine were node's sisters; then the nine became eight, and the eight seven, and the seven six, and the six five, and the five four, and the four three, and the three two, and the two one, and the one none. May this be a medicine to you for kernel and for scrofula and for worm and for every kind of evil; *sing Benedicite nine times.* (as1)

As we replaced the Pater Noster earlier, we shall simply replace singing the nine Benedicite by singing the Futhark nine times, thus obtaining a purely Heathen charm.

Charm against a sudden pain in the body: against a sudden stitch ("Wið foerstice")

Feverfew and the red nettle that grows in through the corn and plantain, boil in butter.

Loud were they, yea loud, when they rode over the hill [grave mound],
were of one mind [fierce] when they rode over the land.
Shield thou now thyself, that thou mayest survive this attack [affliction].
Out, little spear, if thou be herein.
[I] stood under linden, under a light shield,
where the mighty women made ready their powers,
and spears yelling they sent.
I will send another hack to them, a flying arrow in opposition to them.
Out, little spear, if it be herein.
A smith sat, forged a knife;
small the iron, mighty the wound.
Out, little spear, if it be herein.
Six smiths sat, wrought battle-spears.
Out, spear, not in, spear.
If herein be a hit of iron, work of witches, it shall melt.
If thou wert shot in skin, or wert shot in flesh,
or wert shot in blood, or wert shot in limb,
never would thy life be smitten.
If it were shot of gods, or if it were shot of elves,
or if it were shot of witches, now I shall help thee.
This be to thee as a remedy for shot of gods,
this be to thee as a remedy for shot of elves,
this be to thee as a remedy for shot of witches; I will help thee.
Fled there on the mountain top.
Be thou healthy; may the Lord help thee.

Then take the knife, apply the liquid. (as2)

When looking at the original Anglo-Saxon text, this charm seems to be of a complex nature because of the abrupt change of style that happens after verse 17, and verse 24. Verse 17 reads: *haegtessan geweorc, hit sceal gemyltan* while verse 18 is: *Gif ðu waere on lið scoten, naefre ne sy ðin lif ataested.* The style becomes also slightly more emphatic in verses 18-24. One of the scholars translating the AS charms, Rodrigues, suggests that it is actually made up of two charms. I rather believe there is a change in the tone of the galdor and it will have to be sung more slowly at this place. The reason why I don't believe in two distinct galdor lies in the phrase "mighty women that make ready their powers" of the first part, which is also very emphatic.

This very beautiful poem can become the base of many different galdr but I prefer to leave it to the reader.

A charm for gathering herbs

This is a very famous charm. It is often called "the nine herbs charm" because it hallows the gathering of nine different herbs. We have already studied a charm for vervain, so it will not be necessary to cite this very long charm completely. However, some of its verses are specifically relevant, so I include them here:

> A serpent went crawling, it wounded no one.
> Then Woden took nine glorious twigs,
> Struck then that adder so that she flew apart in
> nine pieces.
> There apple and poison made an end
> That she never should dwell in a house. (as3)

As already said, Woden is simply the West-Germanic word for North-Germanic Odin. The allusion to Odin in an Anglo-

Saxon charm shows how important this God was in the pre-Christian European civilization. The end of the charm is particularly poetic:

> Now the nine herbs have power against the nine
> fled from glory,
> Against nine poison and against nine infections,
> Against the red poison, against the foul poison,
> Against the white poison, against the purple
> poison,
> Against the yellow poison, against the green
> poison,
> Against the lurid poison, against the purple
> poison,
> Against the brown poison, against the blue
> poison,
> Against serpent blister, against water blister,
> Against thorn blister, against thistle blister. (as4)

The nine herbs used in this charm remind me of the nine rune songs which were briefly discussed in Chapter 1 and which are analyzed at length on my web-site, under the heading *Sigrdrifumal*. I suggest associating one song to each of the adjectives in the charm, that is: red, foul (that I will equate to black to avoid associating the pejorative 'foul' to a set of runes), white, purple, yellow, green, lurid (that I will equate to orange which is the one of the seven colors which is left out in the charm), brown, and blue. Maintaining both the ordering of the charm and the ordering found in Sigrdrifa's lay, leads us to associate the runes of Joy to red, the runes of Victory to black, the runes of Magic to white, the runes of Protection to purple, the runes of Delivery to yellow, the runes of Undertow to green, the runes of Branches to orange, the runes of Speech to brown, the runes of Spirit to blue.

The charm with its associated galdr will then become:

Nine herbs have power against nine bad ones,
Against nine poison and against nine infections.
Against the red poison, against the black poison,
Jeran! Wunjo! Gebo! Sowelo! Dagaz! Ehwaz!
Thurisaz! Tiwaz!
Against the white poison, against the purple
poison,
Thurisaz! Othala! Naudiz! Algiz! Hagla!
Laukaz! Fehu! Tiwaz! Isaz!
Against the yellow poison, against the green
poison,
Pertho! Berkanan! Ihwaz! Isaz!
Against the orange poison, against the purple
poison,
Kaunan! Uruz! Algiz! Laukaz! Fehu! Tiwaz!
Isaz!
Against the brown poison, against the blue
poison,
Mannaz! Ansuz! Raido! Hagla! Ingwaz!
Against serpent blister, against water blister,
Fehu! Laukaz!
Against thorn blister, against thistle blister.
Thurisaz! Thurisaz!

A charm against fever ("*dweorh*")

The word *dweorh* usually means dwarf, but in medical contexts, it seems to have meant fever since there are Anglo-Saxon translations of a Latin medical text that translate *dweorh* by fever.
The charm begins with the building of an amulet made of wafers, but it is of little interest to us because of its Christian origin. When hanging the amulet, you must sing a charm, first in the left ear, then in the right ear, then over the top of the head.

Here came stalking in a ... creature,

Had his bridle in his hand
Said that you were his steed.
He laid for thee his bond on the neck.
They began to move from the land.
As soon as they came from the land
Then his limbs began to cool.
Then came stalking in the fever's sister.
Then she made an end and swore oaths
That never this should do harm to the sick one
Nor to the one who might get this galdor
Or who knew how to sing this galdor. Amen,
Fiat. (as5)

First, some comments on the translation. There have been many discussions about what kind of creature it could be (a spider, or an "all swathed" one?), which is why I prefer to leave it undecided in the text above. In the second verse, Cameron leaves the word *haman* non translated (*hama* is a dress) but he points out that it has been suggested that it might also mean bridle, which makes a lot of sense here, (especially in view of the following "bond" which can be the same bridle) since 'dress' does not make sense at all. In the fourth verse Cameron translates *legde the* by "I lay," while Rodrigues correctly gives "He laid," as above. I also do not follow Cameron when he translates the Anglo-Saxon *dweores sweostar* by "the animal's sister." It means exactly "the dwarf's sister," as Rodrigues says, but, as explained earlier, I translate it by "the fever's sister." Finally, *Fiat* is a Latin word meaning "let be" as in *Fiat lux*: let the light be.

Even with my translation, which decreases the level of obscurity in both Cameron's and Rodrigues' versions, the text is not altogether clear, so it still deserves some discussion. It speaks of one creature and of its sister. The creature is often referred as by 'he'. I suppose that the fever, i.e. this 'he', is seen as riding the patient. 'He' seems to own the case into which the charm has been put, and which is laid on the neck of the patient. By the departure of the first animal, the limb of the patient starts to cool, that is, his or her fever leaves, as if fever would now start riding the departing animal. Later, the sister arrives, who swears that the fever will never harm the sick one, etc.

Let us stick to the (classical) idea that fever is a spider first reaching and then leaving the patient. We can associate the fever to Kaunan, the rune of internal fire. Isaz, the rune of ice, will be associated to the cooling of the patient's limbs. The 'she' who comes stalking in can be a female aurochs, which gives us the rune Uruz, or also a female elk, and we can also use the rune Algiz, or even a mare, and we would use rune Ehwaz. The swearing of an oath is associated to the runes of Speech, which explains why here I would use Mannaz and Ansuz. Finally, the Christian "Amen. Fiat" which hallows the charm, can be replaced by an evocation of Thor whose hammer represents protection. Therefore, the charm can be chanted in this form:

> Here came stalking in a spider,
> Fever had his bridle in his hand
> *Kaunan! Kaunan! Kaunan!*
> Said that you were his steed.
> He laid for thee his bonds on the neck.
> They began to move from the land.
> As soon as they came from the land
> Then his limbs began to cool.
> *Isaz! Isaz! Isaz!*
> Then came stalking in the animal's sister.
> *Uruz! Algiz! Ehwaz!*
> Then she made an end and swore oaths
> *Mannaz! Ansuz!*
> That never this should do harm to the sick one
> Nor to the one who might get this galdor
> Or who knew how to sing this galdor
> *Thor, come when you are called,*
> *Come in this need, Thor!*
> *Laukaz! Laukaz! Laukaz!*

The amulet will carry the runes Kaunan, Isaz, Uruz, Algiz, Mannaz and Ansuz. Since Mannaz and Ansuz are together here as runes of Speech, they must be bound, as the so-called bind-runes, so that it will look like this:

Obviously, once the runes have been carved, the healer or the patient can color the runes with his or her blood in order to free their magic.

Against the watery Elf-disease ("*woeteroelfadl*")

The next charm describes a medicine made from many herbs, mixed together with holy water. Then this galdor must be sung three times:

> I have bound the wounds with the best of war-bands,
> that the wounds neither burn nor burst,
> nor spread, nor go bad,
> nor throb; nor the injuries increase,
> nor the sores deepen; but the health balance is restored,
> nor will it hurt thee more than *eare* hurts earth.
>
> *Sing this many times*: May the earth destroy thee with all her might and main. *These galdor can be sung on a wound.* (as6)

I follow here (again) Cameron's translation of *woeteroelfadl* because he argues that one often finds remedies against *oelfadl* which designate skin eruptions of various kinds. Hence, *woeteroelfadl* is one kind of *oelfadl*, of a *woeter* (= water) type. The translation for the second half of the fifth line is original. Most translators speak of an unintelligible "health container" rather than my very clear "health balance." I have checked my translation with serious specialists of Old English, and they have accepted it.

There are many possible translations of *eare*, the most probable being 'ears' in the sense of ears of corn. It makes more sense than any other kind of ear since it is a product of the earth. A fancy hypothesis of mine is that *eare* is here the rune of the Earth, Ear, to which Earth should not show any animosity. Anyhow, everyone invokes some object's mildness towards Earth. Grattan and Singer, in their explanation of charm (as5), suggest that Eare might be the name of the Goddess of dawn, evoking yet another mild time.

As you can see, this text actually contains two different charms, both against wounds. The first one is to be sung three times, the second one is very short and is to be sung many times.

Both are very peculiar because they invoke the earth as a positive power that helps the patient. I have seen many charms (especially Lithuanian ones) that speak of the earth in a depreciative way. For instance: "Deep Earth, bad badness, where have you been? why have you been watching from your door? go back where you come from! God help me in my illness' beginning, Lord hurry up to save me!" I see here a Christian influence that puts all the world's sins on the Earth's back. That the Earth is called to save the patient in the Anglo-Saxon charms is thus not at all innocent, it denotes a persistence of Heathen influence.

There are no runes especially devoted to Earth's power. Nevertheless, Jeran ("the good year") evokes the richness of the Earth's gifts, and Pertho, the rune I associate to Frigg, is related to the Earth through her, since Frigg was able to ask all the elements of Earth to refrain from harming her son

Balder (even if Loki's guile ultimately won over Frigg's power in the Nordic myth).

It would be possible to build a runic galdr using this set of runes.

Against a Wen ("Wið wennum")

> *Wen, wen*, little *wen*
> ("Wenne, wenne, wenchichenne [*chicken of a wen*]")
> here thou shalt not build, nor have any abode,
> but thou shalt fare north to the hill hard by,
> where thou hast a brother in misery.
> He shall lay a leaf at thy head.
> Under *uolmes* foot, under eagle's wing,
> under eagle's claw, ever mayest thou fade.
> Shrivel as coal on the hearth,
> shrink as dung on a wall,
> waste away as water in a pail.
> Become as little as a linseed grain,
> and much less also than a hand-worm's hipbone,
> and also become so little that thou become
> naught. (as7)

A wen is a cyst usually occurring on the scalp.
The *uolmes* is usually seen as *uoles* or *wolues* (wolf) but it disrupts the rhythm of the poem where we expect a mention of the eagle three times. Two other Anglo-Saxon poems gather also several beings : *The Wanderer* associates a bird, a wolf, and a human; *The Sea-Farer* associates two eagles. The association of a wolf and of two eagles in the present charm is thus far from being absurd. This is why I follow here those, among them Cameron, who suggest this should be translated by 'the raptor'. Similarly, instead of translating "thou shalt fare north to the hill hard by," some propose : "thou shalt fare north to the hill of the killer" which makes

more sense in a magical perspective. I would counsel those who will use a personal version of this charm, to stick to these two interpretations even though they include two Anglo-Saxon words found nowhere else.

The rune Kaunan is known as torch under its Anglo-Saxon name, Cen, but it is known as boil, or ulcer, under its Scandinavian name Kaun. Although it may seem obscure now, these two forms are in fact related by a complicated past that I won't get into here. The most important etymological dictionary of the German language, by Kluge, suggests Kaunan can be associated to a *wen*, a kind of germ growing under the skin of the skull.

At the beginning of the charm, calling the *wen* three times amounts to calling Kaunan three times. Following the poem exactly would lead to the invocation of Kaunan, Kaunan, Kaunanko (little Kaunan in Old Norse) which is possible if you are familiar enough with this rune. I would make the *wen* fare East rather than North, so that it can go to the land of the Thurs, and the rune Thurisaz can then be used.

The reference to the eagle's wing leads me to believe that Uruz is called for here.

Lithuanian charms

Now we will look at some charms from Lithuania that are completely pagan and unpublished in French, English, or German, to my knowledge. They are the image, hopefully, of the non deformed magical and religious beliefs that I thought were lost forever until I met my Lithuanian friends who have graciously introduced them to me. The only change that I suggest for these poems is to replace the Lithuanian name of a God with one of the Aesir. Other than that, I wouldn't change a single word in these charms. I will, however, add a galdr that can be directly associated to them.[36]

Casting out evil Spirits

> Leave, cursed slug, from man,
> Because you have already dirtied him,
> Now that you live in him,
> You are the cause of great pain.
> The sun hates you, the moon hates you,
> The stars hate you, the stars hate you,
> Man hates you, children hate you,
> The whole family hates you, and me, I hate you.

The slug makes me think of the cold. Thurisaz, dedicated to the frost giants, is perhaps the most aggressive of the runes, and the attitude of the giants towards the Aesir can often be seen as hatred. Therefore, Thurisaz can be used as a helper for eradicating the slug. I do not think the galdr should be sung with hatred, but rather sung in a commanding voice to aggressively order the slug. This poem can be closed by invoking Thurisaz three times.

Charm for banishing sickness
(with an example of the runes we can associate to it)

> Early, I wake,
> *Dagaz!*
> With bitter dew, I wash,
> *Uruz!*
> To the sun, I address myself,
> *Sowelo!*

---

[36] I cannot give precise references for these charms that were translated for me by my Lithuanian informant, and I put them in French and English. General references about these charms are given in the bibliography.

I glorify God.
[Here, I suggest instead:
I glorify Thor]
Laukaz!
Sicknesses facing me,
Go in the dry trees,
The deep swamps,
There where no man walks,
There where no animal wades,
There where no bird flies.
Mannaz! Mannaz! Mannaz!

The first verse of this charm calls on the rising day (Dagaz rune), on the dew descending from the sky (Uruz rune), on the sun (Sowelo rune) and then it glorifies God which would be the rune of Tiwaz for the God of the sky, or any other rune dedicated to one of the Nordic Gods.

The invocation to Mannaz is obviously not attempting to call the Spirits of dry trees and deep swamps; it wouldn't be very wise. Instead the invocation is to the Spirits of human solidarity, of populated places.

Charm banishing fever

In the name of the sun,
Sowelo!
In the name of Perkunas, [*God of thunder and lightning*]
[Here, also, I would replace Perkunas with Thor, since he has the same functions in the Scandinavian mythology]
In the name of Thor,
Laukaz!
By thunder,
Thor!
I command you, fever,
Kaunan!

I hunt you from men, from animals, from birds,
from each living being,
To the green forest, the deep pools, the somber
swamps,
There where the sun does not shine,
Where no man walks,
Where no animal wades,
Where no bird flies.
Mannaz! Mannaz! Mannaz!
If you do not obey me,
I will dry you on the sun's beams,
I will wear you out with the sun's fervor,
I will drown you in the bitter dew,
I will feed you bewitched bread.
Sowelo! Uruz! Gebo!
I order you to leave [*name of the patient*]
To no longer torment him (or her).

The call to Sowelo, Uruz and Gebo should be done in a special way since these runes are being invoked so that they use their power aggressively against the sickness.

Charm to stop bleeding

Valiuli Dievuli, stop the blood!
[*Valiuli Dievuli is best translated as 'all - powerful'*]
Do not hunt the spirit of the body,
So that it does not leave with the blood,
That it does not leave the body alone.
By the hard stone, by the high oak, Valiuli
Dievuli, by the blood,
I order, I contain the blood in the veins.

There is neither a rune for stones, nor a rune for blood. However, there are several runes that evoke the idea of life and heat. If we want to invoke the joy of life with the word 'blood', then the associated rune would be Wunjo. The stone is hard, and its capacity to break is what is being called on, and this is a property of Hagla. The high oak obviously evokes Yggdrasil. So, one possible galdr for this poem would be to sing or to shout Hagla! Ihwaz! Wunjo!

Charm to protect against venomous snakes

> It is by fate that our difference is born, Rue,
> Fate has made us meet, Rue,
> Be not evil, Rue,
> Do not suffer, Rue,
> Show proof of your kindness, Rue. (*repeat three times*)
> Show proof of your kindness from (*present time*)
> From this day,
> From this sigh.
> Show proof or your kindness, Rue,
> We thank you, Rue,
> With our beautiful words, Rue,
> With our beautiful words, Rue.

The rue is a plant holding much meaning in Lithuanian mythology. I can explain it best as my informant did when telling me a personal anecdote. While on a bus, she saw an old woman who was having a difficult time getting off the bus. The old woman turned to her and said, "Please help me, rue." So, she helped her, and the old woman said, "Thank you, green rue." Hopefully, you will now better understand the tenderness that Lithuanian people hold for this herb, and why the healer tries to please the viper by giving it the name 'Rue'. This charm is thus constantly calling upon the power of the green rue to protect one who crosses an adder on his or her path. The three runes that evoke some kind of greenery are Ihwaz (rune of the yew), Berkanan (rune of the birch) and Laukaz (rune of the leek). Therefore, I suggest simply punctuating this beautiful poem with an invocation of these three runes.

Saint Hildegard's Charms and Incantations

As a doctor, Hildegard grouped the charms according to the illness that they were intended for. I have kept her classifications, but it doesn't necessarily mean that we must automatically follow her guidelines for diagnosis.

The first charm is purely Christian and I give it to you here anyway so that I can present all of Hildegard's mystical charms.

Against mental illness

> If someone falls ill with paralysis and one of those sicknesses that increases or decreases according to the moon, as with the case for lunatics, you must find a place where a donkey has been killed or where one has died on its own, or where it is still rolling on the ground: make the patient lie down on the ground for a short time, covered by a blanket; he or she will sleep, if they can; then take his or her hand and say:
>> "Lazareth slept and rested, then he raised; and, just as he was pulled by Christ from his disgusting stench, you also relieve yourself of this harmful sickness and these changing fevers, you who finds yourself in the situation where Christ was found, sitting on the same kind of donkey at the entrance to Jerusalem, before the resurrection of Lazareth, meaning he would redeem man of his sins and would straighten him."

A few minutes later, start over in the same place, and do this three times; then three times the following day or two days later; then three times again the following day or two days later, and he or she will be healed. (hilde2)

Against uncontrolled loves

Now, here is a charm designed for protecting against a troublesome lover.

> And if even the devil pushes a man to desire a woman, to such point that, without magical practices and invocations to demons, he becomes mad with love, and if that is disagreeable for this woman, let her pour a bit of wine on a sapphire three times, each time saying:
>> "I spill this wine on your fiery forces so that, just as God took away your shine when the angel sinned, take away the fiery love that this man feels for me."
>
> If the woman does not want to do this, another man who feels threatened by this love can do it in her place : he will make him drink the wine on an empty stomach or not, whether he tells him or not, and this must last for three days in a row.
> And if it is a woman who has a burning passion for a man, and that, for him, this love is disagreeable, he must act on the woman with wine and a sapphire as I have described it above, and the fire of the passion will burn out. (hilde3)

This charm is quite unexpected from a Christian devotee. Saint Hildegard was a very sick woman throughout her whole life, and she received vision upon vision showing her how the Christian God created the universe. It is all the more surprising that she would be so direct towards sexual problems. For instance, she explains that bears can become sexually excited by a human (of the opposite gender) who is sexually aroused. She says explicitly that in this case, you must either use her remedy or submit to the bear's desires unless you want to be torn to pieces. In the present charm, she says clearly that it is to be used "if that is disagreeable for this woman." Implicitly, it means that if not disagreeable (and if no demons have been involved), then the woman might as well abide to the wishes of her lover. I'll give no charm for this problem since I believe that clearly stating the solid bond, you want to stay faithful to, is the best remedy to discourage an undesired lover.

The following charms have more Heathen content although still hidden by a story which is holy to the Christians.

Remedies and incantations against bewitchments

> If someone has been bewitched by the devil, or by magic, take the same wood that is at the center of this tree [*the cypress*], hollow it out with an auger and then collect, in an earthen jug, water from a living source by making it flow through the hole in the wood. While pouring say:
>
>> "I pour you, water, through this hole and in this virtuous virtue, so that, thanks to the force that is in your nature you flow in this man whose senses are bewitched, and so that you destroy all contradictions that are in him, and that you straighten him, and give him back the just feelings and

just knowledge that God gave him in
the first place."
Let this water be given to drink on an empty
stomach, nine days in a row, because he is
tormented or bewitched by the devil by ghosts or
by magic, and he will get better. And thus,
during nine days, this formula must be uttered in
the same manner. (hilde4)

This charm is mainly calling on the powers of water and the
tree in which water flows. We have yet to interpret "that you
straighten him, and give him back the just feelings and just
knowledge that God gave him in the first place." Nordic
myths associate Tyr with courage since he placed his hand in
Fenrir's mouth to chain it, and also to the idea of justice and
soundness. This is why I again suggest that Tyr replace
Hildegard's God. On the other hand, "the virtuous virtue" of
the charm seems somewhat useless and a bit naive, and so I
will just leave it out. The charm becomes therefore:

"I pour you, water, through this hole so that,
thanks to the force that is in your nature, you flow
in this man whose senses are bewitched, and so
that you destroy all contradictions that are in him,
and that you straighten him, and give him back the
just feelings and just knowledge that Tyr gave him
in the first place."

The water that flows from the sky by passing on the
branches of Yggdrasil is precisely Uruz according to my
interpretation of the Viking runic poem. This charm is
therefore a sort of simulation of the Nordic myth: the power
of water and wood activated again. Therefore, Uruz and
Ihwaz together represent this power. We create a union like
this ᚾ with linked runes when, for example, we want to
denote a dominance of the tree over water, or vice versa ᚾ ,
or even ᚾ when they are considered equally. In any case, the
associated galdr will be made with both Ihwaz and Uruz

without a doubt. This power is then blessed by singing Tiwaz three times.

Another charm against bewitchments

> If someone is bewitched by spells or by magical formulas, to the point that he or she loses reason, you must take hot rye bread and split the crust at the highest part in the form of a cross, without dividing the loaf completely; then slip the precious stone [*the hyacinth*] along the length of the crack and say:
>
>> "Let God, who removed from the devil, when he went against his commandment, the bright light that he pulled from precious stones, pull from you, N..., all the spells and magic formulas, and let him free you from the pain of this madness."
>
> Then, while sliding this same stone from one side of the bread to the other, add:
>
>> "Just as the devil, because of his sin, saw his bright light removed from him, in the same way, let the madness that torments N..., because of spells and magical formulae, be removed by you and disappear."
>
> To end, make the patient eat the part of the bread that is the length of the crack where the hyacinth has been placed. (hilde5)

This is clearly an imitative treatment, according to Frazer's terminology, where the bright light (Lucifer) removed by God is associated to the flash of the precious stone.

In Nordic mythology, there are no equivalents for Lucifer, carrier of light, who revolts against the established order. However, it does tell us that the first light of day transforms dwarves and giants (trolls) into stone. We could, therefore, use a charm such as this:

> "Just as trolls freeze with the dawn, let the
> nightmares of spells and magic formula freeze, let
> Thor free you from the pain of this madness."

The associated galdr would be made up of the runes Thurisaz (trolls), Dagaz (the day), Ehwaz (the nightmare), Laukaz (Thor), and Algiz (madness).

To heal jaundice

> When the leaves of the beech have not yet
> returned completely, go near this tree, seize a
> branch with your left hand, and holding a small
> knife with your right hand, say :
>> "I cut your tartness, because you
>> purify all the humors that lead man on
>> paths of wrong doing and injustice; by
>> the living Word that made man
>> without regret."
> With your left hand, hold a branch while you say
> this, then cut it with a steel blade and keep this
> branch the entire year; and do this each year.
> (hilde1)

> If during the year, someone suffers from
> jaundice, cut some bits of this branch, put them
> in a small vase, sprinkled with a bit of wine
> three times, each time saying these words:
>> "By the holy womb of the holy
>> Incarnation, thanks to which God has
>> made man, take from this man the
>> pain of jaundice."
> Then heat the wine with the small branches that
> you have cut, in a pan or a pot and give this
> drink to the patient on an empty stomach, for

three days, and he will be healed, unless God does not want it. (hilde6)

This charm contains two declamations, one is more of an announcement and the second is a request or command. The first declamation alludes to the power of the branches whose tartness, (that Hildegard often refers to as *viridity*), is the force that makes the sap rise in the branches. It can be translated as:

> "I cut you, branch, to ask for your tartness that purifies the humors that lead man on the paths of wrong doing and injustice; by Yggdrasil, the tree that bears the world."

Therefore, all three runes of Branches will be used, followed by the rune of Yggdrasil, Ihwaz. The associated galdr for cutting the branch would then be: Uruz, Kaunan, Algiz, Ihwaz.

The second declamation, in a very unchristian way, calls on the womb of the holy incarnation by which God has made man and since the following charm does so as well, I'll use the same paganization for both of them.

Against fevers

> If someone has sharp pains, take the fruit of the beech when it starts to grow and put it in pure water while saying:
>> "By the holy womb of the holy Incarnation, thanks to which God has made man, you, sharp pains, and you, fevers, lessen and weaken your cold and your heat in this man."
> Then give him this water to drink. Do this for five days and if he has a daily fever or ague, he will be

quickly relieved; or else God does not want to free him. (hilde7)

This charm is making an explicit allusion to the fact that the patient has been suffering from shivers of cold and at the same time, the burning from fever. The rune of ice is certainly the one that is best to fight fever. However, it cannot act alone because it needs its counterpart, heat. As the rune of internal fire, Kaunan is the one to be invoked here. Also, in the Nordic creation myth, the Gods always existed, but they were frozen in ice, and they only became active after the ice melted. So, I suggest the following version:

"By the ice of the Origin that contained the Gods, by the heat of the Origin that freed them, you, Isaz, bring your cold to soothe this man's burns, and you, Kaunan, soothe his frozen shivers."

The galdr associated with this charm will obviously be made up of Isaz and Kaunan.

To give life to a dying patient

Find a beech root that is breaking through the ground, remove the outer bark of this root and cut it in such a way that you can do it in one cut and say:
"By the first revelation in which God sees a man in the Mambré root (*Genesis,* 18,1), [*or at least Hildegard says so*], break the waves of poison in this man and push death away from him."
Cut as much as you can with a second cut and say the same words; in the same way, make a third cut in this same root, so that it does not fail you during the year, and you will keep it

throughout the year and you will do this each year. And when, during the year, someone has some boilings [*sic*] in their body, take a small piece of these cut roots and put it in a vase. You will then pour a bit of water over it three times, each time saying these words:

> "By the first manifestation during the
> course of which God was baptized in
> the Jordan *(Mark,* 1) push death away
> from this man, thanks to this remedy,
> and remove all of his apparent stains,
> just as the life of Jesus was pure."

Give the water to the patient to drink on an empty stomach for three days, and prepare it each time as was said: he will be thus liberated from these boilings, unless God does not want it. (hilde8)

The first invocation in this charm alludes, for me, to the possibility that humankind might come from a piece of wood carved by the Gods, since the prose Edda says: "The sons of Bur went along the shore, found two tree stumps ... and made human beings."

The sons of Bur are the Aesir, the Gods of Nordic mythology, and therefore 'God' can simply be replaced here by Aesir. The *Völuspa* says that dwarves made human shapes and that the sons of Bur gave breath, senses, blood and life color to them. Thus, the "first revelation" will be for us the gift of the Gods: breath, senses, blood and life color. The first charm then becomes:

> "By the work of the sons of Bur who made human
> beings by giving them breath, senses, blood and
> life color, break these waves of poison in this man
> and push death away from him."

The Aesir corresponds to the whole Futhark, and Mannaz, since it correspond to being a human, will be central to the poem and will be repeated three times in the middle of the other runes.

The second invocation in the charm is making an allusion to the power of water, specifically baptismal water. The Germanic equivalent of baptism is a sort of 'lustral' ceremony; a ceremony using water to purify and acknowledge children. *Havamál* tells us that Berkanan is the rune associated to this. The end of the sentence makes reference to the purity of Jesus. For the Aesir, the symbol of purity is Balder, the son of Odin and Frigg. This now gives us:

> "By the lustral water that parents sprinkle on their children, push death away from this man, thanks to this remedy, and remove all this apparent stain, just as Balder has represented purity."

The runes representing this are Berkanan and Uruz, as in ᛒᚢ.

Traditionally, no rune is associated to Balder. However, since he is always represented as luminous, he can be associated with Sowelo which completes the runic representation of this charm:

> *Berkanan Uruz! Berkanan Uruz! Berkanan Uruz! Sowelo! Sowelo! Sowelo!*

The two runes associated with trees, Ihwaz and Berkanan, could also have been used to compose another galdr. They will be used to make up the galdr for the two next charms.

Against melancholy

> And if someone is, by character, always sad and always in grief and always has a heart full of pain and sorrow, he must collect the mandrake

after it has been uprooted; he must put it in a fountain as we have said, for one day and one night. Once it is out of the water, he must put it in his bed beside him, so that he will be heated by the plant's sweat and he must say:

> "God, you who has created man with
> the silt of the earth without putting
> pain in him, here is what I put beside
> me, this earth, that has never sinned,
> so that the earth, of which I am made,
> knows the state of peace that is in it,
> and in which you have created it."

And if you have no mandrake, take the first shoots of a beech, because they have the same happy virtues in this case. Cut off the branches with a clean cut, without breaking them, keeping them whole; put them in your bed near you so that they warm you and that they absorb your body's sweat. Then, recite the formula stated above: You will find joy, and, in your heart, you will feel calmness. You can also do the same thing with cedar and aspen, and of that, you will find yourself well. (hilde9)

The *Völuspa* hints that the dwarves made the human shapes out of earth and water. The revision of the above formula becomes therefore:

> "As the dwarves shaped humans forms out of
> earth and water, I place you beside me, earth, so
> that its innocence and grounding which are part
> of me might come to the fore."

Against apathy

If someone is completely exhausted and has some kind of paralysis, another man must take a bit of this earth (*green clay*) and put it on the right and the left side of the patient's head, in bed, and, in the same way, put it on either side of the right foot and the left foot; when he digs to get the earth, he must say:

"You, earth, you sleep in this man N..."
Then, after having removed the earth on either side of the head, he must put it under the man's head, just until it becomes warm; in the same way he must put the earth under his feet so that it receives some of the heat: and, when he puts this earth under the head and under the feet, the one putting it there must say:

"You, earth, develop in this man and
be useful for him, so that he receives
your tartness, in the name of the
Father, the Son and the Saint who is
God complete and living."
And it must be done this way for three consecutive days. (hilde10)

I recommend an equivalent ritual replacing the Christian trinity by a Nordic one.

Against possessions

If a man is possessed by a crafty spirit, another man must make a sapphire fall on the earth, then put a bit of this earth in a leather pouch, he must hang it around the patient's neck while saying:

"O you, unspeakable spirit, leave this
man immediately, just as, during your
first fall, the bright light of your
splendor has gone as quickly as
possible far away from you."
This crafty spirit will be violently tortured and distanced from this man (at least if it is not a

very aggressive or very wicked spirit) and the patient will improve. (hilde11)

This charm is very similar to the one against bewitchments that we have already seen and a similar adaptation is easy to imagine.

> If someone is possessed by the devil, spread a bit of water on a chrysoprase and say:
>> "Water, I sprinkle you on this stone with the power by which God has made the sun as well as the wandering moon."
> Then you give the possessed this water to drink, as you can, since he will only drink it if forced to. And all day the devil will struggle in him and will weaken; he will no longer show his strength in him as he did before. You will do this for five days. On the fifth day, using this water, prepare a kind of bread that you will give him to eat, as you can. And, if it is not a persistent demon, it will leave this man. (hilde12)

This time, the power of the water flowing on a precious stone is invoked. This charm really shows its Heathenism. Frazer's work contains many examples of using stones to make rain, but they do not come from the Nordic countries. I also never found an allusion to the power of stones for healing in the Nordic myths. Therefore, I would not use this charm.

Against migraines

> If you suffer, in your head, from several sicknesses and weaknesses, to the point of becoming mad, you must put a piece of sard on

the nape of your neck, in your bonnet, with a linen or leather pouch; and you must say:

> "As God rejected the first angel in the abyss, let him also take away from you, N..., this madness, and let him return to you your good sense."

And you will be healed. (hilde13)

The struggle between the Aesir and the Thurs can be used as a background for an equivalent of Lucifer's fall, which is how he is identified here, rather than by his brilliance. I suggest this adaptation:

> "Just as the Thurs live in cliffs, let the Aesir throw your madness into the abyss; just as they live in the cold, let the hail that hits them hit your madness."

The associated galdr here will be, therefore, made up of Thurisaz, Laukaz, Thurisaz, Hagla.

To ease delivery

> If a pregnant woman, overwhelmed by pains, is not able to deliver, you must rub her thighs with a sard stone and say:
> > "Just as you, stone of sard, have shone on the first angel by the order of God, in the same way, you, child, come shine as a man who lives in God."
>
> Then, she will place this same sard at the baby's exit, to the exit of her sex, and she will say:
> > "Open, paths and doors, just as for the appearance by which Christ, God and man, has appeared and has opened the doors of hell; and you, baby, cross this door without dying and without making your mother die."

At this moment, you must place this stone in a
belt around her, and she will be eased. (hilde14)

The first part of the incantation is making an allusion to
brilliant angels, the role played by Elves in Scandinavian
mythology. The second part is asking the doors to open to
give way to the baby. An equivalent would be to ask for an
easy passage for the baby, in the same way as the Gods
easily crossed the Bifrost bridge which gives them access to
their home.
The revised version gives us:

> My child, as the shining elf,
> Come enlighten us with your justice.
> *Sowelo! Tiwaz! Sowelo!*
> Open paths and roads,
> *Raido!*
> As the Gods crossed Bifrost painlessly,
> *Isaz! Isaz! Isaz!*
> You, my baby, pass the bridge toward life
> Without making us die.
> *Pertho! Pertho! Pertho!*
> *Urdr! Skuld! Verdandi!*

Sowelo is seen as the rune of the hot light, Tiwaz is that of
justice, Isaz of the cold light, Raido of the journey, and
Pertho is the rune of the woman giving birth. The three
Norns represent the terrible aspect of the Powers, but these
Powers also have a more cheerful aspect called the Disir.
They preside over births that also have these two aspects.
They must be evoked here without brutality, otherwise you
risk calling the Norns and not the Disir to attend to the
newborn! This is also why I advise calling the Norns by
their names, rather than by the rune, Naudiz, that contains
their terrible power of deciders of destiny. Pertho represents
the Disir better than Naudiz, and this is why it is invoked
just before the three Norns.

Against madness

> If someone goes mad, or is in some way prey to
> fantasies, you must rub a magnet with saliva,
> and, with the stone, rub the nape of his neck,
> then his forehead while saying:
>> "Bad madness, yield to this power by
>> which God has transformed the devil's
>> power into kindness for man, sent
>> forth from the high sky."
> And the patient will find his spirits. (hilde15)

This incantation is alluding to the fact that a pain
experienced by a celestial creature could become favorable
to humans. In Nordic mythology, Thor's destruction of the
Thurs is the closest myth to this. One possible revised
version could be:

> "Bad madness, just as the giants had to yield to
> the strength of Mjöllnir, yield now to the
> strength of the runes."

Once again, this is a charm based on Thurisaz since it
alludes to the giants. Laukaz will also be used to remind us
that Thor is the destroyer of giants. If you use the Younger
Futhark of 16 runes, then, of course, Laukaz, having lost its
original meaning of 'leek', becomes 'water', and a rune
equivalent to Thurisaz, Thurs, takes on the power of Thor.
This last attribution is the choice of the majority of mystics
using runes today. Remember my attribution of Laukaz to
Thor is very personal, although well-argued in the next
volume, and that my naming Laukaz follows the rather
disputed position of Krause.

Against obsessions

> If a person is disturbed by demonic thoughts,
> night and day, awake or asleep, he must use a

belt made of elk hide, and another of deer skin, and connect them with four small steel points, so that one of the belts is on the stomach, one on the back, and one on each of the sides. When he joins them at the point on the stomach, he must say:

> "By the power of the all-powerful God, I swear to you my protection."

When he puts the point on the back in place, he must say: "By the power of the all-powerful God, I bless you to my protection."
When he puts the point that will be on its straight side in place, he must say:

> "By the power of the all-powerful God, I order and ordain you to my protection."

Finally when he puts the point that will be on his left side in place, he must say:

> "By the power of the all-powerful God, I attach to you my protection."

(hilde16)

This charm is therefore playing on the four sides of the body, and on the four actions giving power to a Spirit: to swear, to bless, to order and ordain (as in: to ordain a priest), and to attach something to a person.
This is very much like the eight operations that one must know to use the runes. The High One asks:

> Do you know how to engrave, interpret, dye the runes, what you must ask the runes, desire from the runes, how to hallow them, send them, sacrifice to the runes? (edda12)

I suggest replacing Hildegard's verb 'to swear' by *engraving*, 'to bless' by *dyeing*, 'to order and ordain' by *hallowing*, and 'to attach' by *sacrificing*. We can also select four Gods. Among the many possible choices, I have chosen the two most important divine couples: Odin and Frigg, Frey and Freya. This gives us the following adaptation of Hildegard's charm:

By the power of the Shouter of the Gods, I engrave you to my protection!
[*Odin is also called the Shouter of Gods*]
Ansuz! Ansuz! Ansuz!
By the power of Balder's mother, I dye you to my protection!
[*Frigg is Balder's mother*]
Pertho! Pertho! Pertho!
By the power of Ingvi Frey, I hallow you to my protection!
[*Frey is often called Ingvi, the king*]
Jeran! Jeran! Jeran!
By the power of brilliant Freya, I sacrifice for my protection!
Berkanan! Berkanan! Berkanan!

The Charms of the Kalevala

Contrary to Hildegard's work, the Kalevala does not give charms associated to specific sicknesses but rather to the expulsion of demons and to asking assistance from Spirits or Gods. The next two charms, intended to ease difficult deliveries, are good examples of the attitude of humility that the healer must show.

Charms to ease delivery

Louhi, the Queen of the North, says this charm when her "horrible daughter" is about to deliver her babies, hidden in a sauna.

Louhi, mistress of the northern land,

The old toothless woman of the North...
Brought her [*daughter*] secretly to the sauna,
In hiding to the bath-hut,
Unnoticed by neighbors;
No word reaching the village.
She secretly heated the sauna,
Preparing her with speed;
She smeared beer on the doors,
Wetted the hinges with ale,
So that the doors would not creak,
Nor the hinges squeak.
Then she put this in words,
She declared, speaking thus: (kal49)

Invocation to mother-nature

Oh Queen, daughter of nature,
Woman in gold, beauty
Who is the most ancient of wives,
The first of matrons:
Run until you wet your knees in the sea
Up to your belt in the waves,
Take the turbot's drool,
The slime of the perch,
Apply it between bones,
Rub along the sides,
To free a girl of tension
A woman of her suffering uterus,
From this tedious pain,
This difficult work in her belly! (kal50)

Invocation to the main God

Oh Old Man, first of Gods,
Come here when you are needed,
Take this way when you are called.

Here there is a girl in bad way,
A woman submitted to the anguish of her belly,
In the middle of the smoke in the sauna,
The village bath-hut.
Take a golden stick
In your right hand
And with it shatter the bars,
And break the doorposts,
Undo Creator's locks,
And slacken the inner bolts,
Let the great pass, let the small pass,
Let the tiny go! (kal51)

Many invocations and charms are given in the Kalevala
through the adventures of Väinämöinen, in his search for
knowledge. His journey takes place in the mouth and the
stomach of the giant, Antero Vipunen, of whom it has been
said that he lies as a hill, covered with trees: "The poplar
grew on his shoulders, the birch on his temples, the alder on
his cheeks, the willow on his beard, the fir on his front, the
wild pine between his teeth."
Here are some of the charms that Väinämöinen learns
along his way.

*General charm for getting rid of bad spirits whose Origin is
known*

Specter go on your way,
Demon of the earth, get out of there,
Before I find your mother,
Oh that I do not summon your honorable parents!
I will tell your mother, speak with her,
Denounce you to your parents.
The work of the mother increases,
Parents are disturbed
When their son behaves wrongly,
Their child acts badly. (kal52)

In the context of the Kalevala, knowing the pain's Origin is what enables the treatment to be made. The rune permitting a struggle against harmful Spirits is Uruz, as we have already discussed, and the rune enabling a fight against bewitchments is Kaunan, according to the words of the High One:

> I know a sixth that saves me when a man, using
> an evil stick, seeks to harm me. His hatred
> returns against him. (edda13)

Therefore, a combination of Uruz and Kaunan can serve as galdr to this poem.

Curses when the Origin of the illness is ignored

> I have no idea
> I can not guess your Origin,
> Hiisi, who has freed you.
> Demon, from where have you come
> To nibble and bite,
> To eat, to chew.
> Are you a sickness coming from the Creator,
> Bane of Jumala,
> Or rather of human origin,
> Fashioned and brought by someone,
> Put in place against payment,
> Raised by money?
> If you are of a human origin,
> Caused by another man,
> Be sure that I will know your family
> That I will find out where you were born! (kal53)

This imprecation is very special since it is being used as more of a threat to the demons rather than as a means to really exorcise them. This type of 'bragging' against so-called evil powers is not rare in primitive behavior, we still see it today. Without repeating this poem word for word, it can be adapted to our vision of magic. Suppose that a treatment using magic has failed, it is not good to leave it there. It is much better indeed to challenge the pain and to promise to never leave it alone in the patient.

Therefore, I would use this type of poem to lessen a failure, and to promise continued support to the patient. I do not give examples of possible adaptations since they would vary strongly according to the patient and his or her pain, and runes to be used will also be variable.

Charm for casting out bad Spirits

> Be calm, Hiisi's dog,
> Soften, Manala's cur
> *[Manala = Tuonela, land of the dead]*
> Leave my lap, scoundrel,
> Grime of the earth, my liver,
> Stop biting the heart of my heart,
> Scratching my spleen,
> Filling my stomach,
> Twisting my lungs,
> Chewing my umbilicus,
> Seizing my intestines,
> Crushing my vertebrae,
> Whipping my sides! (kal54)

All runes of Branches can be used to summarize this poem, therefore Uruz, Kaunan, and Algiz can be used as basis for the galdr associated to it.

Charm to ask for the earth's assistance

> I invoke from the ground the earth matron,

From the field the first masters,
From the earth all warriors,
From the sand all horsemen,
Let them be my force and my power,
My support and my refuge
In this hard work,
In this cruel pain. (kal55)

This is a perfectly Heathen poem, and therefore there is nothing to change. I am content to simply repeat it now with the runes of its galdr.

I invoke from the ground the earth matron,
Pertho!
From the field the first masters,
Othala!
From the earth all warriors,
Tiwaz!
From the sand all horsemen,
Raido!
Let them be my force and my power,
Thurisaz! Othala! Naudiz! Algiz! [runes of Magic]
My support and my refuge
Laukaz! Fehu! Tiwaz! [runes of Protection]
In this hard work,
In this cruel pain.

Charm to ask for the forest's assistance

Rise, Oh forest, you and your peoples
Junipers, you and your people
Pines, you and your household,
Oh still pools, you and your children,
You and a thousand guys of steel,
To use this demon,
To crumple this Troll. (kal56)

Birches and yews will replace juniper and pines, but aside from this, nothing needs to be changed except to add the galdr to this poem.

> Rise, Oh forest, you and your peoples
> Birches, you and your people
> Berkanan!
> Yews, you and your household,
> Ihwaz!
> Oh still pools, you and your children,
> Uruz! You and a thousand men of steel,
> To use this demon,
> To crumple this Troll.
> Laukaz! Laukaz! Laukaz!

Laukaz, rune of Thor, is certainly the rune to use to get rid of the trolls or Thurs.

Charm to ask the water's assistance

This charm does not need to be modified, which is why I give it here with its associated galdr in parentheses:

> Rise from the waters, (Laukaz!) mistress
> From the waters, (Uruz!) that the waves cap in blue,
> Covered by a fine blanket of sludge,
> Face washed of its mud,
> To become the strength of a guy, (Thurisaz!)
> The virility of a small man, (Thurisaz!)
> Let me not be eaten without cause,
> Killed without sickness! (Ihwaz! Isaz!) (kal57)

Here the assistance of all waters is being asked and therefore Uruz, the water falling from the sky, is important, but so is

Laukaz which became the rune of water in the younger Futhark. The virile force is contained in Thurisaz. This is one case, then, where the Thurs can be invoked for assistance. Finally, the runes of Undertow must be invoked here: Ihwaz and Isaz.

Charm to ask for the assistance of Mother Nature

> Oh Queen, nature's daughter,
> Woman in gold, beauty
> Who is the most ancient of wives,
> The first of matrons,
> Come now to calm the pains
> To drive away the bad days,
> To take care of this deal,
> To ward off this attack! (kal58)

Frigg, obviously, has power over the elements of nature, as she clearly shows in her attempt to protect her son Balder from his fate since she was able to make each of the earth's elements swear that they would not harm Balder. This poem is completely dedicated to Frigg, and therefore to the rune Pertho.

Charm to ask for the assistance of the main God

> Ukko, navel of the sky
> At the edge of storm clouds,
> Come here when you are needed,
> Take this way when you are called,
> To undo the miserable deeds,
> To hunt misfortunes,
> With a sword with a proud blade,
> Of a sparkling brand. (kal59)

The main God for us is Odin, but he was never referred to as the "navel of the sky," and he has a lance not a sword. I suggest this alternative instead:

> Odin, horseman of the sky
> Prancing on storm clouds,
> Hail!
> *Odin! Odin! Odin!*
> Come here when you are needed,
> Take this way when you are called
> To undo these wretched facts,
> To hunt misfortunes,
> With the proud Gungnir, [*Name of Odin's lance*]
> *Hagla!*
> And your sharp tongue.
> *Ansuz!*

A runic inscription on a lance reads : "Hagala that breaks helmets!" (rune8) This is why I suggest invoking Hagla as the rune associated to Gungnir.

Charm of banishment

> Yonder I banish you,
> Yonder, wretch, I force you - into
> Old Brunet's house, [*the other name of the bear*]
> The old bear's farm
> To marshy holes,
> To still frozen marshes,
> In living springs,
> In pools
> Without fish, without perch. (kal60)

Once again, Kaunan is the rune for making a curse bounce, sending it back to the one who sent it. Therefore, it will be the basis for the galdr associated to this poem.

Incantation to Ukko, the Old Man

The Kalevala gives us this healing treatment performed by
Väinämöinen:

> Then the old Väinämöinen,
> The eternal man,
> Was going to cover the pains
> And treat these wounds
> With nine balms
> And the eight remedies; (kal61)

He completes this treatment with an invocation to the 'Old
One', the first of Gods, who must obviously be replaced by
Odin in our context. I give the Kalevala's poem in its
original form with the addition of the galdr associated to it.

> Hail Old Man, first of the Gods, (*Odin!*)
> Ancient of the skies (*Odin!*)
> Raise an eastern cloud (*Thurisaz!*)
> Lift a North-west curtain
> And send a breath from the West:
> Let honey rain, let water rain,
> That will be the balms for pains,
> Remedies for the wounds!
> (*Uruz! Uruz! Uruz!*)
> Give me a proud
> Sword, a sparkling brand
> To hold the pains
> To take away the pain forever
> Pains in winds' path
> Sufferings in large clearings
> Yonder I send sufferings ,
> Yonder I banish pains -
> In stone cellars
> And iron mounts
> To make the rock suffer,

To put the rock in pain:
No rock cries of pain
No rock complains of its misfortunes
As much as one piles on them ,
As much as one pours on them. (kal62)
(*Tiwaz! Tiwaz! Tiwaz!*)

Call to the servant of Death

Girl of pains, Tuoni's servant
Sitting on the rock of pains
Where three rivers run,
Where three rivers part,
Turning the mill of pains,
Making the mount of sufferings turn:
Go and gather up the pains
In jaws of the blue rock,
Or rather rolls them in the water,
Throw them to the bottom of the sea
Where the wind will not find them
Nor the sun shine upon them! (kal63)

This last poem is difficult to interpret, but its wild beauty makes it unavoidable. I leave it to each one to associate a galdr to it. Be careful when calling upon the servant of Death!

Conclusion

We have now seen how a galdr can be associated to a healing through the runes. The next chapter will detail the twelve phases of the complete healing treatment that we discovered in Chapter 2. The six main ones are as follows:

- In ordinary reality, you must become informed about the origin of the sickness, gain scientific knowledge about the sickness.

- In non-ordinary reality (that of the shamanic journey), you must journey to the Lower world to find the mystical Origin of the sickness. You must consult your Animal-Spirits on this Origin.

- After this shamanic session, you have to return to ordinary reality, and write a poem that expresses this knowledge, one that is friendly toward the cause of the sickness.

- By alternating between ordinary and non-ordinary reality, search for the runes that you will associate with the poem, and create the galdr that will accompany this poem.

- Again in ordinary reality, engrave this poem in runes in the bark of a branch. Choose a tree that seems most appropriated: oak, birch, yew, ash, hazel, and rowan are the main trees in the mystical sense. The branch you choose must stem from a larger one that grows toward the east, as Sigrdrifa teaches.

Finally, in a state that mixes ordinary and non-ordinary reality at the same time, hallow this poem and the runes in a place that has some 'sacredness' for the patient. There, recite the poem, by howling or singing the galdr that you have associated to it. The last thing you must do is to send the branch carrying the runes back to its element: earth, water, air, or fire.

Chapter 5

GLOBAL PRIMITIVE MEDICINE

The Origin of Sicknesses
It is here that this abomination,
Tuoni's blind girl,
Emptied her stomach, delivered
Her hateful kids,
Under a copper colored coat,
Her bed curtain of linen:
She produced nine sons
In one summer night
In one quiver of vapor,
One wave of heat from the sauna,
A mob come from one single belly,
From her full womb.
And she named her sons,
Prepared her brats,
As each one does with her offspring,
Creatures whose shell she has broken:
She put one to provoke sharp pains,
That one was called colic,
This one she pestered to become gout,
She raised this other one to be rickets,
This one to become the boil,
That one she fixed to become the scabs,
This one she shod in cancer,
That one she hit to be the plague.
One remained nameless, the son
In the bottom of the litter:
This one she sent far away,
To give to the witches of the water,
To the witches of the deep marshes,
And to the jealous that one finds everywhere.
(Kalevala, song 45*)*

I would be very surprised if a patient immediately consulted a healer before having tried everything that modern medicine has to offer. Because modern medicine is indisputably efficient, by the time the patients get to the healer, they have become very sick, even if their symptoms are not very debilitating. Some illnesses, such as cancer and AIDS are fatal and many advances are made in these areas by modern medicine. There are also many chronic sicknesses, not diagnosed as fatal, that defy and, in my opinion, will continue to defy the rational approach to treating them. For example, migraines, poor blood circulation, herpes, poor digestion, depression, anxiety and various other pains seem linked to causes so variable that they can not be made the object of a precise characterization nor a fixed therapy. Even though you can live a long time suffering from these sicknesses, I still consider them very deep illnesses. This last chapter is not trying to describe an ordinary treatment of a sickness that isn't very serious, but one that is deeply anchored in the patient. As I have already said, I would never recommend abandoning modern medical treatments, and this is why I think you could always see, if so desired, magical techniques as a method of accompaniment, in other words, a method that isn't efficient by itself, but that helps the success of another treatment.

This idea is certainly seductive, and it would enable magical methods to 'become respectable again' by finally finding a sort of rational justification: they wouldn't have any 'real' efficiency, but they would offer psychological support to patients allowing them to better accept the scientifically efficient treatment. Admitting this hypothesis would be convenient for me, but it would be dishonest to the readers because I believe that many stages of the mystical treatment are essential conditions for healing, and are as important, perhaps even more so, as the application of efficient medicines. Taking charge of yourself when you are sick, searching for the best healer, discovering the Origin of the sickness, in a practical and mystical sense, carrying out a holistic treatment (not just limited to symptoms), and giving thanks (by both healer and patient), are each of capital importance and must not be forgotten if a complete healing is desired. When such a healing is completed, the patient's state after the sickness is, in some sense, better than before it occurred, even when it leaves visible scars. Odin lost one eye but won knowledge, what he longed for, Tyr lost one hand but won fame, what he seemingly longed for.

THE TWELVE STEPS FOR HEALING PHYSICAL SICKNESS

1 - Self healing
(Patients try to use their own strength to heal themselves)

First I want to really stress the need for the healer to take this step into account. Healers and doctors tend to forget about the amount of effort to self-heal that most patients perform before going to see a doctor. Knowing about these efforts allows the healer to know exactly where he or she must strike the sickness.

Many people tend to confuse being responsible for yourself and 'self-medication', which perhaps explains the fact that modern medicine does not try to encourage patients to become responsible for themselves. When medicines are dangerous, obviously only a specialist can be authorized to administer them. However, with alternative medicines, nothing stops the patient from helping the physician. Especially, when using essential oils and trace elements, patients can use trial and error and feel for themselves which of these medicines work best.

What do I mean by responsibility? This term tends to designate the one who will pay for the disastrous results of making a mistake and, in this sense, everyone is centrally responsible for their own body. The first responsibility of each, and the first way of caring for yourself, can be found in your diet, the air you breathe, and the exercise that you give to your body.

- Diet

Here are, in a few words, the fundamental principles that I believe are useful for patients so that they can help themselves heal through diet.

The problem is that everything and its opposite have been recommended as an infallible diet for treating each illness. Amusingly, we went from the Carton method, pre WWII war (based on very light and cooked foods), to the macrobiotic diet and to the frugivorous techniques (complete foods and/or vintages) postwar. On the other hand, and equally amusingly, the method of food combination (not eating some foods together, starches and proteins, for example) discovered and well-described by Shelton, pre-war, is recommended by crowds of people all claiming to have discovered it, while really, they are only describing Sheltonism in a nice neat package. All this shows very well that fad diets do not hold the answer.

The ideal diet considers that the only illness is too much eating. This is how I explain the success of extreme diets such as macrobiotics, frugivorism and vegetalism. In these diets, you are putting yourself in a partial fast state since you are suppressing an important part of your dietary intake, and since most often the food is not very appetizing, and you eat a lot less. They are harmful in the long run because of the deficiencies that they create, but they are certainly beneficial for short periods of time. I must confess that I prefer partial fasts (taking vegetable juice), which are better adapted to long term fasts, as the Swedes have popularized. The medical risks associated with the strict fast (where only pure water is taken) is practically neutralized because of the daily intake of mineral salts and vitamins, while still maintaining a brutal reduction in the other components of your normal diet. The patient gets used to no longer considering hunger as very important, and can then continue by naturally reducing his or her food consumption. After realizing what your true needs are, the problem is no longer is to reduce certain foods, as the modern nutritionists often advise, but to simply eat enough to avoid deficiencies. Therefore, filling foods, rich in calories and poor in nutritional value, would naturally be eliminated, and fish, for example, richer in nutritional elements with fewer calories, would become preferred to other meats. I often practiced, and I still practice, the strict fast. My reasons for doing this are mystical and I don't do it as an attempt to improve my health. I would never recommend this practice to a patient, but I would to those in good health, and the healthy who are a bit too fat!

The difficulty is being able to feel how our body reacts to each food. I have met many people who are irresponsible, precisely because they exaggerate the attention they give to their body's reactions, or on the contrary, they scorn them. The goal is to refine our own sensitivity, to really feel the reactions without becoming a slave to them. Sickness is a very efficient way to practice our sensitivity, and to show us the path to health. For example, almost all smokers stop smoking when they have the flu; the sickness clearly shows them that it's bad for them. Few, however, actually listen to this teaching.

   - Air

Aside from the classic statement: "Ah, fresh air!" of those who finally get to breathe the air of the mountains or the seaside, I find that most people are hardly sensitive to the quality of the air they breathe. This is again because of their lack of responsibility; they are not sufficiently open to receiving messages from their own body. As with food, we should feel almost at once the effect of a particular atmosphere on our own body.

I can't condemn strongly enough the dreadful stench of our inevitable cars. You smell them as soon as you finally rid your body of their odor, for example by staying in the mountains for several days, far from all roads.

- Exercise

Exercise is also important when you are caring for your health, and again you have to feel responsible. Many people complain of horrible back pain, yet their abdominal musculature is a disaster and their dorsal musculature has practically never existed! Everyone who feels well in their body knows how efficient regular exercise is, and, besides, it takes up so little time to practice! How many of us have refined their reception of their body's messages to the point of finding these daily exercises pleasurable instead of boring? It is a pleasure each morning to feel your muscles and joints stretched, and your muscles slightly exerted. So few people exercise daily that I will allow myself to insist: don't do the exercise to get it out of the way, "because it must be done", but instead try to feel how good your body feels while you exercise. Even the slight burning that normal abdominal exercise provokes should be experienced as a pleasure!

I confess that it seems more reasonable to me, to say the least, to begin with this sort of general body hygiene, before turning to magical practices.

2 - Humility of the patient
(in case of failure, he or she must go to someone able to help, a healer, and ask for help)

Knowing how to take charge is obviously linked to a certain pride, and this pride, necessary in the first stage, does not have to be left because of the humility necessary in this second stage. On the contrary, and despite the necessary awareness of being unable to nurse themselves, the patients seek to create a symbiotic relationship (without abandoning their responsibilities) with a healer. Keeping this in mind, a confident relationship must be established between the healer and the one being healed, and might unfortunately cause problems in modern society. Our society only accepts extremes: so much impersonal contacts that they come close to being indifferent, or completely taking charge as do those that we call gurus.

When he realizes that he is not able to nurse his injury alone, the great Väinämöinen looks for help, as we saw in the Kalevala. To emphasize this aspect of Nordic medicine, here is another version of this search, recorded around 1803, that is different from Lönnrot's version :

> ... He sought a sage on the road,
> a mighty man on the bridge,
> a singer of spells,
> a mutterer over salt
> and a binder of blue threads,
> a speaker of red ribbons. (kuusi3)

The ideal relationship between the healer and the one being healed seems to me to be close to that of teacher-student. Good students do not have to be passive, they must be attentive to the teaching that they receive, and the teacher has to push the students to become independent. Similarly, patients must admit the temporary superiority of their healers who will teach them how to live in good health. All patients must therefore accept, in a sense, their healer as a kind of guru. They must listen to the healer's advice, confide their most intimate secrets, and allow him or her to take care of them for as long as is required. However, contrary to gurus, our healer is aware that the patients are the ones who know their body, and that they must participate in evaluating the treatments' efficiency. Further, the healer must do everything so that the patients become independent again as soon as possible. The patient must also try to lose the least amount possible of their independence, and to help the healer as much as possible.

Therefore, the patients' humility must be sincere, but they must never give up their personality.

All this might seem very obvious, but I want to insist on the importance of this humility. The patient has to ask the healer for the treatment and be happy to receive it, otherwise the healing will be at best incomplete, or at worst, the state of the patient will worsen. I have often refused to work with patients simply because instead of showing a strong will to receive the treatment, they had only a fuzzy wish to be healed. In this case, the sick person could oppose the healer during the treatment, and it would worsen the sickness. Besides, the healer's work becomes totally exhausting. In this case, the normal means of interaction is inverted, and everything goes from bad to worse.

3 - Search for the Origin of the illness
(the healer researches the Origin of the sickness. He or she can ask others for help)

The two points before were about the social environment of the patient, this one deals with the actual treatment.

Finding the Origin is a major undertaking, even from a rational point of view. The irrational Origin of the sickness is a problem that is rarely approached by classical medicine, and very badly handled by soft medicines. Irrational does not mean odd! I have often seen an illness attributed to a completely ridiculous cause in small manuals for alternative medicines. For example, a toothache would be associated to a lack of affection in childhood, and so on. A miserable childhood can obviously cause your toothache, but it cannot be the cause of all toothaches. To state general laws, valid for everyone, is the privilege of the rational approach, and the irrational one should not try to do so. Let us not compete with the strongest points of rationality, but rather address its weakest point, that is, taking into account the causes that are particular to an individual.

A Study of Rational Causes

The causes of a universal nature are those researched by science, and it doesn't do a bad job of its work. Therefore, there is no point in trying to redo this work, but to deepen it by including the individual dimension that science is unable to take into account.

Our study thus consists in deepening rational causes, starting with the universal ones discovered by scientific medicine. Suppose, for example, that rational medicine attributed the cause of a sickness to a microbial infestation. This, in turn, tells us that sickness is a sort of accident, linked to the chances of the patient's life, but without other causality. In this way, all sick people are essentially the same, and the differences among them is the result of the nature of the accident that they have had, chance having decided what microbial infestation they endure.

I know that official medicine keeps files on patients, and that their past is thereby taken into account. But this file deals only marginally with the treatment, except for stating any allergies and other impossibilities for applying a treatment. The cause of the sickness is always considered as essentially accidental, even for genetic sicknesses. For example, cancer has a hereditary component that is taken into account, as much as possible, by modern medicine, which takes it into account only to the point of detecting the sickness, not yet for its treatment. The same applies even to the research programs concerned by detecting specific genetic links with specific sicknesses, with the hope – unfortunately the hope only – of discovering links leading us to new specific treatments. Such discoveries, when and if they take place, will unify a part of the patients' deep nature and the treatment they receive. Nevertheless, the genetic default is an even tinier part of the patient's whole personality.

Alternative medicine leans far more toward the individualization of the patient, by associating him or her to a 'terrain'. The nature of this terrain determines which microbial infestations (by following the same example) will be able to take the best on the patient's organism. In this way, in order to become sick, the patient must be infested and have a terrain that isn't very resistant to this type of infestation. Each patient is therefore classified according to his or her terrain and each terrain requires a particular treatment. Therefore, the terrain is treated rather than the microbial infestation. For example, Shiatsu, although it does not talk about terrain explicitly, detects and processes one possible weakness (or an excess of energy) for each of the twelve meridians of energy. Since more than two sick meridians are rarely detected at the same time, that gives 264 possible combinations, which can be looked at as 264 possible terrains for Shiatsu[37]. The cause of the sickness is determined by which category it belongs to.

---

[37] The number 264 comes from 12 * 11, the number of combinations of 12 meridians 2 to 2 (which is 132), then it is multiplied by 2 to take into account that a meridian can be either too strong or too weak. Of course, if

To summarize this view: for rational medicine, the physical cause of the sickness is to be found in the recent luck, good or bad, that the patient had recently. For alternative medicine, the physical cause of the sickness is to be found in the patient's type or in the terrain associated with him or her.

With mystical medicine, no two patients can be absolutely identical. All this is well-known, but not applied in every day life. Even a practitioner of soft medicine, in that respect, will behave as the standard physicians. For them, a patient carries the sickness which is alien to the patient's body. In primitive medicine, the difference between the sickness and the patient does not exist. The cause of the sickness lies in the patient's whole life, and his or her environment, it integrates the patient's life. Soft medicine does take a good look at the totality of the patient's life to determine what terrain it belongs to, which is for them the deep cause of the sickness. Within traditional medicine, some physicians, especially psychotherapists, also take into account the patient's life, but then this research is made according to conceptual patterns that are fixed in advance. For example, psychoanalysts attribute all causes to early childhood, others go even further to the patient's ancestral past, but no approach examines the conjunction of all causes. The internist physician only considers immediate causes, the psychoanalyst only considers causes linked to early childhood, and, seemingly, the patient has to make the connection among all these approaches. I do not find this attitude, on the part of traditional medicine, very rational.

---

you think that three meridians can be sick at the same time, then the number of possibilities becomes 2640. The maximum number of 'terrains' possible for Shiatsu would therefore be 958 003 200, which is very great, but less than the number of living humans on this planet. Therefore some patients can be identical from the Shiatsu viewpoint, and that happens very often since only 264 combinations are used in practice.

A truly rational approach to sickness, even for those who consider that humans are perfected machines, must take into account two diversities. Firstly, the diversity of the causes must be considered. There is no reason for a sickness to have only one objective cause and, the possible causes are found in the patient's entire past, including the recent past and the very distant past, perhaps even ancestral. All these causes must be hunted out and are equally importantly, the bonds among them must be considered. Secondly, the diversity of the meanings of the symptoms must also be taken into account. The same symptom, active in two different individuals, will not have the same cause for both individuals. The number of weaknesses that our organisms, if seen as engines, can show is great, but not infinite. However, the number of possible causes is infinite. Outside of this argument, (which is a bit formal I must confess), intuition tells us, for example, that two people who each have a cold can have it for different reasons: one for having been exposed to the cold for a long time while being in good shape, the other for having been only slightly exposed to the cold while being in bad shape. It is easy to see how the number of such arguments is unbounded.

Determining the rational origin of the sickness can be done in all sorts of ways in ordinary life: discussions with the patient, with his or her close friends and family, the medical file, etc. The healer must not neglect any information, and he or she must always try to find increasingly distant causes.

Here is a simple example illustrating this attitude. Suppose that a patient suffers from what standard medicine calls hypertension. You have to discuss the possible causes of this hypertension with the patient, and also all the habits of the patient's life. You must note everything that the patient considers as a deviation from the norm, and each of these 'deviations' can be a possible cause of the hypertension. You then help the patient go into a deep state of concentration so that he or she can distinguish among all possibilities those that seem to be behind the pains, including those that are medically 'absurd'. I believe, even though this hypothesis is well-known for being scientifically false, that overindulging in starch can be linked to hypertension - this is only an example. I believe so because it might be that behind this taste stand psychological tensions, and those would be accepted as medically valid causes. Therefore, by noting the opportunities where the patient overindulges on potatoes, you will know when the harmful tensions will appear, which will help you to identify them. Having detected these psychological tensions, you must continue to search behind them for other possible causes even more distant, and go on in this manner. From the classical medicine point of view, knowing if starches can or cannot cause the **sickness** called hypertension is very important. From the mystical medicine point of view, the starches indeed cause problems to the **patient**, who happens to show symptoms of hypertension. That is a matter of fact, not a hypothesis.

The healer's role is to help patients feel and express what can or can't be a cause, to let them reflect, and to push them to always go further in the search for causes. Preconceived ideas, even if they are scientifically proven, systematically prevent patients from expressing themselves. For example, suppose that the real cause of the sickness is found in the patients' adolescence. You could always torture them to find causes in their early childhood, but these causes won't be very useful. On this subject, in any event, you must stop where the patient wants. In fact, it could be that the patient has already found the true causes and it is useless to go further, or the patient is not ready for go further for the moment, and they will interpret your insistence as an attempt to humiliate them. Your role is not to 'push' the patient to some particular place, but to help them to understand themselves and to judge the importance of the various events of their life. It is quite possible that this understanding will evolve over time.

Now let's look at researching the mystical, magical and irrational causes of the sickness. This research uses the communication means of non-ordinary reality, as is commonly practiced in shamanism.

Study of Irrational Causes

In chapter three, I spoke of the Shamanic method of journeying into the patient's past in order to find the missing parts of the patient's soul, whether they were lost by the patient or stolen by someone close to the patient. I suggest that you essentially follow this way, with some important variations that differentiate it from Sandra Ingerman's method.

a. Classic shamanism uses an instrument like the drum, along with accompanying chants to help the journey. Here, the only 'chant' is the beat of the patient's life. Like in Shiatsu, I recommend that you listen to the wave of the patient's energy. You will feel a sort of beating in your own body, and this beating reflects the patient's energy. By following this internal flicker (that, of course, rationalists will attach to the beating of our own blood circulation) you begin the Shamanic journey, in the way that I recommend.

b. The classic Shamanic journey takes place in an 'upper' or 'lower' world in which the shaman's spirit evolves, and where he or she has various encounters and adventures. In our case, the journey happens in the patient's body. The feeling that must be reached is a sort of fusion between the soul of the patient and that of the healer. It is important to note that this fusion is not without danger for healers; they must have learned to preserve their integrity during this experience. I must admit that I have not found the words to express this, but with exercises and explanations adapted to each case, I attempt to teach it in my seminars.

c. Classic shamans do not ask their patients to participate in the experience, but they certainly ask the permission to carry it out. Once this permission is obtained, the shaman goes into non-ordinary reality, interacts with Spirits, but treats the patient as an object to be healed. In my version of the shamanic treatment, the patient has 'opened' his or her soul to the healer, otherwise it would correspond to some sort of aggression of the patient by the healer, and this would lead us to paths of abusive magic. The healer, therefore, must ask the patient to open their soul, and the resulting interaction is a type of fond abstract exchange (and not sexual!), comparable to what is called 'neighborly love', for example.

d. The healer practices seið and not shamanism. Thus, he or she experiences, as passively as possible, a series of adventures, and does not set out as the classic shaman does. The seið is, in my opinion, very close to Zen, as stated earlier, and the journey takes place by quieting the 'voices' in our head and by concentrating on the center of our body, just as in the practice of Zen.

e. We often compare the information from ordinary reality to that of non-ordinary reality. The healer can interrupt his or her journey at any given time to ask a question, give an impression to the patient, or talk with the patient, then return to his or her mystical interaction; this can happen several times during a session. The classic shamanic journey is less easily interrupted.

In summary, the healer has to oscillate between the world of ordinary reality and the world of non-ordinary reality. This oscillation enables a kind of re-rationalization of the irrational due to the fact that the bond between the two realities is constantly kept.

All this lets the healer find the knowledge needed about the Origin, or the genesis, of the sickness that the patient is suffering from.

Finally, as the Canterbury charm shows, finding the 'name' of the deep irrational cause of the sickness is perfectly suitable. This name will be used in the poem addressing the sickness.

4 - Poem and galdr for the Genesis of the sickness

(the healer states the genesis of the sickness in an emphatic way, and this may be accompanied by supplications addressed to the cause of the sickness)

It is not enough to have found the Origin, it must then be stated in a clear and poetic way. Therefore, the healer has to create a poem that describes this genesis. The Kalevala gives us some examples of particularly complex geneses, the iron that injured Väinämöinen and the water dragon that killed Lemminkäinen. In less mythical cases, it's a matter of specifying the genesis that has been discovered. In this way, the patient acknowledges that the healer's words exactly reflect the patient's experience.

Once this poem is composed, the healer will extract a galdr from it, as we have seen in the previous chapter. He or she will sing the galdr, and carve it into a wooden branch.

Should the runes be dyed with blood or not? Indeed, all texts describing the use of runes show them dyed with the sorcerer's blood. However, it was always used for black magic, where the sorcerer is demanding spiritual powers to show themselves immediately. I do not think that it's good to demand a healing and I advise patients to keep the galdr that the healer carved for them. If the opportunity presents itself, and if their blood flows accidentally, take advantage of this to dye the runes with it. It will mark their deep desire to be through with their sickness.

5 - Topical Treatments
(giving first aid care to the wounded: cleaning the wounds, antipyretic, etc.)

Whatever the sickness is, and even for the internal ones, our method, coming from the Kalevala, recommends applying a topical treatment. In the case of an injury, the topical treatment will be the one suggested by modern medicine. More generally, you are specifically treating the symptoms that may seem unrelated to the sickness as they could be being felt some distance away from it. Both cancer and a light indigestion can cause abdominal pains, for example, and you must help the patient get rid of these pains. These topical treatments can therefore be extremely varied. They could include cleaning a wound, administering anti-pain medicine, or giving light massages on the painful areas. The so-called hand-healing treatments, such as Shiatsu or Reiki, usually claim to have a deeper action, but they can be also used efficiently at this stage.

6 - Poem and galdr to the symptoms
(a supplication to the manifestation of the sickness, the symptoms)

Symptoms are, in general, easy to recognize, and they shouldn't be despised. They show how the patient is reacting to the sickness. Therefore, they deserve explicit recognition by a poem and a galdr. The poem of course leads to the galdr, but it also has the role of making sure that the symptoms experienced by the patient have been well noted by the healer.

7 - Preparation of the internal remedy
(the healer makes the remedies from various herbs. Only after several tests does the healer finally find a satisfactory result. He or she then takes a shamanic journey to also get the spiritual ingredients for the ointment)

This part corresponds to the effort of modern medicine to improve how they treat sicknesses, and the Kalevala shows this stage must not be neglected. A physician could have prescribed some medicine for the patient, and my approach is to respect the social effort that is made to create these medicines. The many tests described in the Kalevala correspond to the many tests performed by the laboratories that develop medicines.

The patient, nevertheless, might be a follower of alternative medicine and would rather have a less traumatic medication than the ones classically given. This can be a delicate point because the healer might not necessarily know the details of all alternative medicines. For this stage, I highly recommend collaboration between the healer and a specialist in alternative medicine. These specialists have to recognize the usefulness as well as the limits of their approach. Regardless, alternative medicine is in general less imposing than classic medicine or, at least, it should be, and the preparation of an internal medicine in collaboration with the patient is again recommended. The alternative medicine physician can, for example, suggest an essential oil to use and, according to the reactions and remarks of the patient, try to find the ones that act the best on the patient's terrain.

Some parts of this remedy can also be of a mystical nature, and that mustn't be forgotten. Shiatsu and acupuncture, for example, act on the internal balance of the patient by re-establishing the energy circulation in the patient's meridians. To acknowledge the nature of this mystical remedy, I suggest performing a classical shamanic journey to ask the

Spirits what mystical component must be added to the physical remedies.

8 - Application or ingestion of the remedy
(applying remedies to the patient's entire body after having tasted them. This is no longer a topical treatment)

The Kalevala shows us precisely that this treatment applies a balm on the patient's entire body. This is only one possibility, corresponding without a doubt to the technical possibilities of the time. Similarly, tasting the balm does not seem to be anything else than a rudimentary chemical analysis.

I want to point out that, for reasons that aren't clear to me, modern medicine has favored almost exclusively global treatments which are based on swallowing medications, completely forgetting (except in treating asthma) that the skin (balms) and lungs (inhalations) are, just as much as the intestines, mediators between the external world and the inside parts of the patient.

In this way, all medicines that have a global action are ingested during this eighth stage. With alternative medicine, a complete body massage with an essential oil, for example, is performed.

9 - Poem and galdr on the remedy
(declaim a poem either to the Gods, or to the patient, to insure a successful remedy)

The efficiency of medicine is never absolute, regardless of how good it might be: the patient's receptivity is also very important. With classical medicine, I understand how strange it might seem to write a poem to the glory of some antibiotic or to cortisone: it is difficult to have a valid opinion for all cases and all medicines. Therefore, this is a step during which the healer must act intelligently in order to avoid creating a ridiculous (and useless) ceremony.

Conversely, with alternative medicines, nothing is more normal than to make a poem to the glory of an essential oil and therefore to the kind of plant that produces it. In the case of trace elements, in a similar way, it isn't ridiculous at all to make a poem to the glory of the metal used in the medicine.

10 - Actions to give the patient responsibility
(end the treatment by putting the patient in charge again)

We are now reaching the last three stages of the healing, during which the patient must gain more and more independence from the healer. From the magical viewpoint, this means explaining to patients what 'price' they must pay for the healing. The Spirits or the Gods have done the patients a favor by accepting to heal them, but this favor is never free. During the shamanic journey that the healer made, he or she has been able to discover the nature of the sacrifices that the patient will now have to agree to and it is time to let the patient know. This sacrifice can be a payment in money that the patient must give to the healer (this payment is a particularly efficient way to find independence), but there are other less mercantile aspects: it could be to give up a certain food or activity, to commit to new activities, or perhaps to take on some social initiatives, etc.

For other methods of treating sickness, these actions have a multiple nature according to the sickness and the treatment that has been used. One principle is common to all approaches: the patient must become a sort of expert in the treatment of his or her own sickness. Here are some examples. In classic medicine, the physician can explain to the patient what is known about the sickness, and he or she can show why the remedy given has been chosen. The patient can also get explanations about the secondary effects and consequences that it can have on their future health. Physicians seldom take the time to go as far as I suggest, but I have never seen a good physician that does not take at least a few steps in this direction. In alternative medicine, it is also necessary to give the patient an explanation on how they are going to have to master the treatment during the years to come. With Shiatsu, the patient must be shown what physical exercises will prevent relapses, and what meridians must be worked on regularly.

11 - Poem and galdr to mark the end of the treatment
(a last supplication to the Gods in order to free the patient)

This step does not present any particular problems : the healer makes sure the patient understood why and how the healing occurred.
The healer then asks the patient to perform the twelfth stage.

12 - The patient's poem and galdr after the healing
(the patient is in charge of thanking the Gods for the healing)

The patients are now completely independent from their healer, and they address themselves to the Spirits or the Gods to thank them for their healing. All runes engraved for this healing can be kept on one or several sticks and given to the patients to keep. When they feel it is the right time, for example, after having had the opportunity to dye them with their blood, they will give these sticks back to the element that seems best associated to treating their sickness. They could be given to the Earth (bury them), to the Air (burn them) or to the Water (throw them in some kind of waterway).

All traces of magic will disappear with it, except those kept in the patients' memory who, finally, will be able to consider that they are definitively healed from the sickness they endured.

THE NINE STEPS OF HEALING MENTAL SICKNESS

As we saw in chapter two, healing mental illness can be described in nine stages that I will now discuss in detail. I'm certainly not going to attempt to define, with any precision, what is a mental illness; specialists seem to have enough difficulty trying to agree on this. Simply, and without any more pretense than to use an image to try to evoke reality, we can use the term 'chimera' for the force that drives the mentally ill outside of the norms. In fact, each of us chases after a chimera, that can go from searching for immortality for example, to trying to purchase a more powerful car, and each of us loses a bit of our objectivity when facing our own chimera. In terms of sickness, a mentally ill person is therefore someone who, like everyone, chases after a chimera, but in such an intense manner that it is considered deviant by society. The goal of most of the modern treatments for this sickness is to make the patient abandon this chimera, or at least, to decrease the intensity with which they pursue it. The goal of the treatments I am presenting here is, on the contrary, to provide patients with their chimera. There are, of course, symbolic ways to do this.

The principle of modern treatments demands that the physician does not become 'trapped' by the patient's chimera, and that he or she remains as neutral as possible with respect to the patient. The doctor is meant to understand the patients and to secretly dominate them. Conversely, primitive treatments ask for the healer to become one with the patients, to become the patients, so as to be able to penetrate in their chimera, by being completely partial in favor of them. Healers do not have to understand the patients, but they need to share their feelings; they do not have to dominate, but put themselves exactly at the patient's level.

While I have emphasized a great concordance between modern methods and ancient Nordic methods for treating physical sickness, we will, on the contrary, now emphasize a large disagreement between the two approaches when it comes to mental illness. This is why there were no major problems in applying the ancient method to physical sicknesses, even without informing the physician. On the contrary, I have now to insist on the fact that some phases of the mystical treatment for mental illness might look unacceptable to some qualified psychotherapists. Modern methods share the positive feature of helping to preserve the integrity of the psychotherapist. Ancient methods could certainly become harmful for the healer who can be enticed into the patient's madness. Only individuals with a rare strength, whose integrity is so powerful that they are almost unreachable, can use the old ways.

1 - Discovering the patient's chimera

The chimera is the spiritual Origin of the patient's sickness. As for physical sicknesses, rational and irrational approaches to finding this chimera must be alternated. In particular, some patients who are mentally ill communicate very little with their environment, and observing the patient's behavior can give the healer some crucial rational tracks to follow. There is nevertheless a very important difference with physical illness. During this first stage, the healer does not try to find the deep cause of the sickness, but the manifestation of this deep cause in the patient's mind.

A category of mentally ill are said to be 'borderline', such as those following a psychoanalytical treatment. In principle, they are very eager for contact and are ready to communicate (perhaps even a bit too much so) with their healer. In order to let them concentrate on their deep problems, we can use all sorts of techniques that have become praised by the 'new age' movement, like massage, meditation, 'rebirth', primal scream, etc. In each case, the purpose is to get the patients in contact with themselves to help them find their true problems. Shiatsu, through the deep mental and physical relaxation it brings, can also be very useful to help the patient. Throughout all these phases performed in ordinary reality, the behavior of the healer is very similar to that of a psychotherapist. You cannot improvise so easily with psychotherapy, and therefore, this is not without danger for the patient also. This is why I recommend strongly to those who wish to apply this method, if they are not already trained psychotherapists, that they should work with a person qualified in psychotherapy who has a sufficiently open spirit to accept a mystical continuation by another healer. Therefore, even for cases that aren't very serious, I cannot state strongly enough that the healer must not attempt to play the sorcerer's apprentice in psychotherapy, relative to what is happening in ordinary reality.

Now let's turn to non-ordinary reality, where classic psychotherapy rarely goes. As with physical sicknesses, you can use a classic shamanic journey to go into the patient's past to gather details looked upon as traumatizing, to point at them for the patient and to compare them with the ones he or she remembers. I prefer however to recommend a method that involves the five differences already emphasized when discussing physical sicknesses:
- listen to the beat of the patient's energy and travel on the rhythm of this beat,
- travel in the patient's body and spirit,

- ask the patient to open his or her soul to your soul,
- perform a passive journey where you wait for irrational phenomena to appear to you instead of going in search of phenomena,
- oscillate constantly between the rational and the irrational, now with a marked preference for the irrational.

Since the patients are sick, their rationality is debatable, and it is not wise to have too much confidence in it. Hence the great importance of exploring the patient's non-rational reality.

Serious cases, still under treatment in a psychiatric hospital, are not likely to be encountered often by a healer. Suppose, however, that a family is strong enough to get a patient out of the hospital, and call a healer, what could he or she do? Suppose that verbal communication is totally cut off, but still non-verbal and irrational communication takes place. In this case, in the spirit of what the Kalevala describes, I would recommend that the healer identify with the patient, and interact physically by entering into his or her 'game', in other words by playing a role that goes along with the patient's actions. I am not pretending to describe a new form of therapy: the goal of this role playing is simply to enable the healer to better identify with the patient. Moreno's brilliant method known as 'psychodrama' is practiced by psychotherapists having received a lengthy training (to my knowledge, it applies mainly to subjects who are borderline), and it would be very dangerous to use it without having received this education. The healer must also know what methods to use to be able to quiet the patient down in order to practice seið on him or her, even without having explicit permission. If the patient has moments of lucidity, it is important to explain what you are trying to do with him or her.

When the chimera has been discovered, just as with physical sicknesses, a poem must be written that describes it, and a galdr coming from this poem must be sung. However, this is not done immediately, the chimera should be better understood first.

2 - Recognizing the country where this chimera lives

It is not enough to have recognized the chimera, you must also create a sort of map of its environment. The chimera is quite real in the non-ordinary reality, and it moves about according to rules that must be learned, in a country that depends on the patient. In other words, the same chimera could be found in very different frameworks for two patients, and the treatments would have to be different. Therefore the healer will have to make a lengthy journey in the patients' spirit, going along with their chimera, and see what paths it chooses to follow. Here we find again a difference between those with a major sickness and those with a minor sickness. A patient with a minor illness will be able to give a full description of this environment, while the others will not be able to.

This 'living' with the chimera, acknowledging its existence, can be seen as very harmful by classic psychiatry that tries to push the patient to deny the chimera's existence. Therefore, the healer will have to be cautious in this stage. A slightly hypocritical behavior is possible : tell the classic psychotherapist that you are trying to recognize the chimera's properties, and that you are not accepting its actual existence.

3 - Follow the tracks in the chimera's country

The first two stages had rational equivalents, but in this third stage, we completely leave out the rational.

The search for details about the chimera's nature still goes on. Now, it no longer amounts to simply recognizing places, but also to modifying them by designing new roads where the patient's chimera will be more easily caught. This action on the patients' psychic unconscious can only be done during a shamanic session (or rather seið, as I recommend) in which the shaman identifies so much with his or her patients that the patients' unconscious environment can be modified by the healer.

4 - Explain the problem to the Gods of this country

Poems and galdr are now necessary. They may even have to remain nonverbal, since they are part of non-ordinary reality. The healer composes the poem in non-ordinary reality, then reads it and proclaims it in this reality, and finally also declaims the galdr in this reality. The Kalevala strongly implies this attitude by explicitly showing that the Gods of the chimera's country must be addressed, and not the Gods of our ordinary reality. However, in the case of a minor illness, where interactions between the two realities have been many, compose two poems and two galdr, one for each of the two realities.

5 - Make allies

The exploration of the chimera's universe deepens again. Among the Divinities or Spirits of the chimera's country, some can become favorable to the healer. In this stage, you must find out which of these are ready to help, and also find out how to please them. Obviously only the relatively secondary Spirits are favorable to the healer, otherwise, the healing would be done immediately. This stage can take very long, or perhaps even never end, and in this case, it's a failure of the healer, unable to return the chimera to the patient.

6 - Understand why the divinities do not reply

As I just said, the main divinities are not favorable to the healer; otherwise he or she would have already been able to heal the sickness. This stage recognizes the reasons why the main Divinities refuse to help.

Often people tend to think of healers, and more generally those who practice magic are able to perform miracles on request. We must also acknowledge that some charlatans (in my opinion) do everything to give this very image. Magicians are those who are able to go and ask the Divinities or the Spirits something, but they even do not to try to impose something on them. They are an intermediary between ordinary and non-ordinary reality in the sense that they are messengers between the two realities; they are not workers constructing one from the other. If the Spirits do not want to step in, then the magicians are helpless, and ridiculous if they have been boasting about their power. I think it is important for magicians to even brag about their **lack** of power, if the Spirits refuse to help. I have already said, the healer is only an intermediary, the Spirits heal, the patients might heal themselves, but the healers never do in spite of their name.

Several episodes of the Kalevala and some Anglo-Saxon charms show clearly that the Nordic magicians were well aware of their limits, and that they knew when the Gods could refuse to help them.

7 - Offer a reward.

Here is a second important point of Nordic healing methods: the patient can't be healed without agreeing to some kind of sacrifice. I have already stressed this aspect when dealing with healing physical illness, but then the Kalevala left it implicit. In the case of mental sickness, the sacrifice is explicit because Lemminkäinen offers wealth to the Divinities.

The deep reason for this is that primitive medicine does not believe in accidents, the sickness being physical or psychological. Sicknesses happen for a specific reason, which is connected to the patient's life. For example, people do not catch influenza because they have in contact with the virus (contact with the virus is a condition, never a cause) but because they were weakened in one way or another, and this weakening is the true cause. In this weakened state, if the patient had not been in contact with the influenza virus, they would have caught something else. This weakening could be the result of a something very minor (for example, staying in a draft and catching cold can bring on influenza) or simply of a normal habit (like an unbalanced diet). If this is the result of a minor action, then the sacrifice will be a minor one and easy to determine - avoid drafts of air, for example, which is still a modification, although superficial, of the patient's behavior. If this is the result of a normal habit, the sacrifices can become far more important, as a complete change in diet, for example.

It is quite possible that the healer would receive messages asking for various changes, such as no longer seeing certain people, committing to new activities, giving money to some organization, etc. These life changes deserve discussion because they might provide power to a charlatan over a patient. The life changes suggested by the Spirits constitute a complete and new vision that the patients must integrate into their own world. However, this new vision must never be foreign to the old world. In a few words, I do not believe that magic only obeys the good pleasure of the Spirits, there is a kind of coherence, sometimes not very pleasant to us, in the organization of things, and this coherence has to be found in messages sent by the Spirits. Whenever this coherence is not respected, I would strongly suspect some kind of trickery, even perhaps unwillingly, on the part of the magician. The patient's earlier life was full of errors, indeed, and they explain the sickness, but it also had a type of coherence that mustn't be broken. To go away and leave their worldly wealth to the healer, for example, seems to me to be coming more from human greed than from a Spirit, because it breaks the coherence of the patient's life.

Less dramatic, but nonetheless important, are all the pleasures that the patient was enjoying. Even smoking, drinking or any other harmful habit should not be forbidden. It is up to the clients to reorganize their life, not up to the healer to play the 'bull in a china shop'.

A good example is provided by the habit of smoking. Everyone knows this habit is harmful to the patients. They however started to smoke for some specific reason. This reason might be apparently stupid, it can, however, also be correlated to very deep needs in the patients' lives. Such a seemingly innocuous reason as imitating a parent's behavior can actually be motivated by a deep need of identifying with this parent. The patients themselves can decide if they need to cut into such habit, or find an adequate substitute. The healer should never bully the patients to force them to take a path that the healer thinks is obviously advantageous to the patient, but that can prove disastrous in the long run.

8 - Provide the patient with his or her chimera

The Gods may finally become favorable to helping the healer. The patient's chimera is now so familiar to the healer, that he or she will find an implicit or explicit way to give it to the patient. We are talking about mental illnesses, therefore the chimera in question is in the patient's head more than a physical need. Suppose that a person, Bill, becomes mad because another person, Sue, has rejected him. To provide the chimera to the patient obviously does not consist of offering Sue to Bill on a tray, but instead giving Bill the means to find the love that he expected to receive. Each physical chimera hides a psychological misery that fathers its own chimera, and these last chimera of a psychological nature are the ones that must be provided to the patient as means of healing.

9 - Thank the Gods and give the promised reward

At the end of the treatment, both a poem and a galdr are required. The stick on which the galdr is engraved stays in the patient's possession in order to dye it with his or her blood when the opportunity arises, just as in the case of physical sicknesses.

It must also be noted that the Kalevala insists that the reward must be delivered. The life changes promised during stage 7 must become effective, otherwise the patient might very quickly experience a relapse.

CONCLUSION: MAGIC AND RELIGION

I would now like to offer you one last piece of advice about practicing the kind of magic that asks you to change your life. I have often alluded to the degeneration of magic when applied in a Christian context. For reasons that otherwise escape me, Christianity has become the objective ally of rationalism, thereby helping to construct the system that currently gnaws at its interior. It is very clear therefore that the practice of magic supposes a certain acceptance of Heathenism, in order to, at least take some distance with Christianity.

A great number of movements are devoted to the revival of Heathenism, and the one that I am most interested in, since it is linked to the runes, is the movement that is either called Odinist or Asatru. The difference between the two lies in who is honored. Odinism reveres Odin more specifically, (and, in practice, and for reasons I do not understand, often with a marked racist component), while Asatru more generally reveres the Aesir and/or the Vanir, (and it is strongly anti-racist). Clearly some of these Heathen movements have a strange reputation, but it is also true that the *Asatruer* (members of the Asatru movement (the singular is *Asatruar*) have gained important success in Iceland, where their religion is one of the religions accepted by the government, and in the US where, in some states, their clergy is recognized as well as the Christian clergy. I consider myself to be Asatruar, although informally.

I do not try to find a religion exclusively dedicated to the Mother Goddess, but rather one that gives to her what she deserves. In Asatru, I have found the ancient Nerthus as Mother Goddess, and the Norns who personify the respect of destiny. Nerthus and Njörd form the divine couple that governs our lives. In Thor, I see the God who hallows, who makes things sacred, and who struggles for the due respect to sacredness. In Nordic mythology, described in the next volume of this book, his struggle against the Thurs describes, for me, a fight of the sacred against the unholy, as two types of opposing life. The Thurs are big, beautiful, strong, intelligent, and cultivated, but bad deep down because they refuse to accept the sacred spark of humanity in them, and this is why Thor is in charge of fighting them. It would take a whole book to discuss seriously the point of whether or not the Nordic myths of the struggles between Thurs and Gods are still taking place nowadays. Let me simply state here my belief that the present triumph of rationalism mirrors the many myths in which the Thurs take the upper hand, at least temporarily.

Readers who are interested in the Asatru movement, and who have Internet access, should consult 'Asatru' on the Internet, and they will find several lists and many pages devoted to this movement. My site also has more information : http ://www.nordic-life.org/nmh/

Finally, here is a text by Patrick Buck whose address you will find at the end of the text. Thank you Patrick!

Rebirth of the antique Asatru religion

'Asatru' means *faith in the Aesir*, which are the Gods of pre-Christian Scandinavia. The other Germanic peoples (Goths, Germans, Dutch, Frisians, Anglo-Saxons, etc.) had essentially the same religion. Similar Deities were once worshipped throughout most of Europe, and as far away as India (the Gods of the Rig Veda). Asatru never really quite died out. Medieval Icelandic books of magical spells (galdrabok) show that some were calling upon the Aesir long after Christianity was forced upon the Germanic peoples. In northern Scandinavia, the Lappish (Saami) people were openly celebrating the worship of Thor, which they had learned from their Heathen Scandinavian neighbors in the pre-Christian period, as late as 1800. The modern revival began in the early 1970's. Within a few months of each other and quite unaware of each other's existence, two groups were formed in the USA, one in Iceland, and one in the United Kingdom. Odin, the wanderer, is once again seeking worshippers. Anyone who wishes to join Asatru may do so, regardless of race, ethnicity, sexual orientation, etc. In addition to Thor, the Thunderer, friend of the common folk, and Odin, Allfather, chief God, poet, and wandering wizard, we worship many others, including Tyr, God of war and justice; Ingvi Frey, God of peace, fertility and nature (the European images of the Green Man may be a memory of Frey and similar Gods); Balder, the bleeding God, and Heimdall, the Watchman of Asgard. Nor do we neglect the Goddesses, who are equal in power and holiness to the Gods: Frigga, wife of Odin and Mother of Gods and Humanity; Freya, Goddess of fertility, love, magic, and war; Idunna, Goddess of renewal; Hela, who rules over the place between death and rebirth (most of us believe in some form of rebirth or reincarnation); Nerthus, the Mother Earth Goddess mentioned in Tacitus' Germania, and many others. We also revere the spirits of nature (landvaettir) and various guardian spirits, such as the Disir and Alfar (Elves). Our Gods are friendly, practical, dependable and approachable. Our two main rituals are the blot and sumbel. 'Blot' means *sacrifice*. While scholars debate whether or not it is connected with the word 'blood', we use mead (honey-wine), beer or cider today. The liquid is consecrated to the God or Goddess being worshipped, and we commune with that Deity by drinking a portion of it. The rest is poured as a libation. The Sumbel is a sort of ritualized toasting. The first of the usual three rounds is to the Gods, starting with Odin, who won the mead of poetry from the Giant Suttung. It's good to pour a few drops to Loki the trickster to ward off nasty surprises! The second round is to ancestors and other honorable dead. The third round is open. While devoid of rigid, legalistic rules, ours is by no means an amoral faith. We start out with basic principles, such as the Nine Noble Virtues: courage, truth, honor, loyalty, hospitality, industriousness, perseverance, self-discipline, and self-reliance. From these, individuals can decide the appropriate course of action for a given situation and honor themselves, their families, their communities, and their Gods by striving to do what is right. The Gods organized the Universe from chaotic material (represented by the body of the dead Giant Ymir), which was what was available. A remaining bit of chaos provides a random factor, which helps the Universe and all in it to keep evolving. Not even the Gods are all-powerful or all-knowing, so perfection is neither required nor expected! The Elder and Younger Eddas (also called the Poetic and Prose Eddas) are texts we hold in high esteem for the information on our religion they contain, although most of us do not interpret our myths literally. Both were written down in medieval Iceland. For scholarly research on Asatru, read Myth and Religion of the North by E.O.G. Turville-Petre and the many books on the subject by H.R. Ellis Davidson. Teutonic Religion and Teutonic Magic, both by Kveldulf Gundarsson and published by Llewellyn Publications Inc., PO Box 64383-K069, St.

Paul, Minnesota 55164-0383 USA will give you the best overview of our religious and magical practices. Magical work is a part of spiritual life of many practitioners of Asatru. Magic involves working with natural but unseen forces, including those embodied in the Runes, the indigenous alphabet of the Germanic Peoples, as well as galdra (spellcraft) and seidhr (shamanic-type workings). Magic can help see the probable direction of future events, obtain healing, and help us in all we do, but it does not substitute for 'mundane' efforts! Ours is a practical, active religion! For more information on Asatru, please feel free to write to the address below:

Rev. Patrick "Jordsvin" Buck, Assistant Godhi (priest), Hammerstead Kindred, PO Horse-box 22379 Lexington, KY 40522-2379 USA,
http://users.aol.com/jordsvin/kindred/kindred.htm.

Good health asks for the pride of self-healing together with the humility of accepting a healer. No wonder it is so seldom !

Fare well !

'Chapter 6' : Bibliography

Runic inscriptions

The runic inscriptions reported here are classical and can be found in a score of various books. I found very useful

W. Krause, *Runen*, Sammlung Göschen, 1970. It contains the version given here as rune1, p. 55.

Since Krause is not translated into English (there is however a French translation), the standard reference is rather

Erik Moltke, *Runes and their Origin, Denmark and Elsewhere*, The National Museum of Denmark, 1985, ISBN 87-480-0578-9. It gives a version of all the runic inscriptions cited here: rune1: p. 360, rune2: p. 23, rune3: p.138-140, rune4: p. 142-143, rune5: p. 360, rune6: p. 494-495, rune7: p. 151, rune8: p. 101 & 104 (not completely translated, see Krause, *Die Sprache etc.*, below).

Nevertheless, I think that a deep understanding of the runic inscription demands some knowledge of the three books that provide a vocabulary and a grammar of the runic inscriptions:

W. Krause, *Die Sprache der urnordischen Runeninschriften*, Heidelberg 1971. rune8: p. 153.

E. H. Antonsen, *A Concise Grammar of the Older Runic Inscriptions*, Niemeyer, 1975. Antonsen's reading of rune3 is p.85, the one of rune4 is on p. 87.

E. A. Makaev, *The Language of the Oldest Runic Inscriptions*, Kungl. Vitterhets Historie och Antikvitets Akademien, Stockholm 1996, isbn 91-7402-259-8, (Russian original published in 1965).

Another very classical reference book is:

R. Derolez, *Runa Manuscripta*, The English Tradition, Ed: De Tempel, Tempelhof 37, Brugge, 1954.

Two well-known books represent the English school of runology:

R. I. Page, *An Introduction to English Runes*, Methuen 1973

R. W. V. Elliott, *Runes : An Introduction*, Manchester University Press, 1959.

The French school is represented by

L. Musset, *Introduction à la runologie*, Paris, Aubier 1965.

A very interesting application of runology to otherwise undecipherable inscriptions is found in

Richard A. V. Cox, *The Language of the Ogam Inscriptions of Scotland*, Univ. of Aberdeen, Scotland, 1999, isbn 0 9523911 3 9.

Not specially dedicated to runes, but to all the Old Norse words including the rune names, the Gods' names etc. is

J. De Vries *Altnordisches etymologisches Wörterbuch*, Leiden 1961. No other dictionary reaches the wealth of information contained in this basic book. I must add that it is obviously written in German, and copies can be found in auctions, but they reach astronomical prices.

Readers with an inquisitive mind should be interested in the Hungarian *rovas*, and their possible links with Germanic runes. I recommend consulting my site at:
http://www.nordic-life.org/nmh/rovas

Charms and incantations

The Finnish tradition is illustrated in poems gathered by

Lönnrot, in *Kalevala* and *Kanteletar*. I used them intensively in this volume since these poems can be looked at as a long galdr. A version similar to the citations given here can be found in *The Kalevala*, Oxford University Press (1989 and 1992): kal1: p. 83, kal2: p. 84, kal3 & kal4: p. 86, kal5: p. 88, kal6: p. 89, kal7: p. 95, kal8: p. 95, kal9: p. 97-98, kal10: p. 99-100, kal11: p. 100, kal12: p. 101,kal13: p. 101, kal15: p. 101, kal16: p. 102, kal17: p. 102, kal18: p. 102, kal19: p. 103, kal20: p. 103, kal21: p. 168-169, kal22: p. 174, kal23: p. 174, kal24: p. 174-177, kal25: p. 177, kal26: p. 178, kal27: p. 178, kal28: p. 179, kal29: p. 179-180, kal30: p. 181, kal31: p. 181-182, kal32: p. 183, kal33: p. 183, kal34: p. 184, kal35: p. 203-204, kal36: p. 150, kal37: p. 155, kal38: p. 156, kal39: p. 156, kal40: p. 156-157, kal41: p. 158, kal42: p. 160-161, kal43: p. 161, kal44: p. 161-162, kal45: p. 23, kal46: p. 23, kal47: p. 30, kal48: p. 662-663, kal49: p. 587-588, kal50: p. 588, kal51: p. 588-589, kal52: p. 203, kal53: p. 203-204, kal54: p. 205-206, kal55: p. 206, kal56: p. 206, kal57: p. 206-207, kal58: p. 207, kal59: p. 207, kal60: p. 210, kal61: p. 593, kal62: p. 591-592, kal63: p. 592.

My version is also inspired by

Kalevala, das finnische Epos published by Reclam (1985).

In French, early translations that are very close to the original text, have helped me a lot. The verse version of

Jean Louis Perret, *Le Kalevala*, Stock, Paris 1931 is very faithful. Nevertheless, I recommend, instead, the following work to those who can read French, and are able to find it in a library: Léouzon-le-Duc's ancient prose translation contains many explanations about Finnish culture and society.

Besides the Kalevala itself, the only publication devoted to Finnish folk songs that I have been able to find is:

Matti Kuusi, Keith Bosley, Michael Branch, *Finish Folk Poetry - Epic*, Finnish Literature Society, 1977, ISBN: 951-717-087-4. Citations kuusi1 and 2 are word for word citations from this book, kuusi1 is p. 117, kuusi2 p. 273. This book contains a selection of Finnish folk songs that were collected by ethnologists and published in:

Suonen Kansan Vanhat Runot (Ancient poems of the Finnish people), 1908-1948.

The theme and style of these folk songs are very close to that of the Kalevala. The differences among the several versions are of course very interesting to those researching Nordic pagan culture. The poems published in this work make up only a very small part of all the folk poems collected by ethnologists, but unfortunately most of them have not been translated. There is also an anthology coming from Karelia that I was not able to consult:

Karjalan Kansan Runot (Poems of the Karelian People, 1976).

The version of the *Landnamabok* (Book of Settlements) that I used, above others, is the German translation published by Thule, Band 23, Eugen Diederichs Verlag, under the title of

Islands Besiedlung und älteste Geschichte, 1967.

A selection of texts translated into French can be found in

Landnamabok trans. R. Boyer, Mouton 1973, Card # Lib. Congress: 73 - 79395.

Unfortunately, this edition does not contain S198 which I used in the appendix to chapter 1. The original that I consulted is:

Landnamabok Islands, Einar Arnorsson, Helgafell Reykjavik 1948.

The English translation quoted here is:

The Book of Settlements, translated by H. Palsson and P. Edwards, University of Manitoba Press, 1972, p. 91.

The Rumanian charm cited in this book is published in

S. FL. Marian, *Descântece poporane române*, Suceava, 1886. Translation into French by Dana and Paul Munteanu.

The Lithuanian charms that I quote come from the Museum of the pharmacy of Kaunas and the following books cited by my Lithuanian informant, Neringa Jablonskyté. She owns

P. Dunduliené, *Lietuvos etnologia*,

and at the Town Library in the rare books section, she found:

J. Cicénas, *Daugeliskiniai burtai*,

Y. Lvov, *Zagorovie, oberegi i spasitelnie malitvi*,

B. Meisteré, *Perkuno funkcijos latviu folklore*, and I was able to see photocopies. Each charm is given in the 'classical' ethnological format, with name of informant, place of gathering, and reference to first publication.

The Highland Scotland charms come from:
Mary Beith, *Healing Threads*, Polygon, Edinburgh, 1995. ISBN: 0-7486-6199-9. Citations: scot1: p. 147-148, scot2: p. 195, scot3: p. 196, scot4: p. 192, scot5: p. 198.
Citation scot6 comes from Cameron's book, cited below, p. 151.

The references to Celtic charms come from
Lewis Spence, *The History and origins of Druidism*, Newcastle publishing 1995 (1st edition 1947), celt1: p. 146, celt2: p. 147, and from
The Tain translated by T. Kinsella, Oxford Univ. Press, 1969, celt3: p. 190.

The version of the Danish charms that I used can be found in:
Léon Pineau, *Chants populaires scandinaves*, published in 1898. First citation: "she taught him the runes, upon her white hand" is part of a Danish charm found on p. 29 of this book. The 'official' reference for these chants is:
Danmarks Gamle Folkeviser, collected by Svend Grundtvig. Part 1. Copenhague. Thieles Bogtrykkeri, 1853.

The Anglo-Saxon charms have been published many times. My best source of charms, and of understanding AS medicine is the richly commented and illustrated edition of *Lacnunga* by
J. H. G. Grattan and C. Singer, *Anglo-Saxon Magic and Medicine*, Oxford University press, 1952. They provide a version of the five first AS charms I used, see as1: p. 185, as2: p. 175 and 177, as3: p. 153 and 154, as4: p. 154, as5: p. 163. Reference as8 is p.113 of this book.
I found also useful a more 'literary' edition, by
Louis J. Rodrigues, *Anglo-Saxon Verse Charms, Maxims & Heroic Legends*, Anglo-Saxon Books, 1994, ISBN:

1-898281-01-07, and the following more technical book, whose author is a biologist, not a linguist:

M. L. Cameron, *Anglo-Saxon Medicine*, Cambridge University Press, 1993. Two AS charms come from this book: as6: p. 154, as7: p. 155. The book by

Karen Louise Jolly, *Popular Religion in Late Saxon England*, the University of North Carolina Press, 1996, also contains many charms that are discussed in a religious context rather than a medical context as with Cameron. This work and that of Cameron's complement each other harmoniously.

The works of Hildegard of Bingen on medical knowledge are:

Hildegard of Bingen, *Holistic Healing*, The Liturgical Press 1994.

It contains descriptions of a great number of sicknesses and their remedies, as well as one invocation that I have quoted: hilde16: p. 172-173. This has been translated into English from a German version.

I could not find the following two books in English, therefore I am giving you their French reference only. Notice that the French versions are directly translated from Latin, they do not use German as an intermediary language, and they are thus worth the German versions.

Hildegarde de Bingen, *Le livre des oeuvres divines*, Albin Michel, 1982. It contains the mystical visions of the saint. Some of these visions describe the organic construction of the human body and the interactions among humors.

Hildegarde de Bingen, *Le livre des subtilités des créatures divines*, Jérôme Million 1988. This one contains a description of the medical properties of plants and stones. Most of charms cited here are my translation from the French. The book has two volumes, thus I give the volume followed by the page in this volume: hilde1: p. II, 47, hilde2: p. II, 178-179, hilde3: p. I, 245, hilde4: p. II, 41-42, hilde5: p. I, 236-237, hilde6: p. II, 48, hilde7: p. II, 48, hilde8: p. II, 48-49, hilde9: p. I, 80-81, hilde10: p. I, 220-221, hilde11: p. I, 244, hilde12: p. I, 255-256, hilde13: p. I, 246, hilde14: p. I, 246-247, hilde15: p. I, 264.

For those that can read German, they will find the same charms in

Hildegard von Bingen, *Heilkraft der Natur-, Physica'*, Herder, 1991.

'Everyone' knows that the basic book relative to the Old Germanic beliefs and legends is

Jacob L. C. Grimm *Deutsche Mythologie* published in 1835. The best available version is the English translation *German Mythology*, the second hands versions of which are very expensive. Fortunately, an electronic version, an almost complete one, is available at:
http://www.midhnottsol.org/lore/main.html
You can consult chapter 38 of this book, Spells and Charms, and find there a source of first hand citations, different than the one you found in this *Nordic Healing*.

Note that Grimm, being the scholar he was, spoke many languages, and his book is full of citations in Latin, Old Norse, Old French, Old Spanish etc. You can join the effort in translating all these citations in English by consulting http://www.midhnottsol.org/lore/grimmtran.html.

I must say that I also consulted some works dedicated to charms and incantations coming from mystical literature but I didn't find them very interesting. They would always describe somewhat fixed rituals, without giving their origin. Their approach is different from mine in the sense that I have carefully given the original version of the charm that I am citing (sometimes to the point of proposing an original translation of some words), and I show a possible adaptation, not an immutable and fixed truth.

Shamanism and remains of Paganism

The following book contains the most complete description of shamanic customs, and as well, it is easy to access for the non specialist (but not rigorous enough for the specialist, and somewhat outdated):

Mircea Eliade, *Archaic Techniques of Ecstasy*, Arkana (Penguin), London 1989. Citations from Eliade's book are: eliade1: p. 469, eliade2: p.41. Nevertheless, the basis of chapter 3 of the present book is

Schamanengeschichten aus Sibirien, collected by G. V. Ksenofontov, translated from the Russian by A. Friedriech and G. Buddruss, Clemens Zerling, 1987. Citations from this book: sib1: p. 201-202, sib2: p. 156-157 (this legend is reported by Eliade and is widely cited. The version given here differs slightly from Eliade's and follows strictly the German translation), sib3: p.162, sib4: p. 160, sib5: p. 195, sib6: p. 205-207, sib7: p.187, sib8: p. 186-187, sib9: p. 189, sib10: p. 192, sib11: p. 197. It is quite incredible that such an important book be not translated into English, especially in view of the kind of fashion into which shamanism is presently held.

The works of James Frazer form an incredibly rich source of information on tales, folk customs, and shamanic traditions. The simplest to read is :

James G. Frazer, *The Golden Bough*, abridged edition, Penguin, 1996.

The book of

Max Bartels, *Medizin der Naturvölker, Urgeschichte der Medizin*, Leipzig 1893, Reprint-Verlag Leipzig, ISBN : 3-8262-0204-X, is a unique source of knowledge about primitive medicine from all over the world, except Europe. Once again, I am very surprised that there is no English translation of this important book.

For more particular points, I have also used:

Knud Rasmussen, *Du Groenland au Pacifique*, published by Comité des travaux historiques et scientifiques, 1994 (ISBN 2 - 0285-6).

Ake Hultkrantz, *Native Religions of North America*, Harper Collins, 1987.

Jacobo Grinberg-Zylberbaum, *Rencontre avec des chamans du Mexique*, Le Mail 1994. Translated from the Spanish series of books *Los Chamanes de México*, Mexico University, 1987-1990.

Ruth Beebe Hill, *Hanta Yo*, Doubleday, 1979

Lewis Spence, *North American Indians*, Harrap, 1914.

For modern shamanism, I recommend both of Sandra Ingerman's books:

Soul Retrieval : Mending the Fragmented Self, Harper San Francisco, 1991.

Welcome Home, Following your Soul's Journey Home, Harper San Francisco, 1993.

Anne Ross' article, "The Divine Hag of the Pagan Celts" and H. R. Ellis Davidson's, "Hostile Magic in the Icelandic Sagas," are published in

The Witch in History Venetia Newall (Ed.) Barnes & Noble, NY 1996. ISBN 0-7607-0123-7.

I have the privilege of owning an original edition of De Lancre's famous book which is entitled,

Tableau de l'inconstance des mauvais anges et démons, par Pierre de Lancre à Paris chez Nicolas Buon, 1613. The Old French of his book has been translated into modern English for the quotes I have used.

Old Norse civilization and myths

Early witnessing of Finnish and Lapp civilizations are

Voyage de Laponie by Jean-François Regnard (1681), republished in 1992 by Edition du Griot. Quite often, this author uses an earlier witness in order to describe regions he could not himself observe. Unfortunately, I was unable to put a hand on a translation of this very first witness. Its initial publishing reference is:

Johann G. Scheffer, *Lapponia, id est religionis Lapponum et gentis nova et verissima descriptio*, Frankfurt, 1673. A bit more than one century later, but still very interesting and more detailed is:

Voyage au Cap-Nord, par la Suède, la Finlande et la Laponie, by Joseph Acerbi, Paris, 1804. I could not find the (existing) English version, thus the citations given here are my translation from the French version. I had to hold myself to refrain from giving more details of a pagan way of life that was preserved in these remote countries, in spite of all the efforts of the local clergy, as Acerbi witnesses. I cannot emphasize enough the need of consulting these books for these interested in our pagan Nordic past.

Here are the sagas that I have been consulting. References are given to the place in the English translations that report the same facts than those reported in the present book.

Egil's *Saga*, Penguin Classics, 1976. (saga1): p.191, (saga5): p 148

Eirik the Red and other Icelandic Sagas, World Classics, Oxford Univ. press, 1981. This edition contains *The Vapnfjord men* (saga8): p. 75, *The saga of the king Hrolf and his champions* (saga10) : p. 256, *Gunnlaug Wormtongue* (saga18) : chap. 4, p. 190.

Eyrbyggja saga, Penguin Classics, 1972.

Heimskringla or the Lives of the Norse Kings, Snorre Sturlason, Dover publications, 1990. It contains *The History of Saint Olav* (saga12): p. 460-461. *Ynglinga saga*, (saga14) p. 30 gives a very shortened version of this citation; (saga20) is p. 5.

Hrafnkel's *Saga*, Penguin Classics, 1971

The saga of the Jómsvíkings, translation by L. M. Hollander, University of Texas Press, 1955.

King Harald's *Saga*, Snorri Sturluson, Penguin Classics, 1966

Laxdaela Saga, Penguin Classics, 1969

Njal's *Saga*, Penguin Classics, 1960. (saga17) is p. 223

Orkneyinga Saga, Penguin Classics, 1978. Reference (saga16) is p. 80

Seven Viking Romances, Penguin Classics, 1985. It includes *The saga of Bosi and Herraud* where Busla's curses are to be found (edda1), p. 205-208. I used also Boyer's version of this poem, as given in his *Edda*, p. 579-583, and Genzmer's, p. 174-176. It includes King Gautrek, where something fuzzily equivalent to (saga2) can be found on p. 155; *Egil and Asmund* (saga11): p. 250.

The saga of the Volsungs, translation by J. L. Byock, University of California Press, 1990.

The Vinlands Sagas, Penguin Classics, 1965.

Gautreks saga, translation Robert Nedoma, Kümmerle Verlag, Göppingen 1990.

Die saga vom Grettir Asmundarson, translation R. Simek, Verlag K. M. Halosar, 1981.

La saga des alliés, translation by A. Marez, Editions du Porte-Glaive, 1989.

Sagas islandaises, translated and edited by R. Boyer, La Pléiade, 1987. Among 13 other sagas, it contains *Gisla saga Surssonar* where (saga3) is to be found in chap. 24, p. 611; (saga6) : chap. 18, p. 599. It contains also *Vatnsdoela saga* and reference (saga4) in chap 33, p. 1021. Reference (saga7) is in *Viga-Glúms Saga*, chap 23, p. 1102; *Grettis Saga Ásmundarsonar* contains references (saga9), chap. 82, p. 937 and (saga19): chap. 79, p. 932.

La saga des Féroïens, translation by J. Renaud, Aubier Montaigne 1983.

La saga d'Óláf Tryggvason, translation by R. Boyer, Imprimerie Nationale 1992.

La saga des Ynglingar (Ynglinga saga), de Snorri Sturluson, translation by I. Cavalié, Éditions du Porte-Glaive, 1990.

The name *Edda* covers two very different things.

One is a set of three works by Snorri Sturluson, usually called *Prose Edda*. It is made of *Gylfaginning*, describing the major Nordic myths, the *Skaldskaparmal*, (Language of the scalds) which explains the principles and main features of skaldic poetry, and *Hattatal* (List of verse forms) which gives scores of examples of skaldic verse forms. The French translation by F.-X. Dillmann (Gallimard, 1991) is very precise and wonderfully annotated; the German one, by A. Häny (Manesse Verlag, 1991) is also an excellent reference source. Both however cannot be compared to the English version by A. Faulkes, (Everyman, 1995) because they are not complete, while Faulkes' is. Häny's misses Skaldskaparmal and Hattatal, while Dillmann's shows only the most significant legends contained in Skaldskaparmal. The full work shows a score of names for the Gods, of equivalence between long expressions and a word (the so-called kennings), that enable to understand the word for word versions of Skaldic and Eddic poetry. In spite of all, I found Dillmann's translation so good, it is both precise and simply worded, that I strongly recommend it to any French reading person. It is a shame that the French and German publishers did not ask the translators to complete their job.

The second one, called the *Poetic Edda* is composed of a set of poems. I consulted again mainly three versions: a French version, by R. Boyer (Fayard, 1992), a German version, by F. Genzmer, (Eugen Diederichs Verlag, 1992), and an English one, *Norse Poems* by W. H. Auden and P. B. Taylor (Faber and Faber, 1983). A relatively new English version, due to C. Larrington, Oxford University press, 1996 is more like the French and German editions that provide explanations to their readers. I will however use Auden and Taylor as a reference. (edda2): p. 166; (edda3) is not in Auden & Taylor, see Boyer p. 587, Genzmer p. 172; (edda4): p. 87; (edda5) p. 165; (edda6): p. 166; (edda7): p. 107; (edda8): p. 164; (edda9): p. 211; (edda10): p. 212; (edda11): p. 212.

More scholarly information on Nordic life and beliefs is available in the journal *alvíssmál* which is published online at: http://userpage.fu-berlin.de/~alvismal/
Particularly relevant to this book, I found the papers:
by Alison Finlay, on medieval Icelandic insults,
by Anatoly Liberman who discusses the etymology of ten Scandinavian and North English words, including the word Edda,
by Carolyne Larrington who provides a feminist view of the poem *Skírnismál.*

The ancient texts I used are:
Tacitus, *The Agricola and the Germania*, Penguin Classics, 1970. (taci1): Germania 10, p. 109; (taci2): Germania 45, p. 140.
Bede, *Ecclesiastical History of the English People*, Penguin Classics, 1990, reference (bede1) is on p. 269-270.
Saxo Grammaticus, *Gesta Danorum* (published around 1215), translation by J.-P. Troadec, Gallimard 1995. (saxo1): p. 261. There exists an English translation available on the web, it is provided by The Project Gutenberg. Compare my version to theirs. For instance, in its book 6, it says: "So the peasant's son approached, replaced the parts of his belly that had been torn away, and bound up with a plait of withies the mass of intestines that had fallen out." In this translation, it is also noticeable that all the names given by Saxo have been 'germanized'. For instance, Saxo's Starcatherus becomes Starkad etc.

Jordanes, *The Origin and Deeds of the Goths*, translation by Charles C. Mierow is available on line at www.acs.ucalgary.ca/~vandersp/Courses/texts/jordgeti.html

As I said in the text, I did not use the Galdrabok, book of Icelandic magical charms, because it hardly deals with healing, but nevertheless this work is very interesting :

S. Flowers, *The Galdrabok* , An Icelandic Grimmoire, Samuel Weiser, 1989.

Objective witnessing of modern Paganism

A bit aside from this book, and for those who are interested in the recent history of the political movements dealing with the runes, two books contain all the objective knowledge available, they are:

Nicholas Goodrick-Clarke, *The Occult Roots of Nazism*, NY University Press, 1992.

Jeffrey Kaplan, *Radical Religion in America*, Syracuse University Press, 1997.

Printed in April 2023
by Rotomail Italia S.p.A., Vignate (MI) - Italy